Y0-BQQ-097

WITHDRAWN
L. R. COLLEGE LIBRARY

FACT AND FABLE
IN
PSYCHOLOGY

BY JOSEPH JASTROW
PROFESSOR OF PSYCHOLOGY IN THE UNIVERSITY OF WISCONSIN

BOSTON AND NEW YORK
HOUGHTON MIFFLIN COMPANY
The Riverside Press Cambridge

CARL A. RUDISILL LIBRARY
LENOIR RHYNE COLLEGE

COPYRIGHT, 1900, BY JOSEPH JASTROW

ALL RIGHTS RESERVED

130
J31

130
g 31
cop 1

8167

TO MY HELPMATE

PREFACE

A GROUP of problems that appears conspicuously in the present volume, and in so far contributes to the fitness of its title, has obtained a considerable interest on the part of the public at large. Such interest seems prone to take its clue from the activity of those who herald startling revelations on the basis of unusual psychic experiences, and who give promise of disclosing other worlds than the one with which common sense and common sensation acquaint us, rather than from the cautious and consistent results of serious and professional students in study or in laboratory. The fascination of the unusual over the popular mind is familiar and intelligible, and seems in no direction more pronounced than in matters psychological. So long as this interest is properly subordinated to a comprehensive and illuminating general view of the phenomena in question, it is not likely to be harmful and may prove to be helpful. But when the conception of the nature of our mental endowment and the interest in the understanding thereof are derived from the unusual, the abnormal, and the obscure, instead of from the normal, law-abiding observations systematized and illuminated by long and successful research, there is danger that the interest will become unwholesome and the conception misleading. It is quite natural that the

plain man should be interested in the experiences of
the world of mind which form an intrinsic part of his
common humanity; and it is equally natural that he
should find attraction in less commonplace and seemingly anomalous mental phenomena. If thunderstorms
were as rare as total eclipses of the sun, it is likely
that they would attract equal attention, be looked upon
as terrifying and portentous by superstitious humanity, and be invested by tradition with mysterious significance, under the influence of the interest in the
unusual. The existence of this interest is itself a distinctive trait meriting a psychological interpretation,
and one not likely to be overlooked. Its direction and
regulation become the care of the several departments
of science that deal with the respective subject-matters
involved. And yet in a special way, as expressions of the
popular *esprit*, such interests claim the psychologist's
attention as they do not claim the attention of representatives of other sciences. It may happen that the
astronomer finds an interest in noting popular conceptions in regard to comets and life on other planets
and beliefs about meteors and eclipses, but such interest forms no essential part of his occupation. He
knows very well that the intelligent layman who wishes
to be informed on astronomical matters will turn with
confidence and respect to the accounts of the solar system, which represent the result of generations of scientific research under the guidance of exceptional ability
and devotion. The psychologist is in a less fortunate
position. His topic has neither that exclusive definiteness of content nor that position of hereditary prestige nor the general acknowledgment of its essentially

technical character, which belong to astronomy. All
men have their own psychological experiences and
notions about mental phenomena, but opinions concerning astronomy are admitted to belong to those who
have specially fitted themselves for such pursuits.

There is thus a natural reason why it should be particularly difficult in psychology to bring about a wholesome and right-minded and helpful interest on the part
of the layman, — a difficulty further aggravated by the
encouragement of well-meaning but logically defective
publications claiming to substantiate by quasi-scientific
methods the popular belief in the peculiar personal and
mysterious significance of events. In the face of this
situation, the professional psychologist cannot but take
heed of the dangers which imperil the true appreciation
of his labors and his purpose, on the part of the sympathetic layman. It is a matter of serious concern that
the methods of genuine psychological study, that the
conditions of advance in psychology, that the scope and
nature of its problems should be properly understood.
It is matter of importance that the dominant interest
in psychology should centre about the normal use and
development of functions with respect to which psychology bears a significant message for the regulation
of life. The restoration of a more desirable and progressive point of view requires some examination of
the false and misleading conceptions and alleged data,
which threaten to divert the sound and progressive interest from its proper channels. It is not to be expected, when many who engage public attention speak
in favor of the importance of the unknown and the
mystic in psychology, when the twilight phenomena of

mental life are dwelt upon — and professionally as well
as by amateurs — to the neglect of the luminous day-
light actualities, that the layman will always correctly
distinguish between what is authentically scientific and
in accordance with the advancing ideals of psychology,
and what is but the embodiment of unfortunate traditions, or the misguided effort of the dilettante, or the
perverse fallacy of the prepossessed mystic. Fact and
fable in psychology can only be separated by the logical sifting of evidence, by the exercise of the prerogative of a scientific point of view substantiated and
fortified by the lessons embodied in the history of rational opinion. The cause of truth and the overthrow
of error must sometimes be fought in drawn battle and
with the clash of arms, but are more frequently served
by the inauguration of an adherence to one side and the
consequent desertion of the other. Both procedures
may be made necessary by the current status of psychological discussion.

The present collection of essays is offered as a contribution towards the realization of a sounder interest
in and a more intimate appreciation of certain problems upon which psychology has an authoritative
charge to make to the public jury. These essays take
their stand distinctively upon one side of certain issues,
and as determinately as the situation seems to warrant,
antagonize contrary positions ; they aim to oppose certain tendencies and to support others; to show that
the sound and profitable interest in mental life is in
the usual and normal, and that the resolute pursuit of
this interest necessarily results in bringing the apparently irregular phenomena of the mental world within

the field of illumination of the more familiar and the law-abiding. They further aim to illustrate that misconceptions in psychology, as in other realms, are as often the result of bad logic as of defective observation, and that both are apt to be called into being by inherent mental prepossessions. Some of the essays are more especially occupied with an analysis of the defective logic which lends plausibility to and induces credence in certain beliefs; others bring forward contributions to an understanding of phenomena about which misconception is likely to arise; still others are presented as psychological investigations which, it is believed, command a somewhat general interest. The prominence of the discussion of unfortunate and misleading tendencies in psychological opinion should not be allowed to obscure the more intrinsically important problems which in the main are of a different, though possibly not of an unrelated character. I should be defeating one of the purposes of these essays if, by the discussion of mooted positions, I conveyed the notion that the problems thus presented were naturally the fundamental ones about which advance in psychology may be most promisingly centred. I deeply regret that the dispossession of fable requires more resolute and more elaborate exposition than the unfoldment of fact; but such is part of the condition confronting the critical student of psychological opinion. I must depend upon the reader to make due allowances for this foreshortening of a portion of the composition, and so to bring away a truer impression of the whole than the apparent perspective suggests.

It would not be proper to claim for this budget of

psychological studies a pre-arranged unity of design or a serial unfoldment of argument. They represent the unity of interest of a worker in a special field, who has his favorite excursions and vistas, who at times ventures away from the beaten paths and as frequently returns along those already traversed, but with varying purposes, and reaches the outlook from a different approach. There seems enough of singleness of purpose in the several presentations to warrant their inclusion in a single volume with a common name. There is enough also to make it pertinent to explain that the occasional repetitions of the same line of thought seemed less objectionable than frequent reference from one essay to another.

All of the essays have been previously printed in the pages of various scientific and popular magazines; and I have accordingly to acknowledge the courtesy of the several publishers, which makes possible their appearance in their present form. The essays have, however, been subjected to a critical revision, in the hope of increasing their acceptability in regard to form and material, and of giving them a setting appropriate to the interests of the present-day readers of psychological literature. Both in the selection of the essays from a larger group of published studies, and in their arrangement and elaboration, I have attempted to bear in mind the several current interests in questions of this type, and to direct these interests formatively along lines which seem to me fertile in promise and sterling in value. In the recasting thus made necessary it has come about (markedly in two cases, The Problems of Psychical Research and The Logic of Mental Telegraphy) that some of the essays have been entirely re-written and bear only a generic resemblance to their former appearance.

The several acknowledgments to be recorded are as follows: To the "Popular Science Monthly," for permission to reprint The Psychology of Deception (December, 1888), The Psychology of Spiritualism (April, 1889), A Study of Involuntary Movements (April and September, 1892), The Mind's Eye (January, 1899), The Modern Occult (September, 1900); to the "New Princeton Review," for The Dreams of the Blind (January, 1888); to "Harper's Monthly Magazine," for The Problems of Psychical Research (June, 1889); to "Scribner's Magazine," for The Logic of Mental Telegraphy (October, 1895); to the "Cosmopolitan," for Hypnotism and its Antecedents (February, 1896). The Natural History of Analogy was delivered as a vice-presidential address before the Section of Anthropology of the American Association for the Advancement of Science, and was printed in its Proceedings, vol. xl., 1891. The article, Mental Prepossession and Inertia, appeared in a college publication of the University of Wisconsin, the "Aegis" (April, 1897). I have also to acknowledge my indebtedness to Miss Helen Keller for her very interesting contribution to my presentation of the dreams of the blind. My most comprehensive obligation in the preparation of the volume I have acknowledged upon the dedicatory page.

JOSEPH JASTROW.

Madison, Wisconsin, November, 1900.

CONTENTS

FACT AND FABLE IN PSYCHOLOGY

THE MODERN OCCULT

I

IF that imaginary individual so convenient for literary illustration, a visitor from Mars, were to alight upon our planet at its present stage of development, and if his intellectual interests induced him to survey the range of terrestrial views of the nature of what is "in heaven above, or on the earth beneath, or in the waters under the earth," to appraise mundane opinion in regard to the perennial problems of mind and matter, of government and society, of life and death, our Martian observer might conceivably report that a limited portion of mankind were guided by beliefs representing the accumulated toil and studious devotion of generations, — the outcome of a slow and tortuous but progressive growth through error and superstition, and at the cost of persecution and bloodshed ; that they maintained institutions of learning where the fruits of such thought could be imparted and the seeds cultivated to bear still more richly ; but that outside of this respectable yet influential minority, there were endless upholders of utterly unlike notions and of widely diverging beliefs, clamoring like the builders of the tower of Babel in diverse tongues.

It is well, at least occasionally, to remember that our conceptions of science and of truth, of the nature of logic and of evidence, are not so universally held as we unreflectingly assume or as we hopefully wish. Almost every one of the fundamental, basal, and indisputable tenets of science is regarded as hopelessly in error by some ardent would-be reformer. One Hampden declares the earth to be a motionless plane with the North Pole as the centre; one Carpenter gives a hundred remarkable reasons why the earth is not round, with a challenge to the scientists of America to disprove them; one Symmes regarded the earth as hollow and habitable within, with openings at the poles, which he offered to explore for the consideration of the "patronage of this and the new worlds;" while Symmes, Jr., explains how the interior is lighted, and that it probably forms the home of the lost tribes of Israel; and one Teed announces, on equally conclusive evidence, that the earth is a "stationary concave cell . . . with people, Sun, Moon, Planets, and Stars on the inside," the whole constituting an "alchemico-organic structure, a Gigantic Electro-Magnetic Battery." If we were to pass from opinions regarding the shape of the earth to the many other and complex problems that appeal to human interests, it would be equally easy to collect "ideas" comparable to these in value, evidence, and eccentricity. With this conspicuously pathological outgrowth of brain-functioning,— although its representatives in the literature of the occult are neither few nor far between,— I shall not specifically deal; and yet the general abuse of logic, the helpless flounderings in the mire of delusive analogy, the baseless assumptions, which characterize insane or "crank" productions, are readily found in the literary products of occultism.

The occult consists of a mixed aggregate of movements and doctrines, which may be the expressions of kindred interests and dispositions, but present no essential community of content. Such members of this cluster of beliefs as in our day and generation have attained a considerable adherence or still retain it from former generations, constitute the modern occult. A conspicuous and truly distinctive characteristic of the occult is its marked divergence in trend and belief from the recognized standards and achievements of human thought. This divergence is one of attitude and logic and general perspective. It is a divergence of intellectual temperament, that distorts the normal reactions to science and evidence, and to the general significance and values of the factors of our complicated natures and of our equally complicated environment. At least it is this in extreme and pronounced forms; and shades from it through an irregular variety of tints to a vague and often unconscious susceptibility for the unusual and eccentric, combined with an instability of conviction regarding established beliefs that is more often the expression of the weakness of ignorance than of the courage of independence.

In their temper and course of unfoldment, occult doctrines are likely to involve and to proceed upon mysticism, obscurity, and a disguised form of superstition. In their content, they are attracted to such themes as the ultimate nature of mental action, the conception of life and death, the effect of cosmic conditions upon human events and endowment, the delineation of character, the nature and treatment of disease ; or indeed to any of the larger or smaller realms of knowledge that combine with a strong human, and at times a practical interest, a considerable complexity of basal principles and general relations. Both the temper and the content, the manner and the matter of the occult, should be borne in mind in a survey of its more distinctive examples. It is well, while observing the particular form of occultism or mysticism, or, it may be, merely of superstition and error, which one or another of the occult movements exhibits, to note as well the importance of the intellectual motive or temperament that inclines to the occult. It is important to inquire not only what is believed, but what is the nature of the evidence that induces belief ; to observe what attracts and then makes converts ; to discover what are the influences by which the belief spreads. Two classes of motives or interests are conspicuous: the one prominently intellectual or theoretical, the other moderately or grossly practical. Movements in which the former interest dominates, contain elements that command respect even when they do not engage sympathy ; and that appeal, though it may be unwisely, to worthy impulses and lofty aspirations. Amongst the movements presenting prominent practical aspects are to be found instances of the most irreverent and pernicious, as well as of the most vulgar, ignorant, and fraudulent schemes which have been devised to mislead the human mind. Most occult movements, however, are of a mixed character ;

and in their career, the speculative and the practical change in importance at different times, or in different lands, or at the hands of variously minded leaders. Few escape, and some seem especially designed for the partisanship of that class who are seeking whom they may devour; who, stimulated by the greed for gain or the love of notoriety, set their snares for the eternally gullible. The interest in the occult, however, is under the sway of the law of fashion; and fortunately, many a mental garment which is donned in spite of the protest of reason and propriety, is quietly laid aside when the dictum of the hour pronounces it unbecoming.

II

Historically considered, the occult points back to distant epochs and to foreign civilizations; to ages when the facts of nature were but weakly grasped, when belief was largely dominated by the authority of tradition, when even the ablest minds fostered or assented to superstition, when the social conditions of life were inimical to independent thought, and the mass of men were cut off from intellectual growth of even the most elementary kind. Pseudo-science flourished in the absence of true knowledge; and imaginative speculation and unfounded belief held the office intended for inductive reason. Ignorance inevitably led to error, and false views to false practices. In the sympathetic environment thus developed, the occultist flourished and displayed the impressive insignia of exclusive wisdom. His attitude was that of one seeking to solve an enigma, to find the key to a secret arcanum; his search was for some mystic charm, some talismanic formula,

some magical procedure, which should dispel the mist
that hides the face of nature and expose her secrets to
his ecstatic gaze. By one all-encompassing, masterful
effort the correct solution was to be discovered or revealed ; and at once and for all, ignorance was to give
place to true knowledge, science and nature were to be
as an open book, doubt and despair to be replaced by
the serenity of perfect wisdom. As our ordinary senses
and faculties proved insufficient to accomplish such ends,
supernatural powers were appealed to, a transcendental
sphere of spiritual activity was cultivated, capable of
perceiving, through the hidden symbolism of apparent
phenomena, the underlying relations of cosmic structure and final purposes.   Long periods of training and
devotion, seclusion from the world, contemplation of
inner mysteries, were to lead the initiate through the
various stages of adeptship up to the final plane of communion with the infinite and the comprehension of truth
in all things.   This form of occultism reaches its fullest and purest expression in Oriental wisdom-religions.
These vie in interest to the historian with the mythology
and philosophy of Greece and Rome ; and we of the
Occident feel free to profit by their ethical and philosophical content, and to cherish the impulses which
gave them life.   But when such views are forcibly
transplanted to our age and clime, when they are
decked in garments so unlike their original vestments,
particularly when they are associated with dubious
practices and come into violent conflict with the truth
that has accumulated since they first had birth, — their
aspect is profoundly altered, and they come within the
circle of the modern occult.

III

Of this character is Theosophy, an occult movement brought into recent prominence by the activity and personality of Mme. Blavatsky. The story of the checkered career of this remarkable woman is fairly accessible. Born in Russia in 1831 as Helen Petrovna, daughter of Colonel Hahn, of the Russian army, she was married at the age of seventeen to an elderly gentleman, M. Blavatsky. She is described in girlhood as a person of passionate temper and wilful and erratic disposition. She separated or escaped from her husband after a few months of married life, and entered upon an extended period of travel and adventure. The search for "psychic" experiences and for unusual persons and beliefs seemed to form the *leit-motiv* of her nomadic existence. She absorbed Hindu wisdom from the adepts of India ; she sat at the feet of a thaumaturgist at Cairo ; she journeyed to Canada to meet the medicine man of the Red Indians, and to New Orleans to observe the practices of Voodoo among the negroes. It is difficult to know what to believe in the accounts prepared by her enthusiastic followers. Violations of physical law were constantly occurring in her presence ; and, to borrow a phrase from Mr. Lang, "sporadic outbreaks of rappings and feats of impulsive pots, pans, beds, and chairs insisted on making themselves notorious." In 1873 she came to New York and sat in " spiritualistic " circles, assuming an assent to their theories, but claiming to see through and beyond the manifestations the operations of her theosophic guides in astral projection. At such a séance she met

Colonel Olcott, and assisted him in the foundation
of the Theosophical Society in New York in October,
1875. Mme. Blavatsky directed the thought of this
society to the doctrines of Indian occultism, and reported the appearance in New York of a Hindu Mahatma, who left a turban behind him as evidence of
his astral visit. The Mahatmas, it was explained,
were a Society of Brothers, who dwelt in the fastnesses
of far-off Thibet, and there handed on by tradition the
super-mortal wisdom which their spirituality and con-
templative training enabled them to absorb. Later,
this modern priestess of Isis and Colonel Olcott (who
remained her staunch supporter, but whom she referred
to in private as a " psychologized baby ") exchanged
the distracting atmosphere of New York for the more
serene environment of India ; and at Adyar established
a shrine, from which were mysteriously issued answers
to letters placed within its recesses, from which secret
facts were revealed, and a variety of interesting marvels performed. Discords arose within the household,
and led to the publication by M. and Mme. Coulomb, her confederates, of letters illuminating the tricks
of the trade by which the miracles had been produced.
Mme. Blavatsky pronounced the letters to be forgeries,
but they were sufficiently momentous to bring Mr.
Hodgson to India to investigate for the Society for
Psychical Research. He was able to deprive many of
the miracles of their mystery ; to show how the shrine
from which the Mahatma's messages emanated was
accessible to Mme. Blavatsky by the aid of sliding
panels and secret drawers, to show that these messages
were in style, spelling, and handwriting the counterpart

of Mme. Blavatsky's, to show that many of the phenomena were the result of planned collusion and that others were created by the limitless credulity and the imaginative exaggeration of the witnesses, — "domestic imbeciles," as madame confidentially referred to them. Through the Akasic force, the medium of which was the mysterious world-ether, Akaz, were brought messages that suddenly appeared in space or fluttered down from the ceiling ; yet M. Coulomb explained how by means of a piece of thread, a convenient recess in the plaster of the ceiling, and an arranged signal, the letters could be made to appear at the proper dramatic moment. When a saucer was left standing near the edge of a shelf in the shrine, and the opening of the door brought it to the floor shattered to pieces, the same mysterious force was sufficient to recreate it, without flaw or blemish ; but when Mr. Hodgson finds that at a shop at which Mme. Blavatsky had made purchases, two such articles had been sold at the price of two rupees eight annas the pair, the miracle becomes more intelligible.

In brief, the report of the society convicted "the Priestess of Isis" of "a long continued combination with other persons to produce by ordinary means a series of apparent marvels for the support of the Theosophic movement;" and concludes with these words: "For our own part, we regard her neither as the mouthpiece of hidden seers nor as a mere vulgar adventuress ; we think that she has achieved a title to permanent remembrance as one of the most accomplished, ingenious, and interesting impostors in history." Mme. Blavatsky died in 1891, and her ashes were divided between Adyar, London, and New York.

The Theosophic movement continues, though with abated vigor, owing partly to the above-mentioned disclosures, but probably more to the increasing propagandism of other cults, to the lack of a leader of Mme. Blavatsky's genius, or to the inevitable ebb and flow of such interests. Mme. Blavatsky continued to expound Theosophy after the exposures, and although depressed by their publication still occasionally essayed a miracle. Later, in a moment of confession induced by the discovery of a package of Chinese envelopes ready to serve for miraculous appearances, she is reported to have said, " What is one to do, when in order to rule men it is necessary to deceive them; when their very stupidity invites trickery, for almost invariably the more simple, the more silly, and the more gross the phenomena, the more likely it is to succeed?" Still, even self-confession does not detract from the fervor of convinced believers; and Mrs. Besant, Mr. Sinnett, and others were ready to take up the work at her death. However, miracles are no longer performed, and no immediately practical ends are proclaimed. Individual development and evolution, mystic discourses on adeptship and Karma and Maya and Nirvana, communion with the higher ends of life, the cultivation of an esoteric psychic insight, form the goal of present endeavor. The Mahatmas, says Mrs. Besant, are giving " intellectual instructions, enormously more interesting than even the exhibition of their abnormal powers." " Our European thinkers," thus Mr. Podmore interprets Mr. Sinnett's attitude, " are like blind men who are painfully learning to read with their fingers from a child's primer, whilst these have eyes to see the universe, past, present, and to come. To Mr. Sinnett it had been given to learn the alphabet of that transcendent language." " He could make the most extravagant mysticism seem matter of fact. He could write of *Manvantaras* and *Nirvana*, and the septenary constitution of man, in language which would have been appropriate in a treatise on kitchen-middens, or the functions of the pineal gland. In his lucid prose the vast conceptions of primitive Buddhism were fused with the commonplaces of modern science; and whilst the cosmology which resulted from their union dazzled by its splendid visions, the precise terminology of the writer, and the very poverty of his imagination, served to reassure his readers that they were listening to words of truth and soberness. We were taught to look back upon this earth and all its mighty sisterhood of planets and suns rolling onward in infinite space, through cycle after cycle in the past. We were shown how, through the perpetual flux and reflux of the spiritual and the natural, the cosmic evolution was accomplished, and the earth grew, through the life of crystal, and plant, and brute, to man. We saw how the worlds throbbed in vast alternation of systole and diastole, and how the tide of human life itself had its ebb and flow. And this fugitive human personality — the man who works, and loves, and suffers — we saw to endure but for a short life on earth, and for an age, shorter or longer, in *Devachan*. Memory is then purged away, the eternal spirit puts on a new dress, and a new life on earth is begun. And so through each succeeding reincarnation the goal of the life preceding becomes the starting-point of the life which follows." In such manner the modern Theosophist seeks to appeal to men and women of philosophical inclinations, for whom an element of mysticism has its charm, and who are intellectually at unrest with the conceptions underlying modern science and modern life. Such persons are quite likely to be educated, refined, and sincere. We may believe them intellectually misguided ; we may recognize the fraud to which their leader resorted to glorify her creed, but we must equally recognize the absence of many pernicious tendencies in their teachings, which characterize other and more practical occult movements.

IV

Spiritualism, another member of the modern occult family, presents a combination of features rather difficult to portray ; but its public career of half a century has probably rendered its tenets and practices fairly familiar.[1] For, like other movements, it presents both doctrines and manifestations ; and, like other movements, it achieved its popularity through its manifestations and emphasized the doctrines to maintain the interest and solidarity of its numerous converts. Deliberate fraud has been repeatedly demonstrated in a large number of alleged " spiritualistic " manifestations ; in many more the very nature of the phenomena and

[1] Spiritualism is here considered only in its general bearings upon modern conceptions of the occult ; any consideration of the special phenomena presented under its auspices or of the influences which contribute to a belief in its tenets would lead too far afield. The topic is separately considered from a different point of view in a later essay.

of the conditions under which they appear is so strongly suggestive of trickery as to render any other hypothesis of their origin equally improbable and superfluous. Unconscious deception, exaggerated and distorted reports, defective and misleading observation, have been demonstrated to be most potent reagents, whereby alleged miracles are made to throw off their mystifying envelopings and to leave a simple deposit of intelligible and often commonplace fact. That the methods of this or that medium have not been brought within the range of such explanation may be admitted, but the admission carries with it no bias in favor of the spiritualistic hypothesis. It may be urged, however, that where there is much smoke there is apt to be some fire; yet there is little prospect of discovering the nature of the fire until the smoke has been completely cleared away. Perhaps it has been snatched from heaven by a materialized Prometheus; perhaps it may prove to be the trick of a *ridiculus mus* gnawing at a match. And yet, in this connection, the main point to be insisted upon with regard to such manifestations is that their interpretation and their explanation demand some measure of technical knowledge and training, and of special adaptability to such pursuits. "The problem cannot be solved and settled by amateurs, nor by ' common sense ' that

> ' Delivers brawling judgments all day long,
> On all things unashamed.' "

Spiritualism represents a systematization of popular beliefs and superstitions, modified by echoes of religious and philosophical doctrines; it thus contains factors which owe their origin to other interests than

those which lead directly to the occult. Its main purpose was to establish the reality of communication with
departed spirits; the means, which at first spontaneously presented themselves and later were devised for
this purpose, were in large measure not original. The
rappings are in accord with the traditional folk-lore
behavior of ghosts; their transformation into a signal
code (although a device discovered before) may have
been due to the originality of the Fox children; the
planchette has its analogies in Chinese and European
modes of divination; clairvoyance was incorporated
from the phenomena of artifical somnambulism, as
practiced by the successors of Mesmer; the "sensitive"
or "medium" suggests the same origin as well as the
popular belief in the gift of supernatural powers in
favored individuals; others of the phenomena, such as
"levitation" and "cabinet performances," have their
counterparts in Oriental magic; "slate-writing," "form
materializations," "spirit-messages" and "spirit photographs" are, in the main, modern contributions. Mr.
Lang has attractively set forth the resemblances between primitive and ancient spiritualism and its modern revival; he suggests that "the 'Trance Medium,'
the 'Inspirational Speaker' was a reproduction of the
maiden with a spirit of divination, of the Delphic
Pythia. In the old belief, the god dominated her, and
spoke from her lips, just as the 'control' or directing
spirit dominates the medium." He suggests that it is
for like reasons that "the Davenport Brothers, like
Eskimo and Australian conjurers, like the Highland
seer in the bull's hide," are swathed or bound; he
notes that "the lowest savages have their *séances*,

levitations, bindings of the medium, trance speakers; Peruvians, Indians, have their objects moved without contact;" he surmises that the Fox children, being of a Methodist family, may have been inspired by "old Jeffrey," who haunted the Wesleys' house.

The phenomena now associated with modern Spiritualism, with their characteristic *milieu*, breed the typical atmosphere of the séance chamber, which resists precise analysis, but which in its extreme form involves morbid credulity, blind prepossession, and emotional contagion; while the dependence of the phenomena on the character of the medium offers strong temptation alike to shrewdness, eccentricity, and dishonesty. On the side of his teachings the Spiritualist is likewise not strikingly original. The relations of his beliefs to those that grew about the revelations of Swedenborg, to the speculations of the German "pneumatologists," and to other philosophical doctrines, though perhaps not intimate, are yet traceable and interesting; and in another view the Spiritualist is as old as man himself, and finds his antecedents in the necromancer of Chaldea, or in the Shaman of Siberia, or the Angekok of Greenland, or the spirit-doctor of various savage tribes. The modern mediums are thus simply repeating with new costumes and improved scenic effects the mystic drama of primitive man.

Spiritualism thus appeals to a deep-seated craving in human nature, that of assurance of personal immortality and of communion with the departed. Just so long as a portion of mankind will accept material evidence of such a belief, and will even countenance the irreverence, the triviality, and the vulgarity surrounding the manifestations; just so long as those persons will misjudge their own powers of detecting how the alleged supernatural appearances are really produced, and remain unimpressed by the principles upon which alone a consistent explanation is possible, just so long will Spiritualism and kindred delusions flourish.

As to the present-day status of this cult it is not easy to speak positively. Its *clientèle* has apparently greatly diminished; it still numbers amongst its adherents men and women of culture and education, and many more who cannot be said to possess these qualities. There seems to be a considerable class of persons who believe that natural laws are insufficient to account for their personal experiences and those of others, and who temporarily or permanently incline to a spiritualistic hypothesis in preference to any other. Spiritualists of this intellectual temper can, however, form but a small portion of those who are enrolled under its creed. If one may judge by the tone and contents of current spiritualistic literature, the rank and file to which Spiritualism appeals present an unintellectual occult company, credulously accepting what they wish to believe, utterly regardless of the intrinsic significance of evidence or hypothesis, vibrating from one extreme or absurdity to another, and blindly following a blinder or more fanatic leader or a self-interested charlatan. While for the most extravagant and unreasonable expressions of Spiritualism one would probably turn to the literature of a few decades ago, yet the symptoms presented by the Spiritualism of to-day are unmistakably of the same character, and form a complex as characteristic as the symptom-complex of hysteria or epilepsy, and which, *faute de mieux*, may be termed occult. It is a type of occultism of a particularly pernicious character, because of its power to lead a parasitic life upon the established growths of religious beliefs and interests, and at the same time to administer to the needs of an unfortunate but widely prevalent passion for special signs and omens and the interpretation of personal experiences. It is a weak though comprehensible nature that becomes bewildered in the presence of a few experiences that seem homeless among the generous provisions of modern science, and runs off panic-stricken to find shelter in a system that satisfies a narrow personal craving at the sacrifice of broadly established principles, nurtured and grown strong in the hardy and beneficent atmosphere of science. It is a weaker and an ignorant nature that is attracted to the cruder forms of such beliefs, be it by the impulsive yielding to emotional susceptibility, by the contagion of an unfortunate mental environment, or by the absence of the steadying power of religious faith, or of logical vigor, or of confidence in the knowledge of others. Spiritualism finds converts in both camps and assembles them under the flag of the occult.[1]

[1] To prevent misunderstanding it is well to repeat that I am speaking of the general average of thorough-going Spiritualists. The fact that a few mediums have engaged the attention of scientifically minded investigators has no bearing on the motives which lead most persons to make a professional call on a medium, or to join a circle. The further fact that these investigators have at times found themselves baffled by the medium's performances and that a few of them have announced their readiness to accept the spiritualistic hypothesis, is of importance

The wane in the popularity of Spiritualism may be due in part to frequent exposures, in part to the passing of the occult interest to pastures new, and in part to other and less accessible causes. Such interest may again become dominant by the success or innovations of some original medium or by the appearance of some unforeseen circumstances. The present disposition to take up "spiritual healing" and "spiritual readings of the future" rather than mere assurances from the dead, indicates a desire to emulate the practical success of more recently established rivals. The history of Spiritualism, by its importance and its extravagance of doctrine and practice, forms an essential and an instructive chapter in the history of aberrant belief; and there is no difficulty in tracing the imprints of its footsteps on the sands of the occult.

V

The impress of ancient and mediæval lore upon latter-day occultism is conspicuous in the survivals of Alchemy and Astrology. Phrenology represents a more recent pseudo-science, but one sufficiently obsolete to be considered under the same head; as may also Palmistry, which has relations both to an ancient form of divination and to a more modern development after the manner of Physiognomy. The common characteristic of these is their devotion to a practical end. Alchemy occupies a somewhat distinct position. The original alchemists sought the secret of converting the

in some aspects, but does not determine the general trend of the spiritualistic movement in the direction in which it is considered in the present discussion.

baser metals into gold, in itself a sufficiently alluring and human occupation. There is no reason why such a problem should assume an occult aspect, except the sufficient one that ordinary procedures have not proved capable to effect the desired end. It is a proverbial fault of ambitious inexperience to attack valiantly large problems with endless confidence and sweeping aspiration. It is well enough in shaping your ideas to hitch your wagon to a star, yet the temporary utility of horses need not be overlooked ; but shooting arrows at the stars is apt to prove an idle pastime. If we are willing to forget for the moment that the same development of logic and experiment that makes possible the mental and material equipment of the modern chemist, makes impossible his consideration of the alchemist's search, we may note how far the inherent constitution of the elements, to say nothing of their possible transmutation, has eluded his most ultimate analysis. How immeasurably further it was removed from the grasp of the alchemist can hardly be expressed. But this is a scientific and not an occult view of the matter ; it was not by progressive training in marksmanship that the occultist hoped to send his arrows to the stars. His was a mystic search for the magical transmutation, the elixir of life or the philosopher's stone. One might suppose that, once the world has agreed that these ends are past finding out, the alchemist, like the maker of stone arrow-heads, would have found his occupation gone and have left no successor. His modern representative, however, is an interesting and by no means extinct species. He seems to flourish in France, but may be found in Germany, in England, and in this country. He is rarely a pure alchemist (although so recently as 1854 one of them offered to manufacture gold for the French mint), but represents the pure type of occultist. He calls himself a Rosicrucian ; he establishes a University of the Higher Studies, and becomes a professor of Hermetic Philosophy. His thought is mystic, and symbolism has an endless fascination for him. The recondite significance of numbers, extravagant analogies of correspondence, the traditional hidden meanings of the Kabbalah, fairly intoxicate him ; and verbose accounts of momentous relations and of unintelligible discoveries run riot in his writings. His science is not a mere Chemistry, but a Hyper-Chemistry ; his transmutations are no longer material, but assume a spiritual aspect. Like all adept followers of an esoteric belief, he must stand apart from his fellow-men ; he must cultivate the higher " psychic " powers, so that eventually he may be able by the mere action of his will to cause the atoms to group themselves into gold.

The modern alchemist is apt to be a general occultist ; he may be also an astrologer or a magnetist or a theosophist. But he is foremost an ardent enthusiast for exclusive and unusual lore — not the common and superficial possessions of misguided democratic science. He goes through the forms of study, remains superior to the baser practical ends of life, and finds his reward in the self-satisfaction of exclusive wisdom. In Paris, at least, he forms part of a rather respectable *salon*, speaking socially, or a " company of educated charlatans," speaking scientifically. His class does not constitute a large proportion of modern occultists, but they present a prominent form of its intellectual temperament. "There are also people," says Mr. Lang, "who so dislike our detention in the prison-house of old unvarying laws that their bias is in favor of anything which may tend to prove that science in her contemporary mood is not infallible. As the Frenchman did not care what sort of a scheme he invested money in, provided that it annoys the English, so many persons do not care what they invest belief in, provided that it irritates men of science." Of such is the kingdom of alchemists and their brethren.

VI

Astrology, Phrenology, Physiognomy, and Palmistry have in common a search for positive knowledge whereby to regulate the affairs of life, to foretell the future, to comprehend one's destiny and capabilities. They aim to secure success, or at least to be forearmed against failure by being forewarned. This is a natural, a practical, and in no essential way an occult desire. It becomes occult, or, more accurately, superstitious, when it is satisfied by appeals to relations and influences which do not exist, and by false interpretation of what may be admitted as measurably and vaguely true and about equally important. When not engaged in their usual occupation of building most startling superstructures on the most insecure foundations, practical occultists are like Dr. Holmes's katydid, "saying an undisputed thing in such a solemn way." They will not hearken to the experience of the ages that success cannot be secured nor character read by discovering their unreal or mystic stigmata ; they will not learn from physiology and psychology that the mental capabilities,

the moral and emotional endowment of an individual
are not stamped on his body in such a way that they
may be revealed by half an hour's use of the calipers
and tape-measure ; they will not listen when science
and common sense unite in teaching that the knowledge
of mental powers is not such as may be applied by rule
of thumb to individual cases, but that, like much other
valuable knowledge, it proceeds by the exercise of
sound judgment, and must as a rule rest content with
suggestive generalizations and imperfectly established
correlations.   An educated man with wholesome interests and a vigorous logical sense can consider a possible
science of character and the means of aiding its advance without danger and with some profit.   But this
meat is sheer poison to those who are usually attracted
to this type of speculations, while it offers to the un-
scrupulous charlatan a most convenient net to spread
for the unwary.   In so far as these occult mariners,
the astrologists and phrenologists *et id genus omne*,
are sincere, and in so far represent superstition rather
than commercial fraud, they simply ignore, through
obstinacy or ignorance, the lighthouses and charts and
the other aids to modern navigation, and persist in
steering their craft by an occult compass.   In some
cases they are professedly setting out, not for any har-
bor marked on terrestrial maps, but their expedition is
for the golden fleece or for the apples of the Hesper-
ides ; and with loud-voiced advertisements of their skill
as pilots, they proceed to form stock companies for the
promotion of their several enterprises and to dispose of
the shares to credulous speculators.

It would be a profitless task to review the alleged

data of Astrology or Phrenology or Palmistry, except for the illustrations which they readily yield of the nature of the conceptions and of the logic which command a certain popular interest and acceptance. The interest in these notions is, as Mr. Lang argues about ghosts and rappings and bogles, in how they come to be believed, rather than in how much or how little they chance to be true. It must be remembered also that our present interest is in the occult factors of these composite systems; they each contain other factors, — in part incorporations of vague and distorted scientific truths, in part dogmatic overstatement of results of observation, which, if reduced to the proportions warranted by definite evidence, dissolve into insignificance or intangibility, in part plausible or specious argumentation, and in still greater part mere fanciful assertion. And if we proceed to examine the professed evidence for the facts and laws and principles (*sit venia verbis*) that pervade Astrology or Phrenology or Palmistry or dream-interpretation, or beliefs of that ilk, we find the flimsiest kind of texture, that will hardly bear examination, and holds together only so long as it is kept secluded from the light of day. Farfetched analogy, baseless assertion, the uncritical assimilation of popular superstitions, a great deal of prophecy after the event (it is wonderful how clearly the astrologer finds the indications of Napoleon's career in his horoscope, or the phrenologist reads them in the Napoleonic cranial protuberances), much fanciful elaboration of detail, ringing the variations on a sufficiently complex and non-demonstrable proposition, cultivating a convenient vagueness of expression, together with an apologetic skill in providing for and explaining exceptions, the courage to ignore failure and the shrewdness to profit by coincidences and half-assimilated smatterings of science, and with it all an insensibility to the moral and intellectual demands of the logical decalogue, — and you have the skeleton, which, clothed with one flesh, becomes Astrology, and with another Phrenology, and with another Palmistry or Solar Biology or Descriptive Mentality or what not. Such pseudo-sciences thrive upon that widespread and intense craving for practical guidance of our individual affairs, which is not satisfied with judicious applications of general principles, with due consideration of the probabilities and uncertainties of human life, but demands an impossible and precise revelation. Not all that passes for, and in a way is knowledge, is or is likely soon to become scientific ; and when a peasant parades in an academic gown the result is likely to be a caricature.

VII

To achieve fortune, to judge well and command one's fellow-men, to foretell and control the future, to be wise in worldly lore, are natural objects of human desire ; but still another is essential to happiness. Whether we attempt to procure these good fortunes by going early to bed and early to rise, or by more occult procedures, we wish to be healthy as well as wealthy and wise. The maintenance of health and the perpetuity of youth were not absent from the mediæval occultist's search, and formed an essential part of the benefits to be conferred by the elixir of life and the philosopher's stone. A series of superstitions and extravagant systems are conspicuous in the antecedents and the by-paths of the history of medicine, and are related to it much as astrology is to astronomy, or alchemy to chemistry; and because medicine in part remains and to previous generations was conspicuously an empirical art rather than a science, it offers great opportunity for practical error and misapplied partial knowledge. It is not necessary to go back to early civilizations or to primitive peoples, among whom the medicine-man and the priest were one and alike appealing to occult powers, nor to early theories of disease which beheld in insanity the obsession of demons and resorted to exorcism to cast them out; it is not necessary to consider the various personages who acquired notoriety as healers by laying on of hands or by appeal to faith, or who, like Mesmer, introduced the system of animal magnetism, or, like some of his followers, sought directions for healing from the clairvoyant dicta of somnambules; it is not necessary to ransack folk-lore superstitions and popular remedies for the treatment of disease; for the modern forms of "irregular" healing offer sufficient illustrations of occult methods of escaping the ills that flesh is heir to.

The existence of a special term for a medical impostor is doubtless the result of the prevalence of the class thus named; but quackery and occult medicine, though mutually overlapping, can by no means be held accountable for one another's failings. Many forms of quackery proceed on the basis of superstitions or fanciful or exaggerated notions containing occult elements, but for the present purpose it is wise to limit attention to those

in which this occult factor is distinctive; for medical
quackery in its larger relations is neither modern nor
occult. Occult healing takes its distinctive character
from the theory underlying the practice rather than
from the nature of the practice. It is not so much what
is done, as why it is done, or pretended to be done or not
done, that determines its occult character. A factor
of prominence in modern occult healing is indeed one
that in other forms characterized many of its predecessors, and was rarely wholly absent from the connection
between the procedure and the result; this is the
mental factor, which may be called upon to give character to a theory of disease, or be utilized consciously
or unconsciously as a curative principle. It is not
implied that "mental medicine" is necessarily and intrinsically occult, but only that the general trend of
modern occult notions regarding disease may be best
portrayed in certain typical forms of " psychic " healing.
The legitimate recognition of the importance of mental
conditions in health and disease is one of the results of
the union of modern psychology and modern medicine.
An exaggerated and extravagant as well as pretentious
and illogical overstatement and misstatement of this
principle may properly be considered as occult.

VIII

Among such systems there is one which by its mo-
mentary prominence overshadows all others; and for
this reason, as well as for its more explicit or rather
more extended statement of principles, must be accorded special attention : I need hardly say that I refer
to that egregious misnomer, Christian Science. This

system is said to have been discovered by, or revealed to, Mrs. Mary Baker Glover Eddy in 1866. Several of its most distinctive positions (without their religious setting) are to be found in the writings, and were used in the practice of Mr. or Dr. P. P. Quimby (1802–1866), whom Mrs. Eddy professionally consulted shortly before she began her own propagandum. On its theoretical side, the system presents a series of quasi-metaphysical principles and also a professed interpretation of the Scriptures ; on its practical side, it offers a means of curing or avoiding disease, and includes under disease also what is more generally described as sin and misfortune. With Christian Science as a religious movement I shall not directly deal; I wish, however, to point out that this assumption of a religious aspect finds a parallel in Spiritualism and Theosophy, and doubtless forms one of the most potent reasons for the success of these occult movements. It would be a most dangerous principle to admit that the treatment of disease and the right to ignore hygiene can become the perquisite of any religious faith. It would be equally unwarranted to permit the principles which are responsible for such beliefs to take shelter behind the ramparts of religious tolerance, for the essential principles of Christian Science do not constitute a form of Christianity any more than they constitute a science ; but, in so far as they do not altogether elude description, pertain to the domain over which medicine, physiology, and psychology hold sway. As David Harum, in speaking of his church-going habits, characteristically explains, " the one I stay away from when I don't go 's the Presbyteriun," so the doctrines which Christian Science "stays away from," are those over which recognized departments of academic learning have the authority to decide.

Mrs. Eddy's *magnum opus*, serving at once as the text-book of the "science" and as a revised version of the Scriptures, "Science and Health, with Key to the Scriptures," has been circulated to the extent of one hundred and seventy thousand copies. I shall not give an account of this book, nor subject its more tangible tenets to a logical review; I must be content to recommend its pages as suggestive reading for the student of the modern occult, and to set forth in the credentials of quotation marks some of the dicta concerning disease. Yet it may be due to the author, or mouthpiece, of this system, to begin by citing what are declared to be its fundamental tenets, even if their connection with what is built upon them is far from evident.

"The fundamental propositions of Christian Science are summarized in the four following, to me, *self-evident* propositions. Even if read backward, these propositions will be found to agree in statement and proof : —

"1. God is All in all.

"2. God is good. Good is Mind.

"3. God, Spirit, being all, nothing is matter.

"4. Life, God, omnipotent Good, deny death, evil, sin, disease — Disease, sin, evil, death, deny Good, omnipotent God, Life."

"What is termed disease does not exist." "Matter has no being." "All is mind." "Matter is but the subjective state of what is here termed *mortal mind*." "All disease is the result of education, and can carry its ill effects no farther than mortal mind maps out the way." "The fear of dissevered bodily members, or a belief in such a possibility, is reflected on the body, in the shape of headache, fractured bones, dislocated joints, and so on, as directly as shame is seen rising to the cheek. This human error about physical wounds and colics is part and parcel of the delusion that matter can feel and see, having sensation and substance." " Insanity implies belief in a diseased brain, while physical ailments (so-called) arise from belief that some other portions of the body are deranged. . . . A bunion would produce insanity as perceptible as that produced by congestion of the brain, were it not that mortal mind calls the bunion an unconscious portion of the body. Reverse this belief and the results would be different." " We weep because others weep, we yawn because they yawn, and we have small-pox because others have it; but mortal mind, not matter, contains and carries the infection." " A Christian Scientist never gives medicine, never recommends hygiene, never manipulates." " Anatomy, Physiology, Treatises on Health, sustained by what is termed material law, are the husbandmen of sickness and disease." " You can even educate a healthy horse so far in physiology that he will take cold without his blanket." " If exposure to a draught of air while in a state of perspiration is followed by chills, dry cough, influenza, congestive symptoms in the lungs, or hints of inflammatory rheumatism, your Mind-remedy is safe and sure. If you are a Christian Scientist, such symptoms will not follow from the exposure; but if you believe in laws of matter and their fatal effects when transgressed, you are not fit to conduct your own case or to destroy the bad effects of belief. When the fear subsides and the conviction abides that you have broken no law, neither rheumatism, consumption, nor any other disease will ever result from exposure to the weather." " Destroy fear and you end the fever." " To prevent disease or cure it mentally let spirit destroy the dream of sense. If you wish to heal by argument, find the type of the ailment, get its name, and array your mental plea against the physical.   Argue with the patient (mentally, not audibly) that he has no disease, and conform the argument to the evidence.   Mentally insist that health is the everlasting fact, and sickness the temporal falsity.   Then realize the presence of health, and the corporeal senses will respond, so be it."   " My publications alone heal more sickness than an unconscientious student can begin to reach."   " The quotients, when numbers have been divided by a fixed rule, are not more unquestionable than the scientific tests I have made of the effects of truth upon the sick."   " I am never mistaken in my scientific diagnosis of disease."   " Outside of Christian Science all is vague and hypothetical, the opposite of Truth."   " Outside Christian Science all is error."

Surely this is a remarkable product of mortal mind! It would perhaps be an interesting *tour de force*, though hardly so entertaining as " Alice in Wonderland," to construct a universe on the assertions and hypotheses which Christian Science presents ; but it would have less resemblance to the world we know than has Alice's wonderland.   For any person for whom logic and evidence are something more real than ghosts or myths, the feat must always be relegated to the airy realm of the imagination, and must not be brought in contact with earthly realities.   And yet the extravagance of Mrs. Eddy's book, its superb disdain of vulgar fact, its transcendental self-confidence, its solemn assumption that reiteration and variation of assertion somehow spontaneously generate proof or self-evidence, its shrewd assimilation of a theological flavor, its occasional successes in producing a presentable travesty of scientific truth, — all these distinctions may be found in many a dust-covered volume, that represents the intensity of

conviction of some equally enthusiastic and equally inspired occultist, but one less successful in securing a
chorus to echo his refrain.

The temptation is strong not to dismiss " Eddyism "
without illustrating the peculiar structures under which,
in an effort to be consistent, it is forced to take shelter.
Since disease is always of purely mental origin, it follows that disease and its symptoms cannot ensue without the conscious coöperation of the patient; since
" Christian Science divests material drugs of their
imaginary power," it follows that the labels on the
bottles that stand on the druggist's shelves are correspondingly meaningless. And it becomes an interesting problem to inquire how the consensus of mortal
mind came about that associates one set of symptoms
with prussic acid, and another with alcohol, and another with quinine. Inhaling oxygen or common air
would prepare one for the surgeon's knife, and prussic
acid or alcohol have no more effect than water, if only
a congress of nations were to pronounce the former
to be anæsthetic and promulgate a decree that the
latter be harmless. Christian Science does not flinch
from this position. "If a dose of poison is swallowed
through mistake and the patient dies, even though physician and patient are expecting favorable results, does
belief, you ask, cause this death? Even so, and as
directly as if the poison had been intentionally taken.
In such cases a few persons believe the potion swallowed by the patient to be harmless; but the vast
majority of mankind, though they know nothing of this
particular case and this special person, believe the
arsenic, the strychnine, or whatever the drug used, to

be poisonous, for it has been set down as a poison by mortal mind. The consequence is that the result is controlled by the majority of opinions outside, not by the infinitesimal minority of opinions in the sick chamber." But why should the opinions of οἱ πολλοί be of influence in such a case, and the enlightened minorities be sufficient to effect the marvelous cures in all the other cases? Christian Scientists do not take cold in draughts in spite of the contrary opinions or illusions of misguided majorities. The logical Christian Scientist concludes that he need not eat, "for the truth is food does not affect the life of man;" and yet at once renounces his faith by adding, "but it would be foolish to venture beyond our present understanding, foolish to stop eating, until we gain more goodness and a clearer comprehension of the living God." And the mental physician, to be consistent, must be a mental surgeon also; and not plead that, "Until the advancing age admits the efficacy and supremacy of mind, it is better to leave the adjustment of broken bones and dislocations to the fingers of surgeons."

But it is unprofitable to consider the failings and absurdities of any occult system in its encounters with actual science and actual fact. It is simply as a real and prominent menace to rationality that these doctrines naturally attract consideration. Regarding them as illustrations of present-day occult beliefs, we are naturally tempted to inquire what measure of (perverted) truth they may contain; but the more worthy question is, How do such perversions come to find so large a company of "supporting listeners"? For to any one who can read and be convinced by the sequence of words of this system, ordinary logic has no power, and to him the world of reality brings no message. No form of the modern occult antagonizes the foundations of science so brusquely as this one. The possibility of science rests on the thorough and absolute distinction between the subjective and the objective. In what measure a man loses the power to draw this distinction clearly, and as other men do, in that measure he becomes irrational or insane. The objective exists; and no amount of thinking it away or thinking it differently will change it. That is what is understood by ultimate scientific truth; something that will endure unmodified by passing ways of viewing it, open to every one's verification who comes equipped with the proper means to verify, — a permanent objective, to be ascertained by careful logical inquiry, not to be determined by subjective opinion. Logic is the language of science; Christian Science and what sane men call science can never communicate because they do not speak the same language.

IX

It would be unfortunate to emphasize the popular preëminence of Christian Science at a cost of the neglect of the significance of the many other forms of " drugless healing," which bid for public favor by appeal to ignorance and to occult and superstitious instincts. Some are allied to Christian Science, and like it assimilate their cult to a religious movement; others are unmistakably the attempts of charlatans to lure the credulous by noisy advertisements of newly discovered and scientifically indorsed systems of "psy-

chic force," or of some personal "ism." For many
purposes it would be unjust to group together such
various systems, which in the nature of things must
include sinner and saint, the misguided sincere, the
half-believers who think " there may be something in
it," or " that it is worth a trial," along with scheming
quacks and adepts in commercial fraud. They illustrate the many and various roads traveled in the search
for health, by pilgrims who are dissatisfied with the
highways over which medical science pursues its steadfast though it may be devious course. Among them
there is plausible exaggeration and ignorant perversion
and dishonest libel of the relations that bind together
body and mind. Among the several schisms from the
" Mother Church of Christian Science " there is one
that claims to be the " rational phase of the mental
healing doctrine," that acknowledges the reality of disease and the incurability of serious organic disorders,
and resents any connection with the " half-fanatical
personality worship " (of Mrs. Eddy) as quite as foreign
to its tenets as would be the views of the " Free Religious Association " to the " Pope of Rome." " Divine
Healing " exhibits its success in one notable instance,
in the establishment of a school and college, a bank, a
land and investment association, a printing and pub-
lishing office, and sundry divine healing homes ; and
this prosperity is now to be extended by the foundation of a city or colony of converts, who shall be united
by the common bond of faith in divine healing as transmitted in the personal power of their leader. The official organ of this movement announces that the personification of their faith " makes her religion a business

and conducts herself upon sound business principles;"
their leader publicly boasts of his vast financial returns. With emphatic protest on the part of each
that he alone holds the key to salvation, and that his
system is quite original and unlike any other, comes
the procession of Metaphysical Healer and Mind-Curist
and Viticulturist and Magnetic Healer and Astrological Health Guide and Phrenopathist and Medical Clairvoyant and Esoteric Vibrationist and Psychic Scientist
and Mesmerist and Occultist. Some use or abuse the
manipulations of hypnotism; others claim the power
to concentrate the magnetism of the air and to excite
the vital fluids by arousing the proper mental vibrations, or by some equally lucid and demonstrable procedure; some advertise magnetic cups, and positive
and negative powders, and absent treatment by out-
puts of "psychic force," and countless other imposing
devices. In truth, they form a motley crew, and with
their "Colleges of Fine Forces," and "Psychic Research Companies," offering diplomas and degrees for
a three weeks' course of study or the reading of a book,
represent the slums of the occult. An account of their
methods is likely to be of as much interest to the student of fraud as to the student of opinion.

There can be no doubt that many of these systems
have been stimulated into life or into renewed vigor
by the success of Christian Science; this is particularly noticeable in the introduction of absent treatment
as a plank in their diverse platforms. This ingenious
method of restoring the health of their patients and
their own exchequers appealed to all the band of healing occultists from Spiritualist to Vibrationist, as easily

adaptable to their several systems. In much the same way Mesmer, more than a hundred years ago, administered to the practice which had exhausted the capacity of his personal attention, by magnetizing trees and selling magnetized water. The absent treatment represents the occult extension movement; and unencumbered by the hampering restrictions of physical forces, superior even to wireless telegraphy, carries its influence into the remotest homes. From ocean to ocean, and from North to South, these absent healers set apart some hour of the day, when they mentally convey their healing word to the scattered members of their flock. On the payment of a small fee you are made acquainted with the " soul-communion time-table " for your longitude, and may know when to meet the healing vibrations as they pass by. Others disdain any such temporal details and assure a cure merely on payment of the fee; the healer will know sympathetically when and how to transmit the curative impulses. Poverty and bad habits as well as disease readily succumb to the magic of the absent treatment. Such an hysterical edict as this is hardly extreme or unusual: " Join the Success Circle. . . . The Centre of that Circle is my omnipotent WORD. Daily I speak it. Its vibrations radiate more and more powerfully day by day. . . . As the sun sends out vibrations . . . so my WORD radiates Success to 10,000 lives as easily as to one."

It is impossible to appreciate fully the extravagances of these occult healers unless one makes a sufficient sacrifice of time and patience to read over a considerable sample of the periodical publications with which American occultism fairly teems. And when one has accomplished this task he is still at sea to account for the readers and believers who support these various systems, so undreamt of in our philosophy. It would really seem that there is no combination of ideas too absurd to fail entirely of a following. Carlyle, without special provocation, concluded that there were about forty million persons in England, mostly fools ; what would have been his comment in the face of this vast and universal array of human folly ! If it be urged in rejoinder that beneath all this rubbish heap a true jewel lies buried, that the wonderful cures and the practical success of these various systems indicate their dependence upon an essential and valuable factor in the cure of disease and the formation of habits, it is possible with reservation to assent, and with emphasis to demur. Such success, in so far as it is rightly reported, exemplifies the truly remarkable function of the mental factor in the control of normal as of disordered physiological functions. This truth has been recognized and utilized in unobtrusive ways for many generations, and within recent years has received substantial elaboration from carefully conducted experiments and observations. Specifically, the therapeutic action of suggestion, both in its more usual forms and as hypnotic suggestion, has shown to what unexpected extent such action may proceed in susceptible individuals. The well-informed and capable physician requires no instruction on this point; his medical education furnishes him with the means of determining the symptoms of true organic disorder, of functional derangement, and of the modifications of these under the more or less unconscious interference of an unfortunate nervous system. It is quite as human for the physician as for other mortals to err; and there is doubtless as wide a range among them, as among other pursuits, of ability, tact, and insight. "But when all is said and done," the fundamental fact remains that the utilization of the mental factor in the alleviation of disease will be best administered by those who are specifically trained in the knowledge of bodily and of mental symptoms of disease. Such application of an established scientific principle may prove to be a jewel of worth in the hands of him who knows how to cut and set it. The difference between truth and error, between science and superstition, between what is beneficent to mankind and what is pernicious, frequently lies in the interpretation and the spirit as much as, or more than, in the fact. The utilization of mental influences in health and disease becomes the one or the other according to the wisdom and the truth and the insight into the real relations of things, that guide its application. As far removed as chemistry from alchemy, as astronomy from astrology, as the doctrine of the localization of function in the brain from phrenology, as hypnotic suggestion from animal magnetism, are the crude and perverse notions of Christian Scientist or Metaphysical Healer removed from the rational application of the influence of the mind over the body.

X

The growth and development of the occult presents an interesting problem in the psychology of belief. The motives that induce the will to believe in the several doctrines that have been passed in review are certainly not more easy to detect and to describe than would be the case in reference to the many other general problems — philosophical, scientific, religious, social, political, or educational — on which the right to an opinion is accepted as an inalienable heritage of humanity or at least of democracy. Professor James tells us that often " our faith is faith in some one else's faith, and in the greatest matters this is most the case." Certainly the waves of popularity of one cult and another reflect the potent influence of contagion in the formation of opinion and the guidance of conduct. When we look upon the popular delusions of the past through the achromatic glasses which historical remoteness from present conditions enables us to adjust to our eyes, we marvel that good and great men could have been so grossly misled, that obvious relations and fallacies could have been so stupidly overlooked, that worthless and prejudiced evidence could have been accepted as sound and significant. But the opinions to which we incline are all colored o'er with the deep tinge of emotional reality, which is the living expression of our interest in them or our inclination toward them. What they require is a more vigorous infusion of the pale cast of thought; for the problem of the occult and the temptations to belief which it holds out are such as can be met only by a sturdy application of a critical logic. Only as logical thoroughness comes to prevail over superficial plausibility, as beliefs come to be formed and evidence estimated according to their intrinsic value rather than according to their emotional acceptability, will the propagandum of the occult meet with greater resistance and aversion.

The fixation of belief proceeds under the influence both of general and of special forces ; the formation of a belief is at once a personal and a social reaction — a reaction to the evidence which recorded and personal experiences present, and to the current beliefs of our environment. To an equal extent is the reaction determined by the temperament of the reagent. And although the resulting individual beliefs, however complex, are not matters of chance nor are their causes altogether past finding out, yet some of their contributing factors are so vague and so inaccessible that they are most profitably considered as specific results of more or less clearly discerned general principles ; and in many respects there is more valid interest in the general principles than in the particular results. It is interesting, and it may be profitable, to investigate why this area is wooded with oak and that with maple, but it is somewhat idle to speculate why this particular tree happens to be a maple rather than an oak, even if it chances to stand on our own property, and to have an interest to us beyond all other trees.

Among the more tangible tendencies that in various ways lead to the occult there is distinguishable what may be termed the intensely personal temperament, — the mental attitude that absorbs knowledge only when dissolved in an all-pervading personal medium ; the attitude that finds a paramount significance in the personal interpretation of experiences, and reacts to massive and extensive generalizations most vaguely and impotently ; the attitude that offers a weak and verbal assent to scientific principles and to the realities of nature, but inwardly cherishes an intense belief in the personal purport of the order of events, and earnestly seeks for a precise explanation of individual happenings. "The chronic belief of mankind," says Professor James, "that events may happen for the sake of their personal significance is an abomination." It is this chronic mental habit that broods upon the problem of subjective experiences, and is ready to recognize in signs and omens the guiding principle of rationality; not that this is always done designedly and superstitiously, but the underlying bent obscures the consideration of experience in any other than a personal light, and obstructs that illumination of the concrete by the generic, which constitutes an indispensable factor in the growth of wholesome thought. The victim of this unfortunate habit will remain logically unfit to survive the struggle against the occult. Only in so far as he succeeds in getting away from his personal perspective will he be able to appreciate the true status of the problem which enlists his interest. Above all is it necessary to subordinate explicit individual explanations to the general illumination of well-established principles. It may be interesting to note that the partaking of mince-pie at evening induces bad dreams, but it is hardly profitable to speculate deeply why my dream took the form of a leering demon with the impolite habit of squatting on my chest. The stuff that dreams are made of is not susceptible of that type of analysis. The most generous allowance must be made for coincidences and irrelevancies, and it must be constantly remembered that the obscure phenomena of psychology, and, indeed, the phenomena of more thoroughly established and intrinsically more definite sciences, cannot be expected to pass the test of detailed and concrete combinations of circumstances. In other classes of knowledge the temptation to demand such explicit explanations of observations and experiences is not so strong, because of the absence of an equally strong personal interest; but clearly this does not affect the logical status of the problem.

The reply to this argument I can readily anticipate ; and I confess that my admiration of Hamlet is somewhat dulled by reason of that ill-advised remark to Horatio about there being more things in heaven and earth than are dreamt of in our philosophies. The occultist always seizes upon that citation to refute the scientist. He prints it as his motto on his books and journals, and regards it as a slow poison that will in time effect the destruction of the rabble of scientists, and reveal the truth of his own Psycho-Harmonic Science or Heliocentric Astrology. It is one thing to be open-minded, and to realize the incompleteness of scientific knowledge, and to appreciate how often what was ignored by one generation has become the science of the next; and it is a very different thing to be impressed with coincidences and dreams and premonitions, and to regard them as giving the keynote to the conceptions of nature and reality, and to look upon science as a misdirected effort. Such differences of attitude depend frequently upon a difference of temperament as well as upon intellectual discernment. The man or the woman who flies to the things not dreamt of in our philosophy quite commonly does not understand the things which our philosophy very

medicine presented on purely intellectual grounds. Rationality is doubtless a characteristic tendency of humanity, but logicality is an acquired possession, and one by no means firmly established in the race at large. So long as we are reproved by the discipline of nature, and that rather promptly, we tend to act in accordance with the established relations of things; that is rationality. But the recognition of the more remote connections between antecedent and consequent, and the development of habits of thought which shall lead to reliable conclusions in complex situations; and again, the ability to distinguish between the plausible and the true, the firmness to support principle in the face of paradox and seeming nonconformity, to think clearly and consistently in the absence of the practical reproof of nature — that is logicality. It is only as the result of a prolonged and conscientious training, aided by an extensive experience and by a knowledge of the historical experience of the race, that the inherent rational tendencies develop into established logical habits and principles of belief. For many this development remains stunted or arrested; and they continue as children of a larger growth, leaning much on others, rarely venturing abroad alone, and wisely confining their excursions to familiar ground. When they become possessed with the desire to travel among other cultures, their lack of appreciation of the sights which their journeys bring before them gives to their reports the same degree of reliability and value as attaches to the much ridiculed comments of the philistine *nouveaux riches*.

The survey of the modern occult makes it seem quite

utopian to look forward to the day when the occult shall have disappeared, and the lion and the lamb shall feed and grow strong on the same nourishment. Doubtless new forms and phases of the occult will arise to take the place of the old as their popularity declines; and the world will be the more interesting and more characteristically a human dwelling-place for containing all sorts and conditions of minds. None the less, it is the plain duty and privilege of each generation to utilize every opportunity to dispel error and superstition, and to oppose the dissemination of irrational beliefs. It is particularly the obligation of the torch-bearers of science to illuminate the path of progress, and to transmit the light to their successors with undiminished power and brilliancy; the flame must burn both as a beacon-light to guide the wayfarer along the highways of advance, and as a warning against the will-o'-the-wisps that shine seductively in the by-ways. The safest and most efficient antidote to the spread of the pernicious tendencies inherent in the occult lies in the cultivation of a wholesome and whole-souled interest in the genuine and profitable problems of nature and of life, and in the cultivation with it of a steadfast adherence to common sense, that results in a right perspective of the significance and value of things. These qualities, fortunately for our forefathers, were not reserved to be the exclusive prerogative of the modern; and, fortunately for posterity, are likely to remain characteristic of the scientific and antagonistic to the occult.

THE PROBLEMS OF PSYCHICAL RESEARCH

I

THE division of the sciences reflects the diversity of human interests; it represents the economical adaptation of organized thought to the conditions of reality; and it likewise recognizes the intrinsically and objectively distinct realms and aspects, in which and under which phenomena occur. It is obvious that the sciences were shaped by human needs; that physics and chemistry and geology and biology and psychology do not constitute independent departments of nature's régime, but only so many aspects of complex natural activities; that a cross-section of the composite happenings of a cosmic moment would reveal an endlessly heterogeneous concomitance of diverse forms of energy acting upon diverse types of material; that, as we confine our attention somewhat arbitrarily to one or another component of the aggregate, we become physicists, or chemists, or geologists, or biologists, or psychologists; that, indeed, Nature is all things to all men. There is, furthermore, a community of spirit between the several sciences, as there is a logical unity of method and purpose within the realm of each. However ignorant they may be of one another's facts, the chemist and the psychologist readily appreciate one another's purposes, and find a bond of sympathy in the pursuit of a commonly inspired though differently applied method. The search for objective truth, the extension of the realm of law and regularity, the expansion and organization of the army of facts constantly marshaled and reviewed and made ready for service, the ever widening development of principles and the furthering of a deeper insight into their significance, — these are ideals for the advancement of science, far easier of expression than of execution, but the clear and accepted formulation of which itself attests a highly developed stage of accurate thought.   A clear-cut conception of the purposes and methods of scientific investigation and of the scope of the several sciences is a dearly bought product of generations of well-directed, as also of misdirected, effort.   The path of progress leading to this achievement has been tortuous and indirect; there has been much expenditure of energy that resulted merely in marking time, in going through the movements of locomotion but with no advance, in following a false trail, or, through a loss of the sense of direction, in coming back after a circuitous march to an earlier starting-point.   It is easy, when a certain height is reached, to look down and back, and see how much more readily the ascent might have been accomplished ; but it is a very different matter to form a successful plan for attaining the next higher commanding point. It is inevitable that there shall be differences of opinion as to course and manœuvre, and errors of judgment of commission and omission ; but such diversity is quite consistent with an underlying coöperation and singleness of purpose.   It is in the inspiration and in the execution of that purpose that science becomes differentiated from the unscientific and non-scientific.

Between the organized effort and well-recognized plan of action of science and the chaotic movements of the untutored mind, there is a marked contrast. The savage, like the child, constantly meets with the unexpected ; every experience lying outside his narrow beaten track stirs him with a shock and often fills him with fear — the handmaid of ignorance. He is apt to picture nature as a fearful monster, and to people the world with tyrannical beings. Step by step the region of the known expands, and suggests the nature of the unknown ; men expect, they foresee, they predict. The apparent chaos of mutually inimical forces gives way to the profound harmony of unifying law. And yet the unknown and the borderland that separates it from the known are always near by, to tempt curiosity and the spirit of adventure.

The problem here to be considered relates to the attitude which may most properly and profitably be taken with regard to the outlying phenomena of the mind. Are they outcasts, to be treated in a spirit of charity and forbearance ? Are they the true owners of the land, driven off, like the Indian before the white man, by the relentless march of civilization to a prescribed reservation ? Are they the unjustly deposed and rightful heirs, soon to be restored to their kingdom by a fairer and more searching examination of their title ? Or are they, gypsy-like, of obscure origin, surviving in a civilization which they are in but not of, attempting to eke out an uncertain existence by peddling relics of antiquated lore to the curious and the credulous ?

II

The current usage of the term "Psychical Research" takes its meaning from the Society for Psychical Research, founded in England in 1882. The original programme of the society involved a systematic investigation of "that large group of debatable phenomena designated by such terms as mesmeric, psychical, and Spiritualistic." "From the recorded testimony of many competent witnesses," it is urged, "there appears to be, amidst much delusion and deception, an important body of remarkable phenomena, which are *prima facie* inexplicable on any generally recognized hypothesis, and which, if incontestably established, would be of the highest possible value." The work of investigation of these "residual phenomena" was intrusted to six committees, who were to inquire severally into "the nature and extent of any influence which may be exerted by one mind upon another, apart from any generally recognized mode of perception;" into hypnotism, the so-called mesmeric trance, clairvoyance, and other allied phenomena; to undertake a revision of Reichenbach's researches with reference to discovering whether his "sensitives" possessed "any power of perception beyond a highly exalted sensibility of the recognized sensory organs;" to investigate the reports of apparitions at the moment of death, and of houses reputed to be haunted; to inquire into the causes and general laws of the phenomena of Spiritualism; and to collect material relative to the history of these subjects. It is the investigation of these topics from the point of view prevalent in the publications of this Society that constitutes the definition of Psychical Research. This phrase, which has come into prominence within less than a score of years, has no simple or familiar synonym; it must not be interpreted by the combined connotation of its component words, but must be accepted as the technical equivalent of the trend and content of a certain type of investigation of obscure phenomena or alleged phenomena, in most of which psychological factors are prominent.

If the term may at all be brought within the circle of the sciences, it certainly there assumes a somewhat unique position. It naturally becomes the analogue, or it may be the rival of Psychology; yet its precise status and its logical relations to other departments of scientific research are far from obvious. The modern conception of Psychology is generously comprehensive; it encompasses the endlessly variable and complex processes of human mentality; it pursues with enthusiasm the study of developmental processes of intelligence in childhood, in the animal world, in the unfoldment of the race; it studies, for their own value, the aberrant and pathological forms of mental action, and brings these into relation with, and thus illuminates the comprehension of the normal. It forms affiliations with physiology and biology and medicine, with philosophy and logic and ethics, with anthropology and sociology and folk-lore; it borrows freely from their materials, and attempts to interpret the materials thus borrowed from the psychological point of view and to infuse into them its distinctive spirit. Surely Psychical Research should be able to find a nook in so commodious a home; if the problems of Psychical Research are legitimate members of the psychological family, some provision should be possible for their reception within the old homestead. Nor does this group of problems represent a difference of school, in some such way as the homœopathists represent a secession from the regular school of medicine ; nor can it be regarded as the special study of the unusual and the abnormal in the sphere of mind, and thus stand in the relation which teratology or pathology bears to physiology and anatomy: for in that event it would constitute a simple division of Abnormal Psychology, and although Psychical Research has close alliance with the latter, it cannot be, and is unwilling to be regarded as a subordinate portion of that domain.

From a survey of the literature of Psychical Research one might readily draw the inference that whereas Psychology studies the recognized and explicable phases of mental phenomena, Psychical Research is occupied with the disputed and mysterious. One might also conclude that whereas Psychology is concerned with the phenomena commonly associated with mental activities and their variation under normal as also under unusual and pathological circumstances, Psychical Research is interested in the demonstration of supernormal faculties, and in the establishment of forms of mentality that diverge from and transcend those with which every-day humanity is permitted to become familiar; and that, moreover, in some of its excursions Psychical Research does not limit itself to mental manifestations, but investigates undiscovered forms of physical energy, and seriously considers whether behind and beyond the world of phenomena there is another and a different world, in which the established order and the mental and material laws of this planet do not obtain. But the unwarranted character, not to say absurdity, of such a differentiation or classification is at once apparent, if we attempt to carry it over into other departments of science. Speculations in regard to the constitution of the earth's centre or as to the future of our planet, if legitimate in character, are as readily incorporable into geology as the consideration of more definite and better known phenomena; biologists recognize that there are mythical as well as anomalous portions of their domain, but do not consider that freaks of nature either destroy the validity of anatomical and physiological principles, or demand a totally distinct and transcendent organization or method for their study. The chemist may become interested in the examination of what was really done when it was supposed that other metals were converted into gold; the physicist may become interested in the applications of electricity and magnetism, of optical reflections and images in the production of stage illusions; but the conception of chemistry and of physics naturally embraces considerations of the growth, the errors, and the applications of these sciences. And while these comparisons do not furnish a complete parallel to the relation that seems to pertain between Psychology and Psychical Research, yet it is as true in the one case as in the others, that the differentiation of a group of problems on the basis of unusualness of occurrence, of mysteriousness of origin, of doubtful authenticity, or of apparent paradoxical or transcendent character, is as illogical as it is unnecessary. The legitimate problems of Psychical

Research are equally and necessarily genuine problems of Psychology, that require no special designation. They need not be especially important, nor interesting, nor profitable, nor well comprehended problems of Psychology, but they belong there if they are scientific problems at all. The objection to Psychical Research is not a verbal one; it is an objection to the separation of a class of problems from their natural habitat, an objection to the violent transplanting of a growth from its own environment. It is a protest against the notion that while the psychologist may be listened to with respect and authority in one portion of his topic, the layman and the member of the Society for Psychical Research are equally or more competent to pronounce judgments in a closely allied field. It is a protest against the view that for the comprehension of such processes as sensation and perception a course in Psychology may be useful, but that telepathy may be established by any moderately intelligent but not specially informed percipient and agent; or that the study of hallucinations is indeed a complex and difficult subject, but haunted houses, and phantasms of the living, offer a proper occupation for a leisure hour. All this is wrong and absurd; and yet it is hardly an exaggeration to declare that a majority of those who profess a deep interest in, and express an opinion about the one group of topics, would be surprised to have demanded of them a familiarity with the data of Psychology as a prerequisite to an intelligent co-operation in Psychical Research. If the problems of Psychical Research, or that portion of the problems in which investigation seems profitable, are ever to be illuminated and exhibited in an intelligible form, it will only come about when they are investigated by the same methods and in the same spirit as are other psychological problems, when they are studied in connection with and as a part of other general problems of normal and abnormal Psychology. Whether this is done under the auspices of a society or in the psychological laboratories of universities is, of course, a detail of no importance. It is important, however, what the trend, and the spirit, and the method, and the purpose of the investigation may be; as it is equally important, what may be the training, and the capabilities, and the resources, and the originality, and the scholarship of the investigators.

Is the " psychical researcher " then merely a psychologist gone astray ? Is he a mere dilettante, an amateur collector of curious specimens, or is he something very different from a psychologist ? He is doubtless one or the other or all of these. He may be a psychologist in the truest and best sense of the word ; and as all psychologists have their special interests, so his may be centred in the group of phenomena which have been unwisely separated from their *milieu*, and have been inaptly termed " Psychical Research." I am ready not only to admit but to emphasize that a considerable portion of the influential contributors to Psychical Research are animated by as truly scientific motives, and carry on their work with as much devotion and ability, with as careful a logical acumen, with as shrewd comprehension of the dangers and difficulties of their topic, as characterize the labors of any other field of psychological endeavor. But this state-

ment can by no means be extended to all ; nor does it at
all militate against the opinion that many of those to
whom it does apply, subscribe to illogical and pernicious conclusions, and indirectly encourage a most unfortunate attitude in others.

III

Approaching the matter next from a descriptive
point of view, it becomes pertinent to inquire what
are the actual interests which give vitality to Psychical Research, which support the investigator in his
laborious and tedious collection and compilation of
cases, which provide the membership for the Society
for Psychical Research, and the still wider circle of
interested readers, which induce so many correspond-
ents to record long and painstaking accounts of their
peculiar " psychical " experiences, which make the discussion of these matters a favorite topic of conversation.   That these interests are diverse is obvious ; yet
they fall naturally into a few groups or types, of which
the occult interest is probably the most widespread.
This, in its pronounced form, proceeds upon a suppressed
or acknowledged conviction that the world which science
reveals is but a torso of reality ; that its very head —
that which gives significance and expression to the
whole — may be missing, and can only be restored
from isolated fragments, themselves to be found by
rare good fortune.   The key to the riddle of existence
is to be sought in the personal significance of events ; in
moments of great stress and strain, in critical emergen-
cies when communication between individuals deeply
concerned must be established though the heavens

...ed that the heavens *do* occasionally fall,
... of earth are transcended, and the phan-
... dying are telepathically wafted to the
...nsciousness of the interested kinsman or
...Apparitions and presentiments are interpreted
...ic symbols of the order of events, which cast
...hadows before or coincidently with them. The
intelligence of the departed, likewise, is discerned in
these manifestations; and through haunted houses and
séance chambers, through the inspired utterances of
entranced mediums, messages are revealed that indicate conclusively the impossibility of their transmission
through ordinary channels, or, it may be, their unmistakable "spiritual" origin. The supernormal, transcendent, undiscovered world of the occult shines
through, though fitfully and visible only to those who
have eyes to see, the commonplace, constrained phenomena of earth-bound reality. Variable as may be
the formulation and trend of this interest, yet in some
form this suspicion or quasi-belief (for which the term
"occult" seems appropriate) that there are things undreamt of in our philosophy, that these residual phenomena are profoundly significant and afford a glimpse
of the great unknown, as well as of the fallibility and the
poverty of scientific conceptions, furnishes a very considerable *clientèle* of Psychical Research. The why
and wherefore of this inclination need not here be discussed; its prevalence is unmistakable. And though
it appears now in a crude and superstitious guise,
and again in a more refined and critical attitude, and
more rarely is unwillingly assumed as the only possible
alternative in the face of striking personal and other

evidence, yet there is a sufficient communi
in these several positions to warrant their incl
common though variable type.   As applied to l
cal Research, it is important neither to generalize f
the worst nor from the best expressions of this occu
interest, but to appreciate its range of distribution
amid the diversity of temperament and endowment.

As the occult interest recedes to an obscure position
in the background, and as the foreground and middle
distance come to be suffused with the light of critical
discernment and of the scientific spirit of inquiry, the
"psychical researcher" approximates to the psychological point of view. This essentially psychological interest is necessarily a strong one in some of the distinctive problems of Psychical Research, and often mingles
with other interests to form a curious composite. It
may be a morbid, an uninformed, a misguided, a dilettante interest, but its psychological character may be
noted without implication of any further comment of
approval or disapproval. Favorably interpreted, this
psychological interest is an interest in the intrinsic
nature and analysis of mental processes, — an interest
in tracing the various threads that compose the twisted
strands of consciousness, in following the kaleido-
scopic transformations wrought by attention and association, in observing the play of habit, the subtle processes of illusion and misinterpretation, the unexpected
intrusion of the subconscious, and likewise in the pursuit of these as exemplified in concrete instances ; among
others, in such alleged phenomena as are commonly
described as " mesmeric, psychical, and Spiritualistic."

While this interest may be combined with the occult

interest, the two are not really congenial and are in essence antagonistic. We are all rational only in spots; and many a " psychical researcher " pursues some of his investigations under the guidance of a scientifically psychological interest, while in other directions the occult interest takes the helm. The analysis of the contrast between the two may be helpful in realizing more fully the divergences of Psychology and Psychical Research. The " psychical researcher " wishes to prove or to disprove something; with regard to this or that phenomenon he wishes to know " what there is in it," and is accordingly attracted to phenomena which seem to have something mysterious in them. As soon as he succeeds in finding a consistent and commonplace explanation for a group of phenomena, his main curiosity is satisfied, and he takes to pastures new. When once he has shown that theosophic marvels are the result of trickery and collusion, then the physical appearances of Theosophy have been *explained*. It has been demonstrated that there is "nothing in them," that is, nothing transcendental. The verdict is given, and the court passes on to the next case. But the psychologist's interest in how Mme. Blavatsky performed her astral manifestations was always a very subordinate and incidental one; the logical scientist, whether he happened to be physicist or biologist or psychologist, was quite convinced that Mme. Blavatsky had not discovered the means of carrying ponderables by unseen agencies from " China to Peru " (which, by the way, would, if possible, be a matter for the physicist and not at all for the psychologist to investigate), any more than she had been able to dis-

cover the secret of immortality (which would in turn
be a biological discovery), or had been able to leave
her body in New York, while her "astral" soul in-
spected what was going on in India (which might
indeed be regarded as a psychological feat). The
psychological problem of Theosophy, so far as there is
one, is of a different type; it takes up the inquiry
as to how such marvelous pretensions come to be
believed, by what influences conviction is formed and
doctrines spread. It contributes an incident or an
apt illustration to the psychology of belief, or to the
social psychology of contagion. The psychologist is
interested in the illustration which such a movement
affords of the action of certain mental processes and
influences; and his interest persists, whether there is
presumably "something in it," or not. The resulting
difference in attitude between the psychologist and the
"psychical researcher" is indeed fundamental, and
even more so in principle than in practical issue.

It is desirable but not easy to find parallel illustrations of this difference in attitude in other than psychological discussions; but perhaps the following may
be pertinent. If the widespread interest in the North
Pole were merely that in the possibility of its furnishing the key to the mystery of the northward-turning
magnet, and were at once to disappear upon the removal of the mystery, such an interest would be quite
parallel to that of the "psychic researcher;" but the
interest of the true physicist in any physical phenomenon which in the future may be demonstrated to
exist at the North Pole would be a persistent one, and
one depending for its value on the illlustration thus

revealed, not of mystery but of recognized physical principles. Furthermore, be it observed that however valuable may be the physical facts obtainable by a polar expedition, there is no overwhelming obligation resting upon every physicist to desert his laboratory and embark for the farthest north; but that such expeditions are decided by considerations of general interest, expediency, and importance. There is no obligation resting upon the physicist any more than upon the psychologist to make large sacrifices for the pursuit of ill-defined residual phenomena, and certainly not for the refutal of far-fetched theories and suggested supernatural notions. Physicist and psychologist alike contribute most to the advancement of their science by an open-minded but systematic pursuit of definite, significant, and logically fashioned problems.

Let it not be inferred from the emphasis placed upon this contrast that Psychical Research is in itself to be condemned or to be regarded as useless. Not at all; only in many aspects it is not psychological, and the psychologist is under no obligation to find an interest in, nor to occupy himself with, this aspect of things, if his general trend does not happen to point that way. The physicist may be called upon with equal propriety to aid in many inquiries which the Society for Psychical Research has undertaken. Among the early records of the Society appears an account of a man who presented himself with an iron ring on his arm, far too small to have been slipped over his hand, and who seemed to imply that possibly the spirits put it there, or that it came on through some supernatural agency. This was regarded as a proper case for the Society for Psychical

Research to examine. If it could have been demonstrated that the ring reached its position through the exercise of the will of some living persons or spirits, the phenomenon, I suppose, would in some sense be psychological; if it were demonstrated that it came transported through the fourth dimension of space, it might be termed physical. But in reality it was probably physiological, for there was evidence that it was by the effects of etherization that the hand was contracted and that the ring was forced over it. Surely it is most absurd to designate such an inquiry, however interesting and proper it may be regarded, Psychical Research. It certainly is a highly commendable function for a society to take upon itself the investigation of such claims as theosophy or spiritualism put forward, whenever movements of this type are likely to develop into psychic epidemics or to prove a social menace. Any authoritative body that will exhibit the absurdity of such claims, and expose the true *modus operandi* of the manifestations, will perform an important civic function. Such a function was performed by the Royal Commission of 1784, in exposing the vain pretensions and the insidious dangers of animal magnetism; Mr. Hodgson's investigations of theosophy, the Seybert Commission's report on spiritualism, are both able and useful contributions of the same type; and, at present, an authoritative statement regarding the theoretical absurdity and the practical dangers of Christian Science might prove efficacious. Such special investigations represent the practical application of science to concrete conditions and problems; they are woefully misnamed, and their significance is likely to be misinterpreted, when they are presented as Psychical Research, and are grouped along with other problems of a totally different nature.

I shall next touch briefly upon other diverse yet allied interests in Psychical Research, which may serve to illustrate further the various avenues of approach to this heterogeneous group of problems. I shall speak of these as the explanatory, the investigative, and the anthropological interests. The first is satisfied with finding out how alleged marvels are really performed; it takes up the physical phenomena of spiritualism or theosophy; it investigates conjuring tricks; it discovers the origin of noises in haunted houses; it ferrets out the means whereby mediums obtain knowledge of their sitters' private affairs. This is proper work for experts in prestidigitation and for detectives, — not for all such, for to be successful, the conjurer and the detective must have special knowledge and fitness for this branch of the trade. While the facts thus gathered may be useful as illustrative material to the psychologist, they form no essential part of his profession; nor is there any special reason why he should be best suited to determine the technical *modus operandi* of such manifestations. That some psychologists with a strong interest in this type of phenomena might properly coöperate in such an investigation, if they chose, is too obvious to merit remark; but to trace out and expose trickery cannot be imposed upon the burdensome duties of the psychologist.

With a certain type of " psychical researcher " this explanatory interest is the dominant one; and by dispelling error and replacing false notions by true ones he may perform a useful service to the community.

The explanatory interest is quite certain to be supplemented by the investigative, and that because the latter soon becomes necessary to the former. While the one is concerned with the explanation and description of the actual marvels accomplished, the other must consider also what is reported and what is believed to have been accomplished. The mechanism of a trick, whether brought forward as evidence of spiritualism or not, when clearly exhibited, explains the trick; a loose board under the roof, or the reflection from a lustrous surface, may at once reveal how mysterious noises and lights were really produced. But one must go farther to account for the recognition of relatives in the form of the medium covered with flimsy drapery, for the automatic spelling out of messages, or for the successes of guessing experiments. These two interests thus proceed hand in hand and furnish valuable material which the psychologist is ready to interpret and to utilize; for the study of how false beliefs spread, of how deception proceeds, teems with points of psychological significance. This, however, is by no means a unique characteristic of Psychical Research; there are also interesting psychological points in such diverse occupations as the actor's profession, in juggling and tricks of skill, in advertising, in religious revivals, etc. It is highly desirable that the materials thus gathered should be psychologically utilized, and it is equally desirable that such material should be collected. Many valuable studies in Psychical Research, which owe their origin not to a truly psychological interest but to this general explanatory and investigative interest, have incidentally brought to light material of great suggestiveness for the psychologist, and material which quite possibly would not otherwise have been discovered. I am more than willing to contribute whatever I can to the maintenance of a Coöperative Psychological Investigation Society which shall stand ready to take up the investigation of any phenomena which promise to yield data of psychological interest; which shall, however, keep far removed from any phase of the transcendental or the occult; which shall not feel itself under any obligation to *disprove* any improbable or absurd hypothesis which this or that seeker for notoriety may choose to put forward; which shall not be dominated merely by the spirit of finding out whether there is "anything in" one movement or another, but will simply stand ready to supplement the work of the academic laboratories by undertaking, in the same spirit, a special form of investigation, which, under existing circumstances, such laboratories or their individual directors cannot expediently undertake.

The anthropological interest, above referred to, is to my mind a most valid one, and is best represented in Mr. Andrew Lang's volume, "Cock Lane and Common Sense." Mr. Lang there examines the stories of ghosts and apparitions, and clairvoyance, and spiritual knocks and raps, and strange influences, and haunted places, not at all for determining how little or how much these things are true, but how they come to be believed in. How is it that the same tale is told, the same powers credited, the same manifestations produced, in evidence of the supernatural? In savage as well as in ancient magic, in the stories current in former centuries as well as in our own day and generation, there is a pro-

nounced generic similarity. There is certainly as strong
an interest in the investigation of the growth and
distribution of these beliefs as of the other clusters
of belief which anthropology and folk-lore consider.
And, moreover, recently acquired knowledge of hypnotic and automatic phenomena, of hyperæsthesia and
nervous disease, shed much light on the obscure tales
of the past, and assist the comprehension of how such
beliefs could have originated. In brief, Mr. Lang
outlines the programme for a " Comparative Psychical
Research," and tells us that " we follow the stream of
fable, as we track a burn to its head, and it leads us
into shy and strange scenes of human life, haunted by
very fearful wild fowl, and rarely visited, save by the
credulous. There may be entertainment here, and, to
the student of his species, there may be instruction."
Part of the instruction will consist in gaining an increased familiarity with the psychological conditions
which produce and foster these narratives and beliefs,
and with their social and traditional significance; in
concluding, with Mr. Lang, " that the psychological
conditions which begat the ancient narratives produce
the new legends."

IV

Thus far, our attention has been centred upon the
tendenz, the basis of interest, and the affiliations of
Psychical Research. It will be well to turn to a consideration of the content of the problems. Inasmuch
as the term represents a convenient but arbitrary
designation of a heterogeneous group of phenomena,
we are prepared to find that the data of the several

problems thus collected will be as diverse as their methods of study. We may begin with the group of problems which might properly be considered in the chapter of Abnormal Psychology that is devoted to the milder forms of aberrant or unusual mental phenomena. The study of hypnotism occupies a prominent place in Psychology and in Psychical Research. The remarkable exhibitions of extreme suggestibility, particularly the hyperæsthesia thus inducible, and again the illumination of the subconscious thereby effected, have brought about a realizing sense of how fearfully and wonderfully we are made. Between savage priest and doctor, and Delphic oracle, and mediæval ascetic, and magnetic somnambule, and inspirational medium, there is an irregular connection in their entrance into a trance-like condition involving a readjustment of the strata of consciousness and of the distribution of authority in the hierarchy of the nervous centres. This was and remains one of the gateways to the land of marvel and mystery. The importance of hypnotism in Psychology is in its use, both as a method of exhibiting the relations of processes not otherwise accessible to experiment, and as a demonstration of the actual possibilities of suggestion in health and disease. The hypnotic phenomena are intrinsically interesting and valuable as contributions to the natural history of mentality; the hypnotic method of study offers the experimental psychologist the opportunity to apply his most potent aid to research in precisely that field of inquiry in which the experimental methods of ordinary consciousness are least available.

In this domain, the psychologist and the "psychical

researcher" proceed most amicably; and yet their purposes and points of view lead them frequently to part
company, although it may be only for a brief *au
revoir*. When the "psychical researcher" leaves the
main highway to track a possible "telepathic" hypnotic subject, or one who, while hypnotized, is sensitive to the magnetic current, or who experiences the
characteristic effects of drugs applied in sealed vials to
the back of the neck, or who falls into the hypnotic
condition when handling a "magnetized" doll, — the
psychologist is apt to decline the invitation to join in
the pursuit. I should advise him, however, to go along
for the sake of the excellent illustrations thus obtainable of the effects of unconscious suggestion. From
the time of the first serious investigation of these
phenomena up to the present, unconscious suggestion
has been one of the most potent influences for the production of alleged marvels and pseudo-phenomena.
All the series of experiments brought forward at
irregular intervals during the past century to establish supernormal sensibilities have depended for their
apparent success (apart from trickery) upon unconscious suggestion of the operators, combined with the
shrewd assimilation of the desired or expected result
on the part of the subjects. The transposition of the
senses discovered by Pététin (1787), the hypnotized
subjects who in Braid's day (1850) proved the location of the phrenological organs by the appropriateness
of their actions when certain parts of the head were
pressed, the sensitiveness to magnets and hermetically
sealed drugs brought forward by Reichenbach (1845),
and by Bourru and Burot (1885), and Dr. Luys's

(1890) absurd trifling with puppets, and probably, too, Charcot's sharp differentiation of distinct hypnotic conditions (1882), — all furnish illustrations of the subtle possibilities of unconscious suggestion. Besides adorning an interesting psychological tale, they point a moral to the intending investigator, and open his eyes to the extreme caution necessary to exclude this source of error, and to realize the ever-present possibility that, in spite of the sterilizing apparatus and the other equipments of modern research, the germs of this insidious form of delusion may have been unwittingly introduced.

The application of our knowledge of hypnotism to the explanation of alleged supernormal and unusual sensibilities is particularly interesting to the " psychical researcher " ; the general enlargement of our knowledge of these conditions, irrespective of such an application, represents the aim of the psychologist. The latter may indeed cite Mr. Lang's dictum that " science is only concerned with truth, not with the mischievous inferences which people may draw from truth," as an excuse for his own declination to coöperate in the correction of such mischievous inferences.   But the civic conscience of the psychologist may convince him that the removal of error is often an indispensable requisite to the dissemination of truth.

The study of the subconscious or the subliminal consciousness, of multiple personality, of mental automatisms, of involuntary actions, of induced visualizations, of sporadic hallucinations, may be cited as further illustrations of topics interesting to the "psychical researcher" for their bearings upon the apparent transcendence of the normal, and to the psychologist for illustrations of important groups of mental processes and relations. I must refer to the general literature for descriptions of these several phenomena ; the subtle connection between one hypnotic condition and the next, bridging over a period of normal consciousness with complete forgetfulness of the hypnotic consciousness ; the still more subtle evidence for the latency of impressions thus revivable by an appeal to the subconscious ; the elaboration, in trance experiences, of these nether world phenomena into organized personalities, which in the remarkable case reported by Professor Flournoy expanded from a personification of Marie Antoinette to that of a Martian revisiting Mars, describing Martian scenery and customs, and writing in Martian language, and again to the reincarnation of a Hindu princess of four centuries ago ; the affiliation of these cases to those of spontaneous loss of personality in actual life, like that of the Rev. Ansel Bourne, related by Professor James ; the automatic writings performed by hypnotic subjects and by persons in normal conditions ; the power to induce visions by " crystal gazing," and auditory hallucinations by " shell-hearing " ; the census of hallucinations, together with the very important series of observations relative to the psychology of deception, — these represent the more truly psychological contributions of psychologists and " psychical researchers " to their common domain.

The place which the explanation of spiritualistic and theosophic manifestations occupies in Psychical Research has already been noted ; that of ghosts and rappings and haunted houses and *poltergeists* is quite similar. Not wholly yet measurably different is the status of the study of hallucinations, presentiments, and previsions or premonitions. In this entire group of phenomena, the interests of Psychology and of Psychical Research are in the main distinct. This is readily illustrated with reference to the study of hallucinations. These are interesting to the psychologist quite in the same sense as any other natural product of psycho-physiological action; the prevalence of hallucinations under fairly normal conditions presents one out of a large number of interesting details, and forms a proper investigation for the Society for Psychical Research. Their census of hallucinations hardly bears out the conclusions which have been drawn therefrom, but contains much interesting information. When, however, the emphasis of the investigation is placed upon "veridical" hallucinations, and the establishment of the conclusion that so many more of these hallucinations and presentiments "come true," or have a mysterious significance, than chance would allow, then the psychological interest is quite obscured by an interest of a totally different character. A "veridical" hallucination has little psychological pertinence; for it is equally interesting psychologically whether it happens to come true or not. The bearing of the hallucination upon or its origin in some of the occupations of normal waking life; the possibility of its interpretation as a peculiar retroactive illusion of memory, as Professor Royce has suggested for some cases; its significance as an unconscious perception of the shadow already present, not yet visible to consciousness, but coming before the event, — such are significant characteristics of hallucinations. The results of the study of hallucinations may likewise be applied to a determination of their relation to the sum total of the sequences of consciousness that constitute our mental life ; but there is only a most incidental psychological interest in the apparently personally significant or " veridical " aspect of the phenomena. And furthermore, whether they are truly " veridical " or only seemingly so ; whether, in other words, there is evidence enough in quality and quantity to make it a proper scientific inquiry as to the existence of a cause-and-effect-like relation between presentiment and issue, — this is a logical inquiry, although one which, along with other factors, includes psychological considerations.

We here naturally approach what has, on the whole, formed the most conspicuous problem of Psychical Research — that associated with the term " telepathy." It will contribute to clearness of distinction to consider separately the question, whether the evidence accumulated in any wise justifies the conclusion, that there exists a form of communication occasionally going on between mind and mind apart from the recognized channels of sensation. This, too, is a strictly logical question, and is so presented in the following essay. We are here concerned with the status of telepathy in its relation to Psychology and Psychical Research ; this it is possible to indicate briefly. First, if there really exist this extra-normal, fitful and occasional, uncertain and sporadic form of communication, and if it can be conceived of in psychological terms, it forms an interesting, possibly even a momentous contribution to our knowledge of mental processes.

In the present status of the alleged conditions of operations of telepathy, it will hardly modify seriously the direction or scope of the development of Psychology. It being unnecessary to cross bridges before coming to them, it may be sufficient to observe that up to the present there exists no decided prospect either of the demonstration of the reality of this process or of its psychological formulation ; and far less either of its inclusion within the science of Psychology, or of its practical utilization. When the day comes when the incontestable establishment of telepathy, as indeed of any totally novel contribution to Psychology, shall require a revision of psychological principles, Psychology will certainly have to be revised. What, then, many will retort, can be more important for the psychologist than to devote himself to the investigation of telepathy, to decide whether his Psychology needs reconstruction or not ? The answer is near at hand : there is no obligation upon any science to reconstruct its basal principles whenever it is suggested that these are incorrect or inadequate. It is not the suggestion of their inadequacy that is significant, but the concrete facts and evidence available to prove their inadequacy. If a new view can establish itself by its logical cogency and displace an accepted doctrine, if new facts, adequately established, make necessary a revision of current generalizations, no scientist and no science will protest. The present status of telepathy is simply not a formidable candidate for this distinction.

That the evidence brought forward in proof of telepathy, similarly to that adduced for " veridical hallucinations," is capable of psychological interpretation, and also contains interesting illustrations of obscure and subtle mental processes, becomes evident to the discerning student, and merits an extended demonstration. It is in the pursuit of such a demonstration that the psychologist turns to the records of " phantasms of the living," and of experimental thought-transference, thereby adding to an already significant and extensive collection of material illustrative of the influences of the undercurrents of thought-processes. Yet it is by no means urged that this is the only phase of utility which the study of telepathy holds out. That any one who is convinced of his ability to demonstrate telepathy is free to follow his conviction, will not be disputed; that in the course of his investigations he may succeed in revealing the presence of unrecognized forms of mental action, it would be mere dogmatism to deny. Two things, however, should be clearly understood; the first, that his data cannot claim serious attention before they are strong in their validity, and extensive in their scope, and consistently significant in their structure; then, and not before, are they ready for the crucible of scientific logic, from which they may or may not emerge as standard metal, to be stamped and circulated as accepted coin of the realm. The second point relates to the status of the obligation to disprove the telepathic position. This is more often a question of expediency than of right. If the obligation can readily be discharged, it is usually desirable to do so, for the reason that the removal of actual error and misconception is often one of the methods of advancing science; but there is no burden of disproof resting upon the scientist.

V

That the proceedings of the Society for Psychical Research contain valuable material in creditable quantity is evident to any unprejudiced reader; in many ways they are neither so bad nor so good as they are painted to be. That "psychical researchers," though pursuing their labors with different motives, have in one direction and another contributed to the advance of Psychology, I have attempted to make clear. Furthermore, the activity of this Society has been prominent in making the borderland of science of to-day present a far more hopeful aspect than ever before. It has substituted definiteness of statement, careful examination, recognition of sources of error, close adherence to as carefully authenticated fact as is attainable, for loose and extravagant speculation, for bare assertion and obscuring irrelevancy. It has made possible a scientific statement and a definiteness of conception of problems, even where its proposed solution of them may be thought misleading or inadequate. But in my opinion the debit side of the ledger far outbalances the credit side. The influence which Psychical Research has cast in favor of the occult, the enrollment under a common protective authority of the credulous and the superstitious, and the believers in mystery and in the personal significance of things, is but one of the evils which must be laid at its door. Equally pernicious is the distorted conception, which the prominence of Psychical Research has scattered broadcast, of the purposes and methods of Psychology. The status of that science has suffered, its representatives have been misunderstood, its advancement has been hampered, its appreciation by the public at large has been weakened and wrongly estimated, by reason of the popularity of the unfortunate aspects of Psychical Research, and of its confusion with them. Whatever in the publications of Psychical Research seems to favor mystery and to substantiate supernormal powers is readily absorbed, and its bearings fancifully interpreted and exaggerated; the more critical and successfully explanatory papers meet with a less extended and less sensational reception. Unless most wisely directed Psychical Research is likely, by not letting the right hand know what the left hand is doing, to foster the undesirable propensities of human nature as rapidly as it antagonizes them. Like indiscriminate almsgiving, it has the possibilities of affording relief and of making paupers at the same time. Particularly by the unwarranted acceptance of telepathy as a reality or as a working hypothesis, and the still more unwarranted use of this highly hypothetical process as a means of explaining more complex and obscure phenomena, has it defeated one of the most important purposes which it might have served.

The popular as well as the more critical acceptance of Psychical Research, both of the term and of the conceptions associated with it, has disseminated a totally false estimate on the part of the public at large of the scope and purposes of modern Psychology; and has quite possibly given an unfortunate twist to the trend of recent psychological thought. The right appreciation of scientific aims and ideals by the intelligent and influential public has come to be almost indispensable to the favorable advancement of science. Psychology

can less afford than many another science to dispense
with this helpful influence ; and no science can remain
unaffected by persistent misinterpretation of its true
end and aims.   If Psychical Research is to continue in its present temper, it becomes essential to have
it clearly understood just how far its purposes and spirit
are, and how much farther they are not, in accord with
the purposes and the spirit of Psychology.   The opti-
mistic psychologist anticipates the day when he will no

in low life, as
r of mediums.
Psychical Re-
f the concep-
n, the pursuit
roblems in a
rhaps, most of
hology " from
s of Psychical
tly to be de-

20

5 1 2 6

jastrow

THE LOGIC OF MENTAL TELEGRAPHY

WHAT will be pronounced strange or curious is largely determined by the range and composition of the common body of knowledge to whose laws and uniformities the phenomena in question apparently fail to conform. What is passing strange to one generation may become easily intelligible to the next. We all have eyes that see not for all but a limited range of facts and views; and we unconsciously fill out the blind-spots of our mental retinæ according to the habits and acquisitions of the surrounding areas. We observe and record what interests us; and this interest is in turn the outcome of a greater or lesser endowment, knowledge, and training. A new observation requires, as a rule, not a new sense-organ or an additional faculty, nor even more powerful or novel apparatus, but an insight into the significance of quite lowly and frequent things. Most of the appearances of the earth's crust, which the modern geologist so intelligently describes, were just as patent centuries ago as now; what we have added is the body of knowledge that makes men look for such facts and gives them a meaning. And although "the heir of all the ages," we can hardly presume to have investigated more than a modest portion of our potential inheritance; future generations will doubtless acquire interests and points of view which will enable them to fill some of the many gaps in our knowledge, to find a meaning in what we perchance ignore or regard as trivial, and to reduce to order and consistency what to us seems strange or curious or unintelligible. And future generations, by virtue of a broader perspective and a deeper insight, may give little heed to what we look upon as significant, — much as we pronounce irrelevant and superstitious the minute observances whereby primitive folk strive to attract the good fortunes and to avoid the dangers of human existence.

I

The possibility of the transference of thought, apart from the recognized channels of sensation, has been too frequently discussed, with the suppressed or unconscious assumption that our knowledge of the means whereby we ordinarily and normally, consciously and unconsciously, convey to others some notion of what is passing in our own minds, is comprehensive and exhaustive. Nothing could be farther from the truth. Whenever a mode of perception, no matter how limited or apparently trivial, has been thoroughly investigated, there have been discovered, or at least suggested, unrecognized possibilities of its use and development. And no result of experimental inquiry is more constantly illustrated than the extent to which inferences from sensations and the exercise of faculties may proceed without arousing consciousness of their existence. Many color-blind persons remain quite ignorant of their defect; and it was only after the description of his own notable deficiencies by Dalton (in 1794) that the general prevalence of color-blindness became recognized. The fact that a portion of every one's retina is as blind as his finger-tip escaped observation until about two centuries ago; and this because the normal use of our eyes does not present the conditions of its easy detection; and for a like reason we persistently refuse to see the double images that are constantly formed upon our retinæ. With the same unconsciousness that we receive sensations and draw inferences from them, do we give to others indications of what is going on in our minds, and read between their words and under their expressions what "half reveals and half conceals the thoughts that lie within." It is important to emphasize the serious limitations as yet attaching to our knowledge of the detailed possibilities of normal perception and inference, in order to realize the corresponding hesitancy with which we should regard any series of facts, no matter how apparently inexplicable, as evidence of a supernormal kind of mental telegraphy.

A further principle important in this connection, and one which is likewise borne out by experimental inquiry, is the general similarity in our mental machinery in matters great and small, and the resulting frequency with which similar trains of thought may be carried on by different persons as the outcome of similar but independent brain-functioning. There is a natural tendency to exaggerate the individuality of our own ways of thought and expression; and yet but little reflection is necessary to suggest how easily this fond belief may be at least partially delusive. In certain lines of thought, such as mathematics, we should regard it as strange if two thinkers, starting with the premises determined by the problem in hand, should not reach the same conclusion ; in others, such as economic or political questions, we observe the preponderance of evidence in one direction, and yet can appreciate the grounds of a contrary opinion ; and while in still other cases we regard the verdict as a matter of taste or of individual preference, it may be questioned whether this is so unmotived or lawless a process as is commonly assumed. While we properly expect more mental community in certain lines than in others, we have good grounds for believing that it exists everywhere and only awaits the proper modes of investigation to reveal it in its full extent and significance. With the marvelously increased facilities for the dissemination and transportation of thought, the range of such mental community is certain to be correspondingly extended. Coincidences arising from the bringing together of widely separated and apparently unrelated happenings are sure to multiply, when the means of bringing them together are so vastly increased. Each man's world is enlarged by the enlargement of the whole. It becomes possible for him to come into relation with infinitely more persons and events, and the resulting coincidences are nowadays more likely to be noticed and recorded.

If we consider the logical ease with which the successful solution of one portion of a problem suggests the next step ; how imperceptibly and yet effectively sentiments and points of view and the spirit of the time are disseminated ; how many persons there

are in this busily reflective era occupied with similar
thoughts and schemes, and how readily they may come
into communication ; how many are anxiously study-
ing the popular taste and demand to determine what
literary venture or mechanical invention is likely to be
timely and successful ; how the possession of a common
inheritance, patriotic interests, education, literature,
political arena, social usages, newspaper intelligence,
household conveniences, and the endless everyday factors of our complex, richly detailed existence all contribute to our common life, — shall we wonder that
some two or half a dozen intellects should give expression to similar thoughts at nearly the same time?
Would it not be infinitely more wonderful if such
coincidences did not constantly occur? In the more
original contributions to literature, science, and inventions, such thought-correspondences should be rarer;
and certainly this is true. Contrast the number of
striking similarities in the higher walks of literature
and science with those that occur in small inventions.
Hardly a day passes without the coincidence of two
persons thinking of devices for accomplishing the same
purposes, so essentially similar that patents could not
be given to both. It is certainly not difficult to understand why several different patterns of typewriting machines should be invented nearly simultaneously, and it
would not be altogether mysterious if, at the first, two
inventors had independently reached the idea of a writ-
ing-machine at nearly the same time. The experience
of offering an article to an editor and receiving a reply
to the effect that another article dealing with a similar topic in a similar way was already awaiting the

compositor is not unusual.   It is true that these coincidences are of a minor order, but it seems desirable to
emphasize the frequency of these minor forms in order
to suggest the law-abiding character of the rarer or the
more striking forms; for this is just what the normal
distribution of such phenomena would lead us to expect.

It would be pleasant to believe that the application
of the doctrine of chances to problems of this character
is quite generally recognized; but this recognition is
so often accompanied by the feeling that the law very
clearly applies to all cases but the one that happens to
be under discussion, that I fear the belief is unwarranted.   Moreover, the notion seems to prevail that
these coincidences should occur with equal frequency
to all persons; while, in fact, the law of probability provides for the most various distribution among individuals.   However, the attempt, and it may be the sincere
attempt, to apply proper conceptions of probability
and improbability to such problems often fails, because
of an unfortunate mental attitude which presents, with
an outward acquiescence in the objective view of the
problem, an inward conviction in which the subjective
interpretation is really dominant; for this and other
reasons, this objective method of viewing the matter,
however pertinent, is not the most important.

II

One of the most deplorable attitudes towards the
borderland phenomena of which mental telegraphy or
telepathy forms a type, is that which insists upon an
exact and detailed explanation of concrete personal
experiences, and regards these as so essentially peculiar

that it refuses to consider them in connection with
the many other instances of the same class, without
reference to which a rational explanation is unattain-
able. This tendency, to insist that the laws of science shall be precisely and in detail applicable to
individual experiences possessing a personal interest
for us, has wrought much havoc; it has contributed to
superstition, fostered pseudo-science, and encouraged
charlatanism. To antagonize this tendency it is necessary to insist upon the statistical nature of the inquiry.
We should certainly be familiar in this statistic-filled
age with the law-abiding character of individual happenings when considered in large groups. So many
types of facts depending upon individual and heterogeneous motives shoot together and form curves of
surprising regularity; the number of marriages or of
misdirected letters, the falsification of ages or the distribution of heights of individuals, and countless other
items that in individual cases seem accidental, or capricious, or due to a host of minute and unaccountable
factors, none the less present a striking statistical
regularity. The owners of a gaming-table, counting
upon the statistical regularity of the accidental, are
assured of a steady income; they are interested long
enough to obtain an extensive view of the fluctuations,
and to see the law that guides the whole. Not so the
individual player; he is interested only in that particular portion of the game in which his money is at
stake. He detects mysterious laws of fortune and
freaks of luck; sees in a series of coincidences or mo-
mentary successes the proofs of his pet schemes, and
dismisses the general doctrine of chances with disdain,

because it is not obviously applicable to his case.   This influences the losers as well as the winners ; both are absorbed in their own minute portions of the game, and forget that the law makes distinct provision for temporary losses and gains, great and small, but is as indifferent to the times and order of such occurrences as to the personality of those affected.

The distinction between the individual and the statistical aspect of a problem may be further illustrated in the much-discussed question of the differences in brain characteristics of men and women.   When the claimants for woman's equality point to the acknowledged inability of an anatomist to determine whether a particular brain belonged to a man or a woman as conclusive evidence of their contention, they unconsciously assume that the problem is capable of determination in the individual specimen.   A sounder logic would insure greater caution.   The differences in question may be certainly established and typical, and yet depend upon statistical, not upon individual data.   Give the anatomist a goodly number of fairly selected brains and tell him that all the women's brains are in one group, and all the men's brains in another, and he will tell you which group is feminine, which masculine ; and this more than offsets his failure in the former test.   It establishes a statistical regularity.   Individually we may argue that many women of our acquaintance have larger heads than the men ; that the English are not taller than the French, because the Frenchmen we have chanced to meet have been quite as tall as the Englishmen of our acquaintance ; that the laws of chance do not apply to the gaming-table, because on that basis we should have come out even and not as losers ; and that coincidences cannot explain our strange mental experiences, because they are altogether too peculiar and too frequent. It is only in the most complete stages and in the more definite realms that knowledge becomes applicable accurately and definitely to individual cases. For the present it is well if, with such abstruse or rather indefinite material, we can glimpse the statistical regularity of the entire group of phenomena, trace here and there the possible or probable application of general principles, and refuse to allow our opinions to be disarranged by rather startling individual cases. The explanation of these, however interesting they may be to ourselves or enter-taining to others, is not the test of our knowledge of the subject.

I pick up a stone, and with a peculiar turn of the hand throw it from me ; probably no student of me-chanics can exactly calculate the course of that projec-tile, — nor is it worth while. What he can do is to show what laws are obeyed by ideal projectiles, ideally thrown under ideal conditions, and how far the more impor-tant practical cases tend to agree with or diverge from these conditions. It is unfair to test his science by its minute applicability to our special experiences.

When the problems involved in mental telegraphy come to be generally viewed under the guidance of a sound logic, the outlook will be hopeful that the whole domain will gradually acquire definite order ; and that its devotees, after appreciating the statistical regularity of the phenomena, will come to the conclusion that much of the energy and ability now expended in a search for the explanation of complex and necessarily indefinite individual cases, is on the whole unprofitable. With an infinite time and an infinite capacity it might be profitable to study all things; but, at present, sanity consists in the maintenance of a proper perspective of the relative importance of the affairs of the intellectual and the practical life. It may be that the man who puzzles day and night over some trivial mystery expends as much brain energy as a great intellectual benefactor of mankind; but the world does not equally cherish the two.

III

It becomes important in the further consideration of coincidences to emphasize the great opportunity presented in their description for error, for defective observation, for neglect of details, for exaggeration of the degree of correspondence; and equally demonstrable is the slight amount of such error or mal-observation that is all-sufficient to convert a plain fact into a mystery. Consider the disfigurement that a simple tale undergoes as it passes from mouth to mouth; the forgetfulness of important details and the introduction of imaginary ones, exhibited upon the witness stand; the almost universal tendency to substitute inferences from sensations and observations for the actual occurrences; and add to these the striking results of experimental inquiry in this direction — for example, the divergences between the accounts of sleight-of-hand performances or spiritualistic séances and what really occurred — and it becomes less difficult to understand why we so often fail to apply general principles to individual cases. The cases cannot be explained as they are recorded, because as recorded they do not furnish the essential points upon which the explanation hinges. The narrator may be confident that the points of the story are correctly observed, that all the details are given; and yet this feeling of confidence is by no means to be trusted. It is quite possible that the points that would shed most light on the problem are too trivial to attract attention; a slightly imperfect connection as effectively breaks the circuit and cuts off the possibility of illumination as a more serious disturbance. After the explanation is given or the gap supplied or the break discovered, we often wonder how we could have failed to detect the source of the mystery; but before we know what to observe and what to record and what to be on our guard against, the possibility of error is extremely great, far greater than most of us would be willing to make allowance for; and the strict demonstration as also the refutation of a proposed explanation becomes correspondingly difficult.

IV

I turn to another point, in some respects the most important of all; I refer to the readiness with which we interpret as the remarkable frequency of coincidences what is due to a strong interest in a given direction. Inasmuch as we observe what interests us, a recently acquired interest will lead to new observations — that is, new to us, however familiar they may be to others. Take up the study of almost any topic that appeals to human curiosity, and it takes no prophet to predict that within a short time some portion of your reading or your conversation, or some accidental infor-

mation, will unexpectedly reveal a bearing on the precise subject of your study, often supplying a gap which
it would have been most difficult otherwise to fill; but
surely this does not mean that all the world has become
telepathically aware of your needs and proceeded to
attend to them. Some years ago I became interested in
cases of extreme longevity, particularly of centenarian-
ism, and for some months every conversation seemed to
lead to this topic, and every magazine and newspaper
offered some new item about old people.   Nowadays my
interest is transferred to other themes ; but the para-
grapher continues quite creditably to meet my present
wants, and the centenarians have vanished.   When
I am writing about coincidences, I become keen to observe them ; such for example as this : I was reading
for the second time an article on " Mental Telegraphy "
(by Mark Twain in " Harper's Monthly Magazine,"
December, 1891) ; I was occupied with what is there
described as a most wonderful coincidence, the nearly
simultaneous origination by the author and by Mr. William H. Wright of a similar literary venture, — when
I happened to take my eyes from the page and saw on
my desk a visiting-card bearing the name, " W. H.
Wright."   It was not the same W. H. Wright, but a
gentleman whom I had met for the first time a few
hours before, and have not seen since. Had I not been
especially interested in this article and its subject, the
identity of the names would certainly have escaped my
attention, and there would have been no coincidence to
record. Quite apropos both of coincidences and of
their dependence upon personal interest, I find recorded
in a current magazine the experience of one who

became enthusiastically interested in thoroughbred cats : " Strangely enough — for it is a thing which is recurrently strange — I, who had rarely seen any printed matter relating to cats, now found the word in every newspaper. Adopting a new interest is like starting a snowball ; as long as it moves, it gathers other particles to itself."

It is only necessary to become deeply interested in coincidences, to look about with eyes open and eager to detect them, in order to discover them on all sides ; resolve to record all that come to hand, and they seem to multiply until you can regard yourself and your friends as providentially favored in this direction. If your calling develops a taste for matters of this kind, — for example, if you are a writer, with a keen sense for the literary possibilities and dramatic effects of such coincidences, or if you are of an imaginative turn of mind with a pronounced or a vague yearning for the interesting or the unusual; if you have a more generous or more persistent endowment of the day-dreaming, fantastic, self-dramatization of adolescence, that is half unreal and yet half externalized in the vividness of youthful fancy, — is it strange that you should meet with more of these " psychic experiences " than your prosaic neighbor whose thoughts and aspirations are turned to quite other channels, and to whom an account of your experiences might even prove tiresome ? If you cultivate the habit of having presentiments, and of regarding them as significant, is it strange that they should become more and more frequent, and that among the many, some should be vaguely suggestive, or even directly corroborative of actual occurrences ?

The frequent coincidences, which form so influential a factor in disseminating an inclination towards such an hypothesis as telepathy, are doubtless largely the result of an interest in these experiences. This interest is very natural and proper, and when estimated at its true value is certainly harmless; it may indeed contribute material worthy of record for the student of mental phenomena, — or it may give spice to the matter-of-fact incidents of a workaday existence. To many minds, however, the temptation to magnify this interest into a significant portion of one's mental life, to invest it with a serious power to shape belief and to guide conduct, is unusually strong, in some cases almost irresistible. It is this tendency that is essentially antagonistic to a logical view and therefore to a scientific study of these irregular mental incidents; it is this tendency that is responsible for much of the spurious and the unwholesome interest in the problems of mental telegraphy.

It would naturally be expected that the nature and subject-matter of the more frequent types of coincidences and presentiments would throw some light upon their origin, and would in some measure reinforce the general position above taken. We should expect that such coincidences would relate to persons and affairs that are frequently in our thoughts, and that similarities of thought and presentiments based upon them should occur among persons intimately acquainted with one another's thought-habits, at least in regard to that line of thought to which the coincidence relates; these expectations are fairly well borne out by the facts. It is a commonplace observation that presentiments and unusual psychic experiences most frequently relate to those who are dear to us, or in whom we have a momentarily strong interest; that they deal with events which we have anxiously dreaded or desired, or with matters over which we have puzzled or worried; and again, that they occur under conditions of emotional strain, excitement, or anxiety. In brief, they deal with what is frequently in our minds or what more or less unconsciously furnishes the general emotional and intellectual background which gives character to our mood and to our associations of ideas. I need hardly add that it is the more successful and striking coincidences that we remember and record, and the others that are quickly forgotten. Moreover, so large a share of mental operations of the type in question takes place in the region of the subconscious, that our recollection of what has occupied our thoughts is by no means a final authority. Occasionally we detect these subconscious similarities of mental operations, when after a silence the same question or thought shapes itself on the lips of two speakers at the same time; and here again, are not many of those who give utterance to the same thoughts, or finish one another's sentences, intimate companions in the walks of life? Is it strange that in the daily intercourse with a congenial spirit, they should have absorbed enough of one another's mental processes to anticipate, now and then, a step in their association of ideas?

Still another factor that figures somewhat in coincidences relates to events which are sooner or later very likely or quite certain to occur, and in which the coincidence is confined to the close simultaneity of the action on the part of two or more persons concerned. The crossing of letters is easily the best illustration of this type of occurrence which has the semblance of thought-communication.   It is so easy to fall into the habit of delaying all delayable matters as long as possible that it must frequently happen that your own sense of duty is aroused and your correspondent's patience is exhausted at nearly the same time. If A is to hear from B, or B from A, within a period not very definite but still reasonably limited, every day's delay makes it more and more probable that their letters will cross. The same consideration applies to other affairs of daily life; we delay a matter of business and are just about to attend to it when the other party concerned comes to us, or we delay offering some social attention until just as we are about to do so it is asked of us; and so on.   In brief, we find not only in sickness and death, in family ties and friendships, in travel and adventure, but also in the special and in the complicated interests of our civilized life an abundant opportunity for coincidences; and we find that their frequency is clearly related to the commonness of the event, and to its familiarity and closeness of relation to our habits of thought.

V

Reviewing the arguments which have been presented, we find a tendency to underestimate the possibilities of expression and communication through the normal channels of the senses and the subtle inferences based upon them, and also an insufficient appreciation of the unrecognized but by no means supernormal capabilities,

which special and unusual susceptibility or training of
these same powers of interpretation and thought-revela-
tion may bring about; we find, further, a prevalent
underestimation of the generic and at times the specific
similarity of the products of our several diverse and yet
homogeneous mental equipments, and with it a lack of
consideration of the greatly increased facilities for such
mental community afforded by modern conditions of
rapid transit and rapid sharing of the common benefits
of civilization. We find a misconception of the nature
of the application of the doctrine of chances to mental
coincidences, which brings about an apparent recognition
but an intrinsic belittling of the rôle which chance
really plays in the evidence advanced for telepathy;
we find that this error is probably due to an unfortunate, intensely individual view of the problem, which
insists upon an explanation of personal experiences, and
disregards the essentially impersonal and statistical
nature of the inquiry. This unfair attitude (which is
equally unfair if applied to other and more exact data)
renders difficult, if not impossible, a just appreciation
of the theoretical aspect of the problem and of the
application of theory to practice. We find, furthermore,
that the recorded data are likely to involve an unusual
degree of unreliability owing to such natural psychological tendencies as defective observation, exaggeration,
preconception, and the ordinary limitations and failings
of humanity; nor is any serious amount of such neglect
needed to bridge the gap between intelligible fact and
unintelligible mystery. Finally, it is not sufficiently
borne in mind that the data are in large part created
by the subjective attitude of expectation and interest

in such experiences, and that the nature of the more frequent coincidences furnishes satisfactory evidence of their natural relations to dominant interests and occupations. The concordant suggestion from these various considerations is that a very large part of the experiences offered in evidence of mental telegraphy, finds a much more natural and more consistent explanation when viewed as the complex and irregular results of types of mental processes included within the legitimate and recognized domain of psychology. There is no desire to overlook the loose and distant connection that often pertains between the general considerations and the particular phenomena here relevant; on the contrary, this lack of explicit and intimate connection is a logical characteristic of the relation of theory to practice in dealing with such complex and irregular material, and is likely for a long time to remain so. A more properly cultivated logical sense will bring about a more satisfactory appreciation of and a greater intellectual content with this aspect of the problem; it will be recognized that it is wiser to make the best of actual though admittedly unsatisfactory conditions than to fly to evils that we know not of.

VI

I therefore regard the inclination towards a telepathic hypothesis as the result of a defective logical attitude, which in turn may be regarded as the outcome of a natural but unfortunate psychological tendency. In considering the question, " What is the proper inference to be drawn from the accumulated data apparently suggestive of ' communication between mind and mind otherwise than through the known channels of the senses'?'" we are considering a logical problem — a problem of considerable difficulty, not one to be entered upon without deliberation and preparation. In considering the question, " How is it that such evidence is readily accepted as proof of telepathy? How is it that this hypothesis is favored above others intrinsically no less improbable?" we are likewise entering upon a complex problem, but one that is psychological in scope and nature. It is to a more fundamental consideration of these questions that we now turn.

I have based my discussion of mental telegraphy almost wholly upon the occurrence of coincidences (using that term not as the equivalent wholly of chance occurrences, but including suggestive or interesting conjunctions of circumstances in general), for the reason that coincidences — both those of a commonplace character and those that seem to possess a striking personal significance — have prepared the popular mind for the acceptance of the telepathic hypothesis, and still constitute the most formidable array of evidence presented for that hypothesis. The other class of evidence to be considered is the experimental, which may be said to include as its most distinctive type the results of tests in which intentional attempts at mental telegraphy were made under definite conditions and usually with specially selected subjects ; and as another type, the precise verification and registration of presentiments and peculiar and startling " psychic experiences " with reference to their coincidence with death, accidents, and other serious events in life. It may be admitted that the experimental data are equally worthy with the others of a logical analysis, and indeed that they present in some respects different and more favorable conditions for the application of such an analysis. In general, however (and I desire to confine this discussion to the general principles involved and not to the analysis of special cases), the considerations that determine the logical value, or the lack of it, of the one type of evidence are applicable without undue modification to the other. Nor do I consider that the experimental data have seriously modified the logical status of the problem as a whole; nor that they have, except in relatively few cases, been of themselves sufficient to make converts to a belief in telepathy. They have undoubtedly very much strengthened and disseminated that belief; but this implies that a favorable disposition to the belief was already present. It is because it seems to me that the presence of this favorable disposition, albeit in suppressed or half-acknowledged form, is in most cases due to some phase of the argument from coincidences, that I have made it central in my discussion. I must not fail to point out, however, that experiments in thought-transference have one important, and that a logical, advantage over observations of coincidences; this is the possibility which they present of quite accurately allowing for the effect of chance. In coincidences the estimate of chance as the source of the conjunction of events is frequently, if not always, a matter of complex judgment over which serious differences of opinion will occur. Some of the published quantitative estimates made by serious and able students of such problems, of the probabilities that certain coincidences have been due to chance have been pronounced altogether wide of the mark and even absurd by others. In experiments arranged with due precautions there can be no uncertainty on this point; the proportion of successes, that is, of striking coincidences, may be calculated. If the actual number of chance coincidences appreciably exceeds the calculated proportion, and if the theory on which the calculation was based corresponds to the actual conditions, then the results were not due to chance alone. But whether they were due to fraud, or to some unconscious transference of indications, or to telepathy, or to spirit influence, or to interference of the devil, or to the fact that the participants in the experiment were born when the stars and planets presented certain conjunctions, or to the existence of a totally unrecognized form of mental vibrations, — all these are mere hypotheses which may be strong or weak or absurd, according to their power to really account for the results, to their concordance with the sum total of scientific knowledge in this field and with the logical principles guiding the formation of scientific hypotheses. To jump from the conclusion that the results are not due to chance to the conclusion that they are due to telepathy, is no whit more absurd than the position of the astrologer, or the spiritualistic explanation of conjuring tricks. That there is something in these results to be explained is admitted; whether the results have been obtained and recorded in such a way as to contain the clue to their explanation cannot be affirmed; whether our present state of knowledge enables us to explain them may be argued pro and con; whether they are worth serious attention is also a debatable question; but none of these condi-

tions warrants a resort to the telepathic hypothesis.
That hypothesis as all others must be weighed in the
logical balance without prepossession, and with full
realization of the possibility, that " general appearances
suspicious," or " not proven," or a complete suspension of judgment, may be among the present verdicts.

VII

So far as the strength and weakness of the arguments
for mental telegraphy depend upon the perspective of
value attached to the various data and to the conditions
under which these have been gathered, I have presented
my estimate and indicated the burden of my conclusions.   But I am aware that I may have laid myself
open to the charge — which will be brought not by
the advocates of telepathy, but by its most emphatic
opponents — of a neglect of consideration of the general logical status of telepathy as a germane and
legitimate hypothesis.   That the hypothesis of telepathy when carefully interpreted is capable, if not of
explaining the data, at least of being fitted without
undue straining to a large portion of the data, may
be claimed with some plausibility; that I regard the
hypothesis as unwarranted and unnecessary has been
made sufficiently clear.   But what if the hypothesis
is not a legitimate one, not one which the methods and
spirit of science can properly or profitably consider?
If this be the case, it would seem superfluous to consider whether the hypothesis is warranted by the data
or capable of explaining them.   That it is the policy
of science to allow the utmost latitude of opinion and
theory and to interpret the possible in an unprejudiced

and liberal spirit will readily be conceded. That it is equally the policy of science to demand of all claimants for recognition authentic credentials framed in accordance with the laws of logic and the principles of evidence and probability, is sometimes overlooked. Science cannot possibly consider all hypotheses, but only legitimate ones. To explain coincidences and the success of experiments in thought-transference by assuming that there is a demon, whose special business it is to make people have uncanny feelings when their relatives in distant places are dying or in danger, and to suggest to the guesser what is in the mind of the party of the second part in the experiment, is certainly not an hypothesis worthy of consideration by science ; and incidentally be it noted that this hypothesis may be successfully shaped to fit the facts, and cannot be definitely disproved. Some absurd hypotheses may be readily disproved and others not ; but are scientists really called upon to disprove them? There recently fell under my observation a claim for the theory that when persons felt an unaccountable aversion for one another, either at once or after a time of friendship, it was due to their opposite horoscopic natures, and it would be found that their birthdays were not far from six months apart, that is, nearly as far apart as they possibly could be. Divorces, breaches of promise, family feuds, and antipathies at first sight could thus be accounted for. Now, it would involve no very burdensome undertaking to disprove this theory ; but I should not expect a cordial approval of my efforts on the part of my colleagues if I carried through the investigation. The hypothesis is un-

Lenoir Rhyne College
LIBRARY

scientific, or even anti-scientific, and its examination unnecessary and unprofitable. Yet it is not always possible to render so decisive a verdict; and in the present case, while I incline to the belief that the hypothesis of telepathy is, as usually advanced and in essence, an illegitimate one, I still regard it as possible that in the future some modification of this hypothesis may be framed, which will bring it within the scope of a liberal conception of the scientific. It is important to make this attitude perfectly clear: if telepathy means the hypothesis of a new force, that is, the assumption of an as yet uncomprehended mode of the output of energy, subject rigorously to the physical bonds of material causation which make possible a rational conception of psycho-physiological processes; and if, further, some one will put forth a rational conception of how this assumed action can take place apart from the exercise of the senses, I am prepared to admit that this hypothesis is (not sound, or strong, or in accordance with the facts, or capable of explaining the facts, or warranted by the facts, but) one which it is legitimate, though perhaps not profitable, to consider. If, however, telepathy is put forward as a totally new and peculiar kind of action, which is quite unrelated to the ordinary forces with which our senses and scientific observation acquaint us, and which is not subject to the limitations of the material world of causation; if telepathy is supposed to reveal to us a world beyond or behind or mysteriously intertwined with the phenomena of this world, — a world in which events happen not in accordance with the established physical laws, but for their personal significance even in defiance of those laws, — then it becomes impossible for the scientist to consider this hypothesis without abandoning his fundamental conceptions of law and science.

My defense, therefore, for not beginning and possibly confining this discussion to the question of the scientific legitimacy of the telepathic hypothesis is that, in the present status of opinion, it does not seem to me hopeful to influence belief by such a presentation. It seems to me a far more practical step to present the unwarranted character of the hypothesis and its logical insufficiencies as a means of influencing those who had been, or were likely to be, impressed by coincidences and death-warning experiences and guessing experiments. And, moreover, it is necessary, so long as such experiences have a strong hold on the popular imagination and shape the popular conceptions of the nature both of mental processes and of the field of psychology, to portray as well as may be the natural explanation and significance of the phenomena, and to indicate the general trend of the conceptions under which they may be profitably viewed; and this, even though it be but measurably possible to apply general principles to special cases. This step is an essential part of the logical task here attempted. Under other circumstances it would have been advisable, as it always would be proper, to determine the legitimacy of an hypothesis before considering it as worthy of detailed examination on other counts. But here, as is frequently the case, it is a condition and not one of our own choosing that confronts us.

VIII

What is the logical conclusion to be drawn from the data offerable in evidence of some supersensory form of thought-transference, and whence the disposition to believe in the existence of such a procedure? — these remain the central questions of the discussion. As to the former, I can say no more in dismissing the topic than that to me the phenomena represent a complex conglomerate, in which imperfectly recognized modes of sense-action, hyperæsthia and hysteria, fraud, conscious and unconscious, chance, collusion, similarity of mental processes, an expectant interest in presentiments and a belief in their significance, nervousness and ill health, illusions of memory, hallucinations, suggestion, contagion, and other elements enter into the composition; while defective observation, falsification of memory, forgetfulness of details, bias and prepossession, suggestion from others, lack of training and of a proper investigative temperament, further invalidate and confuse the records of what is supposed to have been observed. Many of the reported facts are not facts at all; others are too distortedly and too deficiently reported to be either intelligible or suggestive; some are accurately observed and properly recorded, and these sometimes contain a probable suggestion of their natural explanation, sometimes must be put down as chance, and more often must be left unexplained. To call this absence of an explanation telepathy is surely no advance; to pose this hypothetic process as the *modus operandi* of any result that can be even remotely and contingently otherwise accounted for seems superfluous;

to actually use this hypothesis to account for still more obscure and more indefinite and less clearly established phenomena is a most egregious logical sin.

As to the natural tendency to believe in telepathy, it may be regarded as part of the anthropocentric and egocentric view of the universe and its happenings, and as an exemplification of the persistence of the mystical view of mundane events, — both of which are dominant in primitive philosophy, remain conspicuous wherever superstition still has a hold, flourish in pseudo-science and in esoteric cults, and will probably never become wholly obsolete. Mr. Clodd's remarks concerning the general notions underlying "sympathetic magic" may be applied to the bias in favor of the telepathic theory: "The general idea has only to be decked in another garb to fit the frame of mind which still reserves some pet sphere of nature for the operation of the special and the arbitrary." However difficult it may be to realize fully and in detail that the objective order of things is not arranged for our several personal benefits, that conclusion is inevitably forced upon us by a true insight into the inexorable logic of events, and harmonizes with the reflections of our more logical moods. Whatever tide there may be in human affairs is largely of our own making; there is nothing to mark the flood except our own judgment and insight. We may select and arrange and adapt circumstances according to our needs, but the selection is made by us and not for us: "We must *take* the current when it serves." Some effort is necessary, some schooling must be gone through with, to enforce this attitude and to give it the practical effectiveness of a living conviction. The attitude of conformity with current belief, the easy acceptance of the plausible, the avoidance of careful and questioning analysis, are far more inviting and less exacting than the regulation of belief by the logic of matured principles. The strenuous life has quite as important a mission in intellectual as in practical affairs. It will be a decided advance when it becomes generally acknowledged that the discussion of such an hypothesis as telepathy presupposes an intimate acquaintance not merely with the facts concerned, but with the logical aspects of their interpretation; that the probability of forming a sound opinion on such matters is measured not by the fervor of the interest in them, but by the intellectual requisites necessary to steer one's way among the intricacies and dangers of such an expedition. No persons are more deeply interested in the successful issue of a voyage than the passengers; but this interest does not qualify them to form an intelligent opinion upon the proper direction of the machinery or the setting of the course, — much less does it fit them to take an active part in the actual navigation. Yet there are always those who confidently criticise the actions of captain and pilot, and are anxious to display their ability to form opinions of their own in regard to the intricate navigation over nature's highways. The most efficient antidote to the too ready inclination towards the popular or the superficial interpretation of the phenomena involved in mental telegraphy is doubtless the cultivation of the logical vigor and prudence so frequently referred to; and next to this is an appreciation of the marvelous complexity and unfathomable subtlety of mental operations.

THE PSYCHOLOGY OF DECEPTION

THE saying that appearances are deceptive is an inheritance from ancient times; to Oriental and to Greek philosophers the illusory nature of the knowledge furnished by the senses was a frequent and a fertile theme of contemplation and discussion. The same problem stands open to the psychologist of to-day; but, profiting by the specialization of learning and the advance of technical science, he can give it a more comprehensive as well as a more practical answer. The physiological activities underlying sense-perception are now fairly well understood; the experimental method has extended its domain over the field of mental phenomena; and in many ways have we become more expert in addressing our queries to the sphinx, Nature, so as to force a reply. To outline the position of modern psychology with reference to this interesting problem of deception is the object of the present essay.

I

In a sense-impression we recognize a primitive element in the acquisition of knowledge. The deprivation of a sense even under most favorable circumstances leaves some traces of an incomplete mental development. This is due, not to the mere sense-impressions that the organ furnishes, but to the perception and co-ordination of these by inferential processes of a more complex nature. It is not the eye of the eagle, but the brain directing the human eye, that leads to intellectual supremacy. Physiology recognizes this distinction as one between lower and higher brain-centres. A man may have his retina or his optic nerve injured, and so be blind in the ordinary sense of the word. He is prevented from acquiring further knowledge by this avenue; but, unless he become blind in early childhood, he will retain a memory for visual images, will be able more or less clearly to imagine pictorially the appearances of objects from verbal descriptions, and in the free roamings of his dream fancy will live in a world in which blindness is unknown. On the other hand, there is a condition resulting from the disintegration of certain portions of the finely organized cortex of the brain, in which the patient may retain full sight and understanding, but be unable to derive any meaning from what he sees. The same cluster of sensations that enables us to recognize a book, a picture, a face, and to arouse all the numerous associations attaching to these, is as unmeaning to him as the symbols of a cipher alphabet. This condition is termed "psychic blindness;" and what is there lost is not the power of vision, but of interpreting, of assimilating, of reading the meaning of visual sense-impressions. It is this interpreting and assimilating process that is largely concerned in the formation of illusions.

In the experiences of daily life we have to do not with simple sensations, but with more or less complex inferences from them; and it is just because these inferences go on so constantly and so unconsciously that they are continually and persistently overlooked. It

is an occasional experience in raising a water-pitcher
to have the vessel fly up in the hand in a very startling
manner, — the reason for this being that the pitcher,
which one is accustomed to find well filled, happens to
be empty. This experience shows that we unconsciously estimate the force necessary to raise the vessel,
but only become conscious of this train of inference
when it happens to lead to conclusions contradictory of
the fact. The perception of distance, once thought to
be as primitive a factor in cognition as the impression
of a color, is likewise the result of complex though un-
realized inferences; and the phenomena of the stereo-
scope, by imitating the conditions of the perception of
solidity and thus making us see as solid the flat representations of a pair of diagrams or photographs, furnish
a brilliant illustration of the variety and complexity of
such unconscious reasonings. As for essential purposes normal persons have a common anatomy, a common physiology, and a common psychology, it results
that we draw these unconscious inferences after the
same pattern; and so completely are they the outcome
of the normal reactions to our common environment,
that we need not be, and as a rule are not, aware of
their existence until — and probably with some little
effort — our attention is directed to them. Unconsciously and spontaneously we learn to see, — that is, to
extract meaning out of the sense-impressions that fall
upon the retina.

The simplest type of a deception occurs when an inference or an interpretation of this type, owing to an
unusual disposition of external circumstances, leads
to a conclusion which other and presumably superior

testimony shows to be false. Thus, in the observation which Aristotle knew and described, that a pea or other round object held between two fingers crossed one over the other seems double, it is the unusual position of the fingers that induces the illusion. Under ordinary circumstances a sensation of contact on the left side of one finger and on the right side of the finger next to it (to the right) could only be produced by the simultaneous application of two bodies. We unconsciously and naturally make the same inference when the fingers are crossed, and thus fall into error — an error, it is important to observe, which we do not *outgrow* but *antagonize* by more convincing evidence. The pea held between the crossed fingers continues to *feel* like two peas, but we are under no temptation to *believe* that there really are two peas.

The limitations of our senses lead directly to the possibilities of their deception, which may in turn be realized inadvertently or utilized intentionally. We appreciate how defective is our localization of sound when we attempt to find a cricket by locating whence proceeds its chirp; the same difficulty lends uncertainty to the determination of the direction of fog-horn signals of passing steamers. This uncertainty coöperates in the illusions of ventriloquism; it is involved in the smack which one clown gives another, but which is really the clapping of the hands of the supposed victim; it produces a realistic effect when a cannon is fired on the stage, for it is necessary only to show the flash while the noise is produced behind the scenes. Again, the stimulation of the retina is ordinarily due to the impinging upon it of light-waves emanating from an external object. Accordingly, when the retina is disturbed by any exceptional cause, such as a blow on the head or an electric shock to the optic nerve, we have a sensation of light projected outward into space. The perception of our own locomotion, which is likewise a highly inferential process, offers illustrations of casual illusion and of artificial deception. When on a train, it is by the passing-by before our eyes in the opposite direction of trees and posts and other features of the landscape, that we realize that we are moving forward ; accordingly, when a train alongside moves out before our own train has started, we have a distinct realization that we are moving backwards so long as we look at the forward-moving train. There is an illusion devised for amusement called the "Magic Swing," in which one is apparently swung to and fro with wider and wider excursions until a complete revolution is apparently made from a vertical to a horizontal, through the antipodal position, back to the horizontal and the normal. In reality, only a slight motion is imparted to the swing, but the inclosing walls, which are painted to represent a forest scene, are themselves revolved forward and then backward about the axis from which the swing is suspended. As, however, we have no experience with oscillating trees, we unconsciously infer the oscillations to be and feel them in our own persons. In another application of the same illusion we seem to be let down into the bowels of the earth ; but after a slight actual descent the car remains stationary while the illuminated sides of the shaft, which are suitably painted, are moved panorama-like in an upward direction. In brief, we are creatures of the average ; we are adjusted for the most probable event ; our organism has acquired the habits impressed upon it by the most frequent experiences ; and this has induced an inherent logical necessity to interpret a new experience by the old, an unfamiliar by the familiar. In describing illusions of the above type, Mr. Sully aptly says that they " depend on the general mental law that when we have to do with the unfrequent, the unimportant, and therefore unattended to, and the exceptional, we employ the ordinary, the familiar, and the well known as our standard." Illusion arises when the rule thus applied fails to hold ; and whether or not we become cognizant of the illusion depends upon the ease with which the exceptional character of the particular instance can be recognized, or the inference to which it leads be opposed by presumably more reliable evidence.

II

To make things seem more wonderful than they are, to possess knowledge and exhibit power beyond the ken of the multitude, has exercised a fascination upon the human mind in all its stages of development. The primitive conjuring of the ancient priest or of the savage medicine-man, the long tradition of Oriental legerdemain, and the stage performances of the modern prestidigitateur are all connected with deep-seated human instincts. It has even been suggested [1] that

[1] By Norman Triplett, " The Psychology of Conjuring Deceptions," *American Journal of Psychology*, xi. 4, July, 1900. This most recent and extensive treatment of this topic furnishes a well-selected storehouse of fact, together with suggestive and able interpretations of the

the mimicry and death-feigning instincts of animals, though essentially biological in type, are yet related to the psychological instincts of deception which make their first clear appearance in the higher animals and assume a distinctive position in the psychological equipment of childhood. The conjuring tricks or paradoxes which apparently contradict or rise superior to ordinary experience, furnish the most various types of illustration of the psychology of deception. Whether presented as miracle by priest or by thaumaturgist or by expounder of the black art, or presented as proof of spirit agency by the modern spiritualistic medium or his less pretentious predecessors, or by the stage performer for entertainment, the analysis of what was actually done, and the accounts of what the spectators saw or believed that they saw, illuminate with striking brilliancy the *modus operandi* of the processes whereby appearance takes the semblance of reality and observation is shrewdly led astray. The conjurer thus becomes a suggester and an actor, not a mere exhibitor of his manipulative skill.

As our present purpose is to investigate the nature of real deception, of the formation of false beliefs which may in turn lead to unwise action, it will be well to note that even such elementary forms of sense-deceptions as those just noted may fall under this head. No one allowed the use of his eyes will ever believe that the pea held between the crossed fingers

material of conjuring deceptions. I shall draw from this material in several portions of this essay, without further detailed acknowledgment.

is really double, but children often think that a spoon half immersed in water is really bent. Primitive peoples believe that the moon really grows smaller as it rises above the horizon; and the ancients could count sufficiently upon the ignorance of the people, to make use of mirrors and other stage devices for revealing the power of the gods. The ability to correct such errors depends solely upon the possession of certain knowledge or of a confidence in its existence.

Continuing with deceptions dependent upon exceptional external arrangements, we may find in conjuring tricks simple and complex illustrations in great perfection. When wine is turned into water, when two half-dollars are rolled into one, when a box into which an article has just been placed is immediately opened and found to be empty, when a handkerchief is torn and made whole again, when the performer drives a nail through his finger, when a coin suddenly appears out of space at the end of a wand, when a card which you have just assured yourself is the ace of hearts on second view is the king of spades, when a bowl filled with water in which goldfish are swimming is produced from under a handkerchief, when a child rests horizontally in mid-air supported only on one elbow, — you are misled or mystified or deceived in so far as you are unaware that the wine was potassium permanganate and sulphuric acid, and was clarified by sodium hyposulphite; that the one half dollar is hollow and the solid one fits into it; that the box has a double bottom controlled by a secret spring; that the real handkerchief was not torn but another substituted for it; that the nail has been replaced by one that fits around the finger; that the wand is hollow, and a spring controls the appearance or withdrawal of a split coin at its other end; that one half of the card is printed on a flap which, by falling down, shows another aspect; that the bowl covered with a rubber cap was secreted under the coat of the performer; that the child wears a steel suit fitted with joints that lock and become rigid. All these are technical devices which amuse us by the ingenuity of their construction, and, though they may be most baffling, provoke about the same type of mental interest as does a puzzle or an automaton. Ignorance of this technical knowledge or lack of confidence in its existence may convert these devices into real deceptions by changing the mental attitude of the spectator. However, the plausibility of such performances depends so much upon their general presentation that they seldom rely for their effectiveness solely upon the objective appearances presented. They are given a dramatic setting, or put forward as examples of newly discovered forces or of magical control; and this makes them far more effective than this bare account would suggest.

Asking the reader, then, to bear in mind the very great number and ingenuity of such devices, and insisting once more that the only complete safeguard against being misled by them to the extent of forming false conceptions of their *modus operandi*, is the acquisition of the purely technical knowledge that underlies their success, I shall cite in detail a trick combining illustrations of several of the principles to be discussed. Several rings are collected from the audience upon the performer's wand; he takes the rings back to the stage and throws them upon a platter; a pistol is needed, and is handed to the performer from behind the scenes; with conspicuous indifference he hammers the precious trinkets until they fit into the pistol. A chest is hanging on a nail at the side of the stage; the pistol is fired at this chest, which is thereupon taken down and placed upon a table towards the rear of the stage. The chest is unlocked and found to contain a second chest; this is unlocked and contains a third; this a fourth. As the chests emerge they are placed upon the table; and now from the fourth chest there comes a fifth, which the performer carries to the front of the stage and shows to contain bonbons around each of which is tied one of the rings taken from the audience. The effect is most startling. This is the appearance of the trick from the audience. Now let us consider what really takes place. In the hand holding the wand are as many brass rings as are to be collected. In walking back to the stage the genuine rings are allowed to slip off the wand and the false rings to take their places. This excites no suspicion, as the walking back to the stage is obviously necessary, and never impresses one as part of the performance. The pistol is not ready upon the stage, but must be gone for; and as the assistant hands the performer the pistol, the latter transfers to the assistant the true rings. The hammering of the false rings is now deliberately undertaken, thus giving the assistant ample time to tie the true rings to the bonbons; and, while all attention is concentrated upon the firing of the pistol, the assistant unobtrusively pushes a small table on to the rear of the stage. This table has a small fringe hanging about it, certainly an insignificant detail, but none the less worth noting. The chests are now opened, and, after having shown the audience that the second chest comes out of the first, the third out of the second, and so on, the performer can very readily and quickly draw the last, smallest chest from a groove *under* the table, where it was concealed by the aforesaid fringe, and bring it forward as though it *had come* out of the next larger chest; this smallest chest is opened and the trick is accomplished. So thoroughly convinced is the observer by the correctness of his first three inferences that the last box came out of the one before it, that I venture to say this explanation does not occur to one person in many thousand, and that most of the audience would have been willing to affirm on oath that they saw the last box so emerge. The psychology of the process, then, consists in inducing the spectator to draw the natural inference, which, in this case, it has been carefully arranged shall be a wrong one.

Deception becomes real according to the skill with which the conditions of reality are imitated. The dexterity and training of the professional conjurer are measured by the fidelity with which he mimics the movements which are supposed to be done. The life-likeness of the movement with which the late Hermann could take up an imaginary orange with both hands from a table (the orange was really let down in a trap on the table as the hands were placed over it), and carry it over to another table where it mysteriously disappeared or passed through a hat, was quite irresistible. Equally so was his palming, or his production of objects from his person, or out of the

air, or in out-of-the-way places. The mimetic movements accompanying these actions were so vividly realistic, the misdirection of the attention was so perfect,
as to produce a complete hallucination of the appearance of objects from places from which they never
emerged. When this was preceded by an actual
sleight-of-hand movement, a true hallucination resulted; for example, in the trick of the flying cards
which were skilfully thrown to all parts of the audi-
torium, a card was occasionally thrown which seemed
to disappear mysteriously in mid-air; but in reality no
card had been thrown but only the movements of
throwing it imitated. A rabbit was tossed up in the
air two or three times, and then disappeared at the
report of a pistol; in reality the rabbit was not tossed
at all on the last apparent throw, but was slipped into
the hollow of the table.[1]

The more closely the conditions that lead to correct
inferences in ordinary experiences are imitated, the
more successful will be the illusion; and a useful principle of conjuring illusions is to *first actually do* that
which you *afterward* wish the audience to *believe that*

[1] Mr. Triplett went through a similar performance with a ball in the
presence of school children; and of 165 children, 78 described how they
saw the ball go up and disappear; of those who were thus hallucinated
40 per cent. were boys and 60 per cent. were girls. Hallucinations of
perfumes in children were obtained by another experimenter when water
was sprayed from bottles labeled as perfumes; 76 per cent. of 381
pupils saw a toy camel move when a crank attached to the camel by
a string was turned, although the camel remained quite motionless.
The experimental tests, though rather cold and lifeless when compared with the dramatic stage deceptions, illustrate the same process,
and make possible a comparative study of the degree of deception in
different individuals and under different circumstances.

you continue to do. Thus, when coins are caught in mid-air and thrown into a hat, a few are really thrown in ; but the others are palmed in the hand holding the hat, and allowed to fall when the other hand makes the appropriate movements. Some of the rings to be mysteriously linked together are given to the audience for examination and found to contain no opening, the audience at once concluding that the rings which the performer retains are precisely like them. In general, to gain the confidence of the person to be deceived is the first step alike in sleight-of-hand and in criminal fraud.

III

As we turn from the objective to the subjective conditions of deception, we enter the true domain of psychology ; for the most scientific deceiver is he who employs least external aids, and counts most upon his power of captivating the intellect. Just as we interpret appearances by the forms they most commonly assume, so it is our average normal selves that interpret them. A variation in our sense-organs or in our judging powers will lead to illusion. The effects of contrast may serve as apt illustrations. When passing from a dark to a light room the light seems glaringly bright; a hand immersed in hot water and then in lukewarm water will feel the latter as cold ; when accustomed to the silence of the country the bustle of the city seems unusually noisy. Fatigue produces similar results. Fatigue the eye for red, and it sees white light as green ; the last mile of a long walk seems the longest ; the last hour of a long wait, the most tedious.

So long as we recognize our unusual condition and allow for its effects, we are not deceived; but under the influence of emotion this power is readily lost, as it may be permanently lost in the insane. The delusions of the insane are often influenced by misinterpretations of real but abnormal sensations under the guidance of a dominant idea. On the basis of an anæsthetic skin a patient may come to believe that he is made of glass or stone; subjective noises in the ear, due to disturbances of the circulation, are transformed into the jeers and taunts of an invisible persecutor. But for the present we will assume that the judging powers do not vary beyond their normal limits.

In every perception two factors contribute to the result. The one is the nature of the object perceived, the other that of the percipient. The effect of the first factor is obvious and well recognized; the importance of the second factor is more apt to be overlooked. The sunset is a different experience to the artist from what it is to the farmer; a piece of rocky scenery is viewed with quite a different interest by the artist and the geologist. The things that were attractive in childhood have lost their charm; and what was then, if noticed at all, considered stupid, has become a cherished hobby. Even from day to day, our interests change with our moods, and our views of things brighten with the weather or the good behavior of our digestive organs. Not only will the nature of the impression change with the interests of the observer, but even more, whether or not an object will be perceived at all, will depend upon the same cause. The naturalist sees what the stroller entirely overlooks; the sailor detects a ship in the distant horizon where the landsman sees nothing; and this is not because the naturalist and the sailor have keener vision, but because they know what to look for. Whenever an impression is vague, or an observation made under poor conditions, this subjective element comes to the front. Darkness, fear, any strong emotion, any difficulty in perception reveal the same influence. "La nuit tous les chats sont gris." Expectation, or expectant attention, is doubtless the most influential of all such factors. When awaiting a friend, any indistinct noise is readily converted into the rumbling of carriage - wheels; the mother hears in every sound the cry of her sick child. After viewing an object through a magnifying-glass, we detect details with the naked eye which escaped our vision before. In spite of the fact that the answer in the book happens to be wrong, a considerable proportion of the class succeeds in reaching it. Everywhere we are apt to perceive what we expect to perceive, in the perception of which we have an interest. The process that we term "sensation," the gathering of evidence by the senses, is dual in character, and depends upon the eyes that see as well as upon the things that are present to be seen.

Accordingly, the conjurer succeeds in his deception by creating an interest in some unimportant detail, while he is performing the real trick before our eyes without our noticing it. He looks intently at his extended right hand, involuntarily carrying our eyes to the same spot while he is doing the trick with the unobserved left hand. The conjurer's wand is extremely serviceable in directing the spectator's atten-

tion to the place where the performer desires to have
it.[1] A call upon the attention in one direction prevents
its dispersion in another. When engrossed in work,
we are oblivious to the noise of the street or even to
the knock at the door. An absent-minded person is
one so entirely " present-minded " to one train of
thought that other stimuli go unperceived. The pickpocket is psychologist enough to know that at the rail-
way station, the theatre, or wherever one's attention is
sharply focused in one direction, is he apt to find the
psychological moment for the exercise of his pursuit.
It is in the negative field of attention that deception
effects its purpose. Houdin, the first of the famous
prestidigitateurs (died 1871), gives it as one of his
rules never to announce beforehand the nature of the
effect which you intend to produce, in order that the
spectator may not know where to fix his attention.
He also tells us that whenever you count " *one, two,
three,*" as preliminary to the disappearance of an object, the real vanishing must take place before you say
" *three,*" — for the audience have their attention fixed
upon " *three,*" and whatever is done at " one " or
" two " entirely escapes their notice. The " patter "
or setting of a trick often constitutes the real art of its
execution, because it directs or rather misdirects the
attention. When performing before the Arabs, Houdin

[1] " Again, a mere tap with the wand on any spot, at the same time
looking at it attentively, will infallibly draw the eyes of a whole company in the same direction." — *Houdin.*

Robert Houdin, often termed " the king of the conjurers," was a
man of remarkable ingenuity and insight. His autobiography is
throughout interesting and psychologically valuable, and his conjuring precepts abound in points of importance to the psychologist.

produced an astounding effect by a very simple trick. Under ordinary circumstances the trick was announced as the changing of the weight of a chest, making it heavy or light at will. The mechanism was simply the attachment and disconnection of an electro-magnet, in those days a far less familiar affair than now. To impress the Arabs he announced that he could spirit a man's strength away and restore it again at a moment's notice. The trick succeeded as usual, but was changed from a mere trick to sorcery — the Arabs declaring him in league with the devil.

The trick, above cited, of supporting a child in mid-air, was performed by Houdin at the time when the inhalations of ether for purposes of insensibility were first introduced. This idea was in the minds of the audience, and magical effects were readily attributed to etherization. Accordingly the trick was announced as " suspension in equilibrium by atmospheric air through the action of concentrated ether," and so successfully was this aspect of the trick accepted that protests were sent in against " the unnatural father who sacrificed the health of his poor child to the pleasures of the public." In the same way, Kellar introduces a " thought-reading " performance, by going through the movements of hypnotizing the lady who assists in the trick ; this enables him to present the phenomenon in a mysterious light, and incidentally his manipulations furnish the opportunity to connect the end of a speaking-tube concealed in the lady's hair with another portion attached to the chair. In brief, the effect of a trick depends more upon the receptive attitude of the spectators than upon what is really done. "Conjuring," Mr. Triplett observes, "is thus seen to be a kind of game of preperception wherein the performer so plays upon the psychical processes of his audience that the issues are as he desires."

There is, too, a class of tricks which illustrate a process, the reverse of this; and which depend for their éclat upon making the issues coincide with the apparently freely expressed choice of the spectator, while really the performer as rigidly determines the result as in all other cases. One of the best of these proceeds by collecting some eight or nine questions prepared by as many persons in the audience, then placing them in a hat, drawing out one at random, and finding the answer to the question thus selected written on the inside surfaces of a pair of slates. The deception begins in the substitution for the collected slips of paper, of the same number of slips all containing the same carefully prepared question; the production of the writing on the blank slate is a chemical technicality. It is a similar result that is obtained in forcing a card; or when the conjurer asks the audience to select one of a group of similar objects, and then himself decides whether the selected object shall be used for the trick or discarded; likewise, when a magic bottle is presented from which any desired variety of liquor may be produced, it is easy to suggest the choice according to the available possibilities. There is thus an imitation of the psychological factors as well as of the objective factors of real experience; and both are utilized in the deceptions of the professional conjurer.

The art of misleading the attention is recognized as *the* point of good conjuring, the analogy of the diplo-

macy that makes the object of language to conceal
thought; and many appropriate illustrations of this
point may be derived from this field.   The little flourishes, tossing an object up in the air, ruffling or
springing a pack of cards, a little joke — all these
create a favorable opportunity, a *temp* when the attention is diverted and the other hand can reach behind
the table or into the " pocket."   It is not necessary to
pursue further these details of technique ; it will suffice
to analyze the points of interest in the chest-and-
ring trick described above.   Here the moment for the
exchange of the rings is the one which is least suggestive of its being a part of the performance, and therefore least attended to.   The preparations for the shooting absorb the attention and allow the introduction of
the small table at the rear to pass unnoticed ; while
the series of drawings of the chests so entirely prepare
the spectator for the appearance of the last chest from
the one preceding, that he actually sees the chest emerge
from where it never had been.

It is necessary, however, not only to provide an
opportunity for non-attention or misdirected attention,
but to be able to take advantage of it when the proper
moment arrives.   Here enters the dexterity alike of
pickpocket and of conjurer.   The training in quickness
and accuracy of motion, in delicacy of touch, in the
simultaneous perception of a wide range of sense-impressions, are among the psychological requisites of a
successful conjurer.   He must dissociate the natural
factors of his habits, actually doing one thing while
seemingly attending to another ; at the same time his
eyes and his gestures and his " patter " misdirect the

attention to what is apparently the essential field of operation, but really only a blind to distract attention away from the true scene of action. The conjurer directs your attention to what he does not do ; he does not do what he pretends to do; and to what he actually does he is careful neither to appear to direct his own attention nor to arouse yours.

IV

There is, however, one important factor lacking in the conjurer's performance to illustrate completely the psychology of deception ; it is that the mental attitude of the observer is too definite. He knows that he is being deceived by skill and adroitness, and rather enjoys it the more, the more he is deceived. He has nothing at stake ; his mind rests easy without any detailed or complete explanation of how it was done. Quite different must have been the feeling of the spectator before the necromancer of old, in whose performance was seen the evidence of secret powers that could at a moment's notice be turned against any one to take away good luck, to bring on disease, or even to transform one into a beast. When magic spells and wonder-working potions were believed in, what we would now speak of as a trick was surrounded with a halo of awe and mystery by the sympathetic attitude of the spectators. The most complete parallel to this in modern times is presented by the physical phenomena of Spiritualism ; and so many of the manifestations presented by performing mediums in evidence of Spiritualism have been exposed and proven to be conjuring tricks, that it is no longer an assumption to consider them in this connection.

Spiritualistic phenomena present a perfect mine for illustrations of the psychology of deception, and it is these that I shall consider as the final topic in this cursory view.

The first general principle to be borne in mind is that the medium performs to spectators *in doubt* as to the interpretation to be placed upon what they see, or more or less prepared or determined to see in everything the evidence of the supernatural. This mental attitude on the part of the spectators is worth more to the medium than any single factor in the performance. The difference between such a presentation and one addressed to persons cognizant of the conjuring element in the performance and interested in its detection, cannot be exaggerated. It is this that makes all the difference between the séance swarming with miracles, any one of which completely revolutionizes the principles of science, and the tedious dreariness of a blank sitting varied only by childish utterances and amateurish sleight-of-hand. Careful observers often report that the very same phenomena that were utterly beyond suspicion in the eyes of believers are to unprejudiced eyes so apparent " that there was really no need of any elaborate method of investigation "; close observation was all that was required, and Mr. Davey, who conducted an admirable investigation of the reliability of accounts of sleight-of-hand performances, has experimentally shown that of equally good observers, the one who is informed of the general *modus operandi* by which such a phenomenon as "slate-writing" is produced will make much less of a marvel of it than one who is left in doubt in this regard.

With these all-powerful magicians — an expected result and the willingness to credit a marvel — clearly in mind, let us proceed from those instances in which they have least effect up to the point where they form the chief factor. First come a host of conjuring tricks performed on the stage in slightly modified forms, but which are presented as "spiritualistic." So simple a trick as scratching a name on one's hand with a clean pen dipped in water, then writing the name on a slip of paper, burning the slip and rubbing the part with the ashes, thus causing the ashes to cling to the letters formed on the hand and reveal the name, has been offered as a proof of spirit agency. Whenever an article disappears or rapidly changes its place, the spiritualist is apt to see the workings of hidden spirits; and over and over again have the performances of professional conjurers been declared to be spiritual in origin in spite of all protest from the conjurers themselves. Here everything depends upon the possession of certain technical knowledge; judging without such knowledge is apt to be mere prejudice. Another very large class of phenomena consists of those in which the performer is placed in a position apparently inconsistent with his taking any active part in their production; rope-tying tests, cabinet séances, the appearance of a "spirit-hand" from behind a screen, locking the performer in a cage, sewing him in a bag, and so on. The psychologist has very little interest in these; their solution depends upon the skill with which knots may be picked, locks unfastened, and the other devices by which security may be simulated. The chief interest in such performances is the historical one, for these have done perhaps more than anything else to convince believers of the truth of Spiritualism. Here, where everything depends upon the security of the fastenings (for once free, the medium can produce messages from the spirit-land limited only by his ingenuity and boldness), upon the particular moment when the examination was permitted or the light turned down, upon the success with which an appearance of security and intactness of seals and knots may be simulated, it might be supposed that all possible precautions had been taken to control and eliminate these possibilities ; while, as a matter of fact, the laxity of most investigators in this regard is well known. These performances deceive because people overlook the technical acquisitions needed to pronounce upon the possibility or impossibility of a fastening having been tampered with and apparently restored without detection. If manufacturers of safes were equally credulous, and gave equally little time to the study of the security of locks, " safe " would be an ironical expression indeed.

Passing next to the most interesting of spiritualistic manifestations, those in which self-deception comes to the foreground, I need hardly dwell at length upon the tilting of tables, the production of raps by movements of which the sitters are unconscious ; for these have been so often and so ably presented that they must now be well understood. Suffice it to say that it has been objectively proven that it is almost impossible not to give some indication of one's thoughts, when put upon the strain ; and that under excitement, these indications may become palpably plain and yet remain unperceived by the individual who gives them. The extreme subtlety of these indications is met by the unusual skill of the professional mind-reader, who takes his clue from indications which his subject is "absolutely confident he did not give." The assurances of sitters that *they know* they did not move the table are equally valueless ; and nothing but objective tests will suffice. The most wholesome lesson to be derived from the study of these phenomena is the proof that not all our intentions and actions are under the control of consciousness, and that, under emotional or other excitement, the value of the testimony of conciousness is very much weakened. Again, it is almost impossible to realize the difficulty of accurately describing a phenomenon lying outside the common range of observation. Not alone that the knowledge necessary to pronounce such and such a phenomenon impossible of performance by conjuring methods is absent, but with due modesty and most sincere intentions the readiness with which the observing powers and the memory play one false is overlooked. In the investigation of Mr. Davey, above referred to, the sitters prepared accounts of the " slate-writing " manifestations they had witnessed, and described marvels that had not occurred, but which they were convinced they had seen — messages written on slates utterly inaccessible to Mr. Davey, and upon slates which they had noticed a moment before were clean. The witnesses are honest; how do these mistakes arise? Simply a detail omitted here, an event out of place there, an unconscious insertion in one place, an undue importance given to a certain point in another place — nothing of which any one needs feel ashamed, something which it requires unusual training and natural gifts to avoid. The mistake lies in not recognizing our liability to such error.

If, however, the spectator is once convinced that he has evidence of the supernatural, he soon sees it in every accident and incident of the performance. Not only that he overlooks natural physical explanations, but he is led to create marvels by the very ardor of his sincerity. At a materializing séance the believer recognizes a dear friend in a carelessly arranged drapery seen in a dim light. Conclusive evidence of the subjective character of such perceptions is furnished by the fact that the same appearance is frequently recognized by different sitters as the spiritual counterpart of entirely different and totally dissimilar persons. A "spirit-photograph" is declared to be the precise image of entirely unlike individuals. In the "Revelations of a Spirit Medium," we read that a wire gauze mask placed in front of a handkerchief, made luminous by phosphorus, and projected through the opening of the cabinet, was "recognized by dozens of persons as fathers, mothers, sisters, brothers, cousins, sweethearts, wives, husbands, and various other relatives and friends." Each one sees what he expects to see, what appeals to his interests the most intensely. What the unprejudiced observer recognizes as the flimsily disguised form of the medium, the believer transforms into the object of his thoughts and longings. Only let the form be vague enough, the light dim enough, the emotions upon a sufficient strain, and that part of perception in which the external image is deficient will be readily supplied by the subjective tendencies of each individual. In the presence of such a mental attitude the possibilities of deception are endless; the performer grows bolder as his victim passes from a watchful, critical attitude to one of easy conviction, and we get scientific proofs of the fourth dimension of space, of the possibility of matter passing through matter, of the levitation or elongation of the medium's body, of the transcendence of the laws of gravity. And the same performance that convinced Professor Zoellner of the reality of the fourth dimension of space would prove to the spiritualist the intercourse with deceased friends, would convince the theosophist of the flight of the performer's astral body; and, it may not be irrelevant to add, it was the same type of performance that served and yet serves to terrify the minds of uncultivated and superstitious savages. All depends not upon what is done, but upon the mental disposition of the spectator. Little by little, through neglect, through mal-observation and lapses of memory, through an unwillingness to mistrust the reports of an excited consciousness, caution is abandoned and credulity enters. Mediums are actually seen flying out of one window and in through another. The wildest and most far-fetched fantastic explanation is preferred above a simple one; the bounds of the normal are passed; real hallucinations set in; conduct becomes irrational, and a state hardly distinguishable from insanity ensues. If this seems improbable, turn to the records of witchcraft persecutions and read upon what trifling and wholly imaginary evidence thousands of innocent lives were sacrificed; and this not by ignorant, bloodthirsty men, but by earnest, eminent, and religious leaders. A child is taken sick, is remembered to have been fondled by an old woman ; therefore the woman has put the child under a spell and must be burned. A man sees an old woman in the woods, and, on turning about, the old woman is gone and a hare flies across his track ; he concludes that she turned herself into a hare, and the witch test is applied. When the personal devil was believed in, he was seen daily clothed in the garments that imagination had given him, and engaged in mischief and villainy of all kinds. When witchery was the dominant superstition, all things gave evidence of that. So long as Spiritualism forms a prominent cult with a real hold upon the beliefs of its adherents, the number of mediums and manifestations will be correspondingly abundant. Create a belief in the theory, and the facts will create themselves.

V

In the production of this state of mind a factor as yet unmentioned plays a leading rôle, the power of mental contagion. Error, like truth, flourishes in crowds. At the hearth of sympathy each finds a home. The fanatical lead, the saner follow. When a person of nervous temperament, not strongly independent in thought and action, enters a spiritualistic circle, where he is constantly surrounded by confident believers, all eager to have him share their sacred visions and profound revelations, where the atmosphere is replete with miracles, and every chair and table may at any instant be transformed into a proof of the supernatural, is it strange that he soon becomes affected by the contagion of belief that surrounds him ? He succumbs to its influence imperceptibly and hesitatingly at first, and perhaps yet restorable to his former modes of thought by the fresh air of another and more steadfast mental intercourse, but more and more certainly and ardently convinced the longer he breathes the séance atmosphere. No form of contagion is so insidious in its onset, so difficult to check in its advance, so certain to leave germs that may at any moment reveal their pernicious power, as a mental contagion — the contagion of fear, of panic, of fanaticism, of lawlessness, of superstition, of error. The story of the witchcraft persecutions, were there no similar records to deface the pages of history, would suffice as a standing illustration of the overwhelming power of psychic contagion. To illustrate with any completeness its importance in the production of deception or in the dissemination of error, would carry us beyond the proper limits of the present discussion. It enters at every stage of the process and in every type of illusion. Although it has least effect when deception is carried on by external arrangements, by skilful counterfeits of logical inferences, yet even then it enters into the distinction between a critical, skeptical, and irresponsive body of spectators, and one that is sympathetic, acquiescent, and cordial; it renders it easier to effect bold and striking impressions with a larger audience than with a smaller one; its power is greatest, however, where the subjective factor in deception is greatest, more particularly in such forms of deception as have been last described.

In brief, we must add to the many factors which contribute to deception the recognized lowering of critical ability, of the power of accurate observation, indeed of rationality, which merely being one of a crowd induces. The conjurer finds it easier to perform to large audiences because, among other reasons, it is easier to arouse their admiration and sympathy, easier to make them forget themselves and enter into the uncritical spirit of wonderland. It would seem that in some respects the critical tone of an assembly, like the strength of a chain, is that of its weakest member. "The mental quality of the individuals in a crowd," says M. Le Bon, "is without importance. From the moment that they are in the crowd the ignorant and the learned are equally incapable of observation."

VI

In this review of the types of deception I have made no mention of such devices as the gaining of one's confidence for selfish ends, preying upon ignorance or fear, acting the friend while at heart the enemy, planned connivance and skilful plotting, together with the whole outfit of insincerity, villainy, and crime. It is not that these are without interest or are unrelated to the several types of deception above considered, but that they are too complex and too heterogeneous to be capable of ready or rigid analysis. When deception becomes an art of life, consciously planned and craftily executed, there must be acting and subterfuge and evasion to maintain the appearance of sincerity. The psychology of the processes therein concerned is almost coincident with the range of social, intellectual, and emotional influences. Complex as these operations may be, they have, in common with the less intricate forms of deception, the attempt to parallel the conditions underlying the logical inferences which it is desired to induce. If we add this great class of deceptions to those already enumerated, we may perhaps realize how vast is its domain, and how long and sad must be the chapter that records the history of human error.

Ethics is so closely related to psychology — right knowing to right doing — that a brief *hœc fabula docet* by way of summary may not be out of place. We find, first, a class of sense-deceptions which are due to the nature of our sense-endowment, and deceive only so long as their true character remains unknown. These are neither pernicious nor difficult to correct. Next comes a class of deceptions that deceive because we are ignorant of the possibilities of technical devices, such as those used in legerdemain, and pronounce upon the possibility or impossibility of a certain explanation in advance of complete knowledge. But still another class, and that the most dangerous and insidious, are the deceptions in which self-deception plays the leading rôle. The only safeguard here is a preventive; the thorough infusion of sound habits of thought, a full recognition of the conditions under which the testimony of consciousness becomes dubious, an appreciation of the true value of objective scientific evidence, and an inoculation against the evils of contagion by an independent, unprejudiced, logical schooling. When once the evil spirit of self-deception, fed by the fire of contagion and emotional excitement, begins to spread, reason has little control. As Tyndall tells us, such " victims like to believe, and they do not like to be undeceived. Science is perfectly powerless in the presence of this frame of mind. . . . It [science] keeps down the weed of superstition, not by logic, but by slowly rendering the mental soil unfit for cultivation." With the spread of an education that fosters independence and self-reliance, with the growth of the capacity to profit by the experiences of others, with the recognition of the technical requisites that alone qualify one for a judgment in this or that field, with a knowledge of the possibilities of deception and of the psychological processes by which error is propagated, the soil upon which superstitions, psychic delusions, mental epidemics, or senseless fads are likely to flourish will gradually be rendered unfit.

THE PSYCHOLOGY OF SPIRITUALISM

I

IN 1848, from the town of Hydeville, New York, came the somewhat startling announcement that certain knockings, the source of which had mystified the household of one of its residents, seemed to be intelligently guided and ready to appear at call. Somewhat later, communication was established by agreeing that one rap should mean *no*, and three raps *yes;* to which was afterwards added the device of calling off the alphabet and noting at which letters the raps occurred. In this way, the rapper revealed himself as the spirit of a murdered peddler. Within a short period the news of this simple and childish invention had called into existence thousands of spirit-circles; had developed wonderful " mediums " to whose special gifts the manifestations were ascribed; had amassed a vast store of strange testimony; had added to the rappings such performances as moving tables, causing objects to be mysteriously thrown about, playing on instruments by unseen hands, materializing spirit flowers, producing spirit forms and faces, gathering messages from spirits on sealed slates, and so on. In brief, the movement became an epidemic; and that despite the fact that from the beginning and continuously satisfactory and rational explanations were offered of what really occurred, and that mediums were constantly detected in the grossest fraud. So early as 1851 the peculiar rappings occurring in the presence of the Fox sisters, the originators of the movement, were conclusively traced to the partial dislocation and resetting of a joint of the knee or foot; and the raps failed to occur when the girls were placed in a position in which the leverage necessary for this action was denied them. Many years thereafter, in 1888, Margaret Fox (Mrs. Kane) and Katie Fox (Mrs. Jencken) publicly confessed that the raps to which they as children gave rise were produced by dislocation of the toes; and one of them added to their confession a demonstration of how this was done. It is unfortunate alike that the character of the confessers leaves much to be desired, that the confession was both belated and made under sensational surroundings, and that the sinners have no better excuse to offer for their long silence than that the movement was started when they were too young to appreciate what was being done, and that when they realized the fraud which they were fostering and the success with which they were meeting, it was too late or too difficult to retract. None the less, these circumstances do not destroy the interest in tracing the evidence of deception and the presence of a moral taint to the very starting-point of one of the most widespread delusions of modern times.

The psychological aspect of the phenomena of Spiritualism may be presented in a consideration of these questions: How is it that the manifestations produced in evidence of spirit-control carry conviction? What is the origin of this mass of testimony in favor of spiritualistic marvels? Whence this general tendency to

believe in the reality of spirit-influence as thus manifested? For the purposes of these inquiries it will be
profitable to consider a few typical manifestations and
to observe their true inwardness. Among the most
influential mediums was Henry Slade; through him
many were converted to Spiritualism, including the
famous Zöllner coterie, for whom he gave a spiritual
demonstration of the reality of the fourth dimension of
space. After all the prominence which has been given
to the Zöllner sittings and the importance attached to
them by reason of the eminence of the participants, it
is somewhat unexpected to read in the report of a reliable observer who interviewed Zöllner's associates, that
"of the four eminent men whose names have made
famous the investigation, there is reason to believe
one, *Zöllner*, was of unsound mind at the time, and
anxious for an experimental demonstration of an
already accepted hypothesis (the fourth dimension of
space); another, *Fechner*, was partly blind, and believed because of Zöllner's observations; a third,
Scheibner, was also afflicted with defective vision, and
not entirely satisfied in his own mind as to the phenomena; and a fourth, *Weber*, was advanced in age,
and did not even recognize the disabilities of his associates." None knew anything about conjuring, and,
deservedly honored as these men were in their own
specialties, they were certainly not fitted to compete
with a professional like Slade. One of Slade's standard performances was the production of communications on a slate held beneath a table, in answer to
questions asked by his sitters verbally or in writing,
the writing in some cases being concealed in folded

slips of paper. In his performances before the Seybert Commission it was soon discovered that the character of the writing on the slates was of two kinds. The long messages were neatly written, with the i's dotted and the t's crossed, and often produced unasked, or not in direct answer to a question; while the short ones in prompt answer to direct questions were scrawled, hardly legible, and evidently written without the aid of the eye. The many methods of producing the short writings were repeated by a professional prestidigitateur much more skillfully than by Slade. The commission distinctly saw every step in Slade's method on one occasion or another, but were utterly baffled by the conjurer (Mr. Harry Kellar), who subsequently revealed his methods to one of their number. The long messages were written beforehand, on slates to be substituted at a favorable opportunity for the ones supplied to the medium. At the last séance with Dr. Slade, two prepared slates were resting against a table behind him, and one of the investigators kept a sharp watch upon these slates. "Unfortunately, it was too sharp; for one second the medium saw me looking at them. It was enough. That detected look prevented the revelation of those elaborate spirit messages. But when the séance was over, and he was signing the receipt for his money, I passed round behind his chair and pushed these slates with my foot, so as to make them fall over, whereupon the writing on one of them was distinctly revealed." The medium at once pushed back his chair, snatched the slates, hurriedly washed them, and could with difficulty regain sufficient composure to sign the receipt for the exorbitant payment of his services. Another observer says with regard to Slade: "The methods of this medium's operations appear to me to be perfectly transparent, and I wish to say emphatically that I am astonished beyond expression at the confidence of this man in his ability to deceive, and at the recklessness of the risks which he assumes in the most barefaced manner. The only reason of our having any so-called 'manifestations,' under the circumstances, was because of the fact that the committee had agreed in advance to be entirely passive, and to acquiesce in every condition imposed." Mrs. Sidgwick, an able English observer, detected the fraudulent character of Slade's performances from the beginning. She points out five important grounds of suspicion: "His conjurer-like way of trying to distract one's attention, his always sitting so as to have the right hand to manipulate the slate, the vague and general character of the communications, his compelling one to sit with one's hands in a position that makes it difficult to look under the table, and his only allowing two sitters at a time."

The Seybert Commission, it should be explained, owes its origin to the bequest of an ardent believer in Spiritualism, Mr. Henry Seybert, to the University of Pennsylvania; which was coupled with the condition that this university should appoint a commission to investigate modern Spiritualism. It is from their report[1] that several of my illustrations are taken. The

[1] *Preliminary Report of the Commission appointed by the University of Pennsylvania to investigate Modern Spiritualism*, Philadelphia, 1887, Lippincott, pp. 159. The members of the commission were: Dr. William Pepper, Dr. Joseph Leidy, Dr. G. S. Koenig, Prof. R. E. Thompson, Prof. G. S. Fullerton, Dr. H. H. Furness, Mr. Coleman Sellers, Dr. J. W. White, Dr. C. B. Knerr, and Dr. S. Weir Mitchell.

members of this commission began their investigations with an entire willingness to accept any conclusion warranted by facts; and their chairman, Dr. Horace Howard Furness, confessed "to a leaning in favor of the substantial truth of spiritualism." They examined many of the most famous mediums and the manifestations that contributed most to their fame. Their verdict, individually and collectively, is the same regarding every medium with whom they saw anything noteworthy: gross, intentional fraud throughout. The mediums were treated with the utmost fairness and courtesy; their conditions were agreed to and upheld; every one, in each kind of manifestation, was caught in the act of trickery, or else the trick was repeated and explained by one of the commission. This testimony goes far to justify the substitution of "trick" for "manifestation," of "senseless cant" for "spiritualistic explanation," of "adroit conjurer" for "medium." While the accumulative force of this conclusion can only be appreciated by a reading of the report itself, a few further illustrations will contribute to a realization of the nature of the "manifestations" and their typical *milieu*. Mrs. Patterson, medium, gives a performance similar to that of Slade. Dr. Knerr had a sitting with her, and adjusted a mirror about his person so as to reflect whatever was going on beneath the table. "In the mirror I beheld a hand . . . stealthily insert its fingers between the leaves of the slate, take out the little slip (containing the question), unfold and again fold it, grasp the little pencil . . . and with rapid but noiseless motion . . . write across the slate from left to right a few lines; then the leaves of the slate were closed, the little pencil laid on the top," and the spirits were graciously invoked to send a message.

The monotony of the narrative of somewhat vulgar deception is agreeably relieved by the entertaining account given by Dr. Furness of his experiences with mediums. He sent out sealed letters, the contents of which certain mediums claimed to be able to read and to answer by the aid of spirits, and found the seals tampered with, and mucilage and skill used to conceal the crime; he asked the same question of various mediums and received hopelessly contradictory answers; he detected the form of the medium in her assumed materializations, and found the spirit ready to answer to any and every name in fiction or reality, from "Olivia" of "The Talking Oak" to Shakespeare. One of the questions asked by Mr. Furness related to the ownership in life of a skull in his possession, used for a long time as the "Yorick's skull" at a Philadelphia theatre. He was told by one medium that it was "Marie St. Clair," by another that it was "Sister Belle." Hence these remarks: "Marie St. Clair, who, on spiritual authority as I have shown above, shares the ownership with Sister Belle of 'Yorick's' skull in my possession, has never failed to assent whenever I ask a Spirit if it be she. To be sure, she varies with every different medium, but that is only one of her piquant little ways, which I early learned to overlook and at last grew to like. She is both short and tall, lean and plump, with straight hair and with curls, young and middle-aged, so that now it affords me real pleasure to meet with a new variety of her." Equally amusing is the conversation with a Spirit who was led to assent to the suggestion that she was "Olive," and at length was addressed thus: "'Oh, Olive, there's one thing I want so much to ask you about. . . . What was the matter with you that afternoon, one summer, when your father rode his hunter to the town, and Albert followed after upon his; and then your mother trundled to the gate behind the dappled grays? Do you remember it, dear?' 'Perfectly.' 'Well, don't you remember, nothing seemed to please you that afternoon, you left the novel all uncut upon the rosewood shelf, you left your new piano shut, some-thing seemed to worry you? Do you remember it, dear one?' 'All of it; yes, yes.' 'Then you came singing down to that old oak, and kissed the place where I had carved our names with many vows. Tell me, you little witch, who were you thinking of all the time?' 'All the while of you,' she sighed. 'And do you, oh, do you remember that you fell asleep under the oak, and that a little acorn fell into your bosom and you tossed it out in a pet? Ah, Olive dear, I found that acorn, and kissed it twice and kissed it thrice for thee! And do you know that it has grown into a fine young oak?' 'I know it,' she answered softly and sadly, 'I often go to it.' This was almost too much for me, and as my memory, on the spur of the moment, of Tennyson's 'Talking Oak' was growing misty, I was afraid the interview might become embarrassing for lack of reminiscences;" so the materialization of a very human form was brought to a close. To this may be added — to illustrate the barefacedness of the medium's business — the fact, com-municated to me by Dr. Furness, that a noted medium had visited a professional juggler, and, "making no secret to him of his trickery as a medium for independent slate-writing, had purchased from the juggler several other tricks with which to carry on his spiritualistic trade."

There is both entertainment and instruction in Dr. Knerr's account of a séance in which the spirit of an Indian and the mysterious use of a drum were to form parts of the performance. He tells of his success in getting some printer's ink on the drum-sticks just before the lights were lowered, and of the bewildered astonishment (when the lights were turned up after the Indian had manifested) at the condition of the medium's hands. "How in the world printer's ink could have gotten smeared over them while under the control of 'Deerfoot, the Indian,' no one, not even the medium, could fathom." We may read how a medium who professed to materialize a "spirit" right-hand while apparently holding his sitter's hand or arm with both his own, was shown to imitate this double grip with one hand and to do the hocus-pocus with the other. We may vary the nature of the fraud almost indefinitely and observe how universal, how coarse, how degrading it is, and how readily it may be induced to leave its hiding-place to snatch at a cunningly offered bait, — until in the end, if it were not so sad, it would be only ridiculous.

In the reports of the investigations of mediums, published by the Society for Psychical Research (vol. iv.), we find accounts of the performances of one Englinton, also with slate-writing, and whose success, as described by enthusiastic sitters, does not fall short of the miraculous. Yet the description of this wonder-worker's doings by a competent observer, Professor Carvill Lewis, renders the manifestations absolutely transparent. He sat intently watching Englinton for an hour, and nothing happened; fearing a blank séance, he purposely diverted his attention. The moment he looked away the manifestations began, and he could see "the medium look down intently toward his knees and in the direction of the slate. I now quickly turned back my head, when the slate was brought up against the table with a sharp rap." The manœuvre was repeated with the same result; and while the writing was going on, Professor Lewis distinctly saw "the movement of the central tendon in his wrist corresponding to that made by his middle finger in the act of writing. Each movement of the tendon was simultaneously accompanied by the sound of a scratch on the slate." Again, for the answer to the request to define "Idocrase," Englinton required the use of a dictionary, and left the room for a minute; the answer was then written just as it is given in Webster's dictionary; but, unfortunately, *albumina* was read for *alumina*. When the slate, which acts with a spring, was to be closed, Englinton suddenly sneezed; when the writing was small and faint, he shifted his position until he came within a few inches of it; a postage stamp secretly glued across the two leaves of the double slate prevented all manifestations; a double fee immediately caused further manifestations, when, owing to the exhaustion of power, such had just been declared to be impossible; and the writing on the slates was identified by an expert as that of Englinton. It was the same Englinton who was convicted of connivance with Mme. Blavatsky in the production of a spurious theosophic marvel; and it is to him that the following story, supplied by Mr. Padshah and indorsed by Mr. Hodgson (the exposer of Mme. Blavatsky), relates: Mr. Padshah and a friend had asked for Gujerati writing at a séance, but without success. Mr. Padshah (without informing his friend) sent anonymously to Englinton a poem in Gujerati; and the friend received from the medium a minutely faithful copy of the same on a slate, as the direct revelation of the spirits!

II

But all this accounts for only part of the problem. To convict every medium of fraud is not a complete explanation of the appearance which this belief presented in its most characteristic form some decades ago, and still presents. It remains to account for the great success of the movement; for the fact that so many have been deceived and so few have really understood; to show why we are to believe the Seybert Commission, and not credit the countless miracle-mongers. This is psychologically the most interesting portion of the problem, and has been very successfully treated by Mrs. Sidgwick, Mr. Hodgson, and Mr. Davey, of the Society for Psychical Research.

There is a very broadspread notion that anybody can go to a spiritualistic séance and give a reliable opinion as to whether what he or she may chance to see is explicable as conjuring or not. Especially where the right to one's opinion is regarded as a corollary to the right of liberty, does this notion prevail. It is probably not an exaggeration to maintain that most such claimants are about as competent to form a trustworthy opinion on such a subject as they are to pronounce upon the genuineness of a Syriac manuscript. The matter is in some aspects as much a technical acquisition as is the diagnosticating of a disease. It is not at all to the discredit of any one's powers of observation or intellectual acumen to be deceived by the performances of a conjurer; and the same holds true of the professional part of mediumistic phenomena. Until this homely but salutary truth is impressed with all its importance upon all intending investigators, there is little hope of bringing about a proper attitude towards these and kindred phenomena. We believe that there will be an eclipse of the moon when the astronomer so predicts, not because we can calculate the time or even understand how the astronomer does it, but because that is a technical acquisition which he has learned and we have not; and so with a thousand other and more humble facts of daily life. Spiritualism, to a large extent, comes under the same category; and observers who have acquainted themselves with the possibilities of conjuring and the natural history of deception, who by their training and endowment have fitted themselves to be competent judges of such alleged ultra-physical facts — these persons have the same right to our confidence and respect as a body of chemists or physicians on a question within their province. It by no means follows that all scientists are fitted for an investigation of this kind, nor that all laymen are not; it does follow that a body of trained and able observers, who are aware of the possibilities of faulty observation and of the tendency to substitute hasty inference for fact, who know something about deception as a psychological characteristic, who have acquired or call to their aid the technical requisites for such an investigation, are better fitted to carry it to a logical outcome than are others, equally distinguished in other directions and equally able, if you will, but who have not these special qualifications. It follows that it is not fair for you to set up what you think you have seen as overthrowing their authority; even if you happen to be an unprejudiced and accurate observer and have weighed the probability of your observations being vitiated by one or other of the many sources of error in such observation, it is only a small fact, though of course one worthy of notice. There is no good reason why the average man should set so much store by his own impressions of sense, when the fallibility of other witnesses is so readily demonstrable.

Whatever of seeming dogmatism there is in this view is removed by the experimental demonstration furnished by Messrs. Hodgson and Davey, that the kind and amount of mal-observation and faulty description which an average observer will introduce into the account of a performance such as the medium gives, is amply sufficient to account for the divergence between his report of the performance and what really occurred. The success of a large class of tricks depends upon diverting the observer's attention from the points of real importance, and in leading him to draw inferences perfectly valid under ordinary circumstances but entirely wrong in the particular case. It must be constantly remembered that the judging powers are at a great disadvantage in observing such performances, and that it is a kind of judgment in which they have little practice. In the intercourse of daily life a certain amount of good faith and of confidence in the straightforwardness of the doings of others prevents us from exercising that close scrutiny and suspicion here necessary. We know that most of our neighbors have neither the intention nor the sharpness to deceive us, and do not live on the principle of the detective, who regards every one as dishonest until proven to be otherwise. This attitude of extreme suspicion is indispensable in dealing with the phenomena now under discussion. It follows, therefore, that the layman cannot serve as a pilot for himself or for others in such troubled waters. This, however, if duly recognized, need not be a matter of concern. " This unpreparedness and inobservancy of mind in the presence of a conjurer," says Mr. Hodgson, is not " a thing of which any one who is not familiar with the tricks already need be ashamed." Even a professional may be nonplussed by a medium's performance, if he have no experience in the special kind of sleight-of-hand required for the trick. This is the experience of Mr. Harry Kellar; he at first declared himself unable to explain slate-writing as a trick, but now can repeat the process in a variety of ways, and with far greater skill than is shown by the mediums. We may therefore approach Mr. Davey's investigation with the assurance that, in all probability, we too should have failed to detect what was really done, and should have rendered quite as erroneous account of what we saw as did his actual sitters; and according to our training and temperament we should have drawn our several conclusions, and all of them variously wide of the mark.

Mr. Davey (who, by the way, was at one time deceived almost into conversion by spiritualistic phenomena, and who, before he took up the matter seriously, recorded his conviction that "the idea of trickery or jugglery in slate-writing communications is quite out of the question") was an expert amateur conjurer, and repeated the slate-writing performances of such as Englinton with at least equal skill. He arranged with Mr. Hodgson to give sittings to several ladies and gentlemen, on the condition that they send him detailed written accounts of what they had seen. He did not pose as a medium nor accept a fee, but simply said that he had something to show which his sitters were to explain as best they could, and with due consideration of trickery as a possible mode of explanation. The "medium" has here a decided advantage over Mr. Davey, because his sitters come to him with a mental attitude that entertains, however remotely, the possibility of witnessing something supernatural; and this difference is sufficient to create an adjustment of the powers of observation less fitted to detect trickery than if the performer refrains from announcing himself as the go-between of the supernatural. This is well illustrated in the reports of Mr. Davey's sitters; for a few friends who were told beforehand that they were to witness a sleight-of-hand performance, or were strongly led to believe it such, made much less of a marvel of the performance than those who had not been thus enlightened. "Nevertheless"

(I am citing from Mr. Podmore's résumé), " the effect produced was such that a well-known professional conjurer expressed his complete inability to explain the results by trickery; that no one of his sitters ever detected his *modus operandi;* that most were completely baffled, or took refuge in the supposition of a new form of electricity, or 'a powerful magnetic force used in double manner: (1) a force of attraction, and (2) that of repulsion'; and that more than one spiritualist ascribed the phenomena to occult agency, and regarded — perhaps still regard — Mr. Davey as a renegade medium."

Mr. Davey's performances, *as described* by many of his sitters, like the descriptions of the performances of many a medium, are marvelous enough to demand the hypothesis of occult agency: " Writing between a conjurer's own slates in a way quite inexplicable to the conjurer; writing upon slates locked and carefully guarded by witnesses; writing upon slates held by the witnesses firmly against the under-surface of the table; writing upon slates held by the witnesses above the table; answers to questions written secretly in locked slates; correct quotations appearing on guarded slates from books chosen by the witnesses at random, and sometimes mentally, the books not touched by the 'medium'; writing in different colors mentally chosen by the witnesses, covering the whole side of one of their own slates; messages in languages unknown to the 'medium,' including a message in German, for which only a mental request had been made, and a letter in Japanese in a double slate locked and sealed by the witness; the date of a coin placed by the witness in a sealed envelope correctly written in a locked slate upon the table, the envelope remaining intact; a word written between slates screwed together and also corded and sealed together, the word being chosen by the witness after the slates were fastened by himself, etc., etc. And yet, though 'autographic' fragments of pencil were 'heard' weaving mysterious messages between and under and over slates, and fragments of chalk were seen moving about under a tumbler placed above the table in full view, none of the sitters witnessed that best phenomenon, *Mr. Davey writing*."

It must not be supposed that the errors of maldescription and lapse of memory thus committed are at all serious in themselves; on the contrary, they are mostly such as would be entirely pardonable in ordinary matters. Mr. Hodgson places them in four classes. In the first, the observer *interpolates* a fact which really did not happen, but which he was led to believe had occurred; he records that he examined the slate, when he really did not. Secondly, for similar causes, he *substitutes* one statement for another closely like it; he says he examined the slate minutely, when he really only did so hastily. Thirdly, he *transposes* the order in which the events happened, making the examination of the slate occur at a later period than when it really took place. Lastly, he *omits* certain details which he was carefully led to consider trivial, but which really were most important. Such slight lapses as these are sufficient to make a marvel of a clever piece of conjuring ; add to this the increased temptations for mal-observation afforded by the dim light and mysterious surroundings of the medium, as well as by the sympathetic attitude of the sitters, and the wide divergence between the miraculous narratives of spiritualists and the homely deceptions which they are intended to describe, is no longer a mystery.

It cannot be too strongly insisted upon how slight may be the clue that holds the key to the explanation, how easy it is to overlook it, how mysterious the performance becomes without it.   It may be the difference between placing the slate in a given position and starting to do so when the hand of the medium naturally comes forward to receive it; it may depend upon whether the slates were examined just before or just after a certain detail in the performance which was carefully not made prominent; it may depend upon the difficulty of really seeing a quick and unexpected sleight-of-hand movement on the part of a skilled performer; it may depend upon whether the question asked was really of your own choosing, or was deftly led up to; it may depend upon a score of other equally insignificant details upon which the assurance of the average person, that such mal-observation or misdescription did not occur, is almost worthless.   These are some of the slighter factors in the case; there may be much more serious ones which lead not merely to exaggeration but to elaborate falsification and distortion of truth, and to the emphatic assertion of the most extravagant miracles, coupled usually with the assurance that there was no possibility or room for deception. Mr. Davey's performance was relatively a matter-of-fact test with critical and intelligent sitters; hence we should expect the divergence between report and reality to be far less serious than when the question at issue is the demonstration of the supernatural by an appeal to the religious fervor and to the emotional susceptibilities of would-be believers and sympathetic propagandists. I shall return to this difference of attitude in discussing the prepossession in favor of the belief in Spiritualism ; for the present, it is sufficient to notice that under the most favorable combination of circumstances — that is, an able, educated, and experienced observer witnessing a definite performance in a calm, critical mood, and carefully preparing a written account of his observations — the difference between actual fact and the testimony of the witness is still considerable, and the divergence often upon essential points. We are accordingly justified in making allowance for double or treble or a hundredfold more serious divergence between fact and report, when we pass to decidedly less favorable conditions, such as those of the ordinary spiritualistic test or séance ; for these surely present conditions least conducive to accuracy of observation or of record.

It is seldom that so direct and forcible an application of experimental results to actual mental experiences occurring under familiar circumstances can be made, as is the case in regard to this noteworthy investigation of Messrs. Hodgson and Davey. This investigation, almost at one stroke, throws a blinding light upon the entire field of the phenomena ; accounting in large part for the vast aggregate of testimony in favor of miracles by actual witnesses, demonstrating the readiness with which we may unwittingly deceive ourselves by false observation and others by lapses of memory, as to what we actually witnessed ; and again presenting the nature of these fallible characteristics of sense-perception and memory, of inference and judgment, so strikingly and tangibly as to serve as a classic illustration for the psychologist.   The practical import of these considerations has been quite generally disregarded by upholders of the spiritualistic hypothesis, and has by no means been fully appreciated by those who lay claim to an opinion upon the significance of spiritualistic manifestations, and who discuss the psychological questions which they involve.

It is pertinent to add that after Mr. Davey's death, Mr. Hodgson felt free to publish a precise account of what Mr. Davey actually did during the slate-writing séances.[1]   The description from before the footlights may thus be compared with the account from behind the scenes ; and although verbal accounts must always be weak and lack the realistic touch of the *mise en scène*, yet this account makes possible a kinetoscopic reproduction, as it were, of the original sitting; we may observe the point at which the several sitters committed their faults of defective observation or report ; we may examine at leisure the several steps in the performance which the eyes overlooked in the hasty single glimpse afforded by the sitting itself; we may attend to details which in the original sitting reached only the outlying and evanescent phases of consciousness.   But, on the whole, the psychological comprehension of the " séance " was sufficiently manifest without this disclosure of the *modus operandi ;* the disclosure has its value, however, in removing the pos-

[1] *Proceedings of the Society for Psychical Research*, vol. viii. 253.

sibility of certain forms of criticism of the results, in presenting data by which the specific nature of mal-observation may be more concretely studied, and in convincing the more obstinate and skeptical of how natural it is to err in matters beyond the range of one's intimate experience.

A corroborative illustration of the subjective contribution to deceptions of this type — the part that " always comes out of our head," in Professor James's phrase — is furnished by M. Binet's series of photographs, taken at the rate of ten or twelve per second, of the hands of the performer during a sleight-of-hand performance; for the photographs do not show the essential illusion which the eyes seem to see, but which is really supplied by the fixed interpretative habits of the spectators.

The conclusion thus experimentally arrived at by Messrs. Hodgson and Davey is reinforced by other investigators. After witnessing a séance that was merely a series of the simplest and most glaringly evident tricks, Mrs. Sidgwick was expected to have had all her doubts entirely removed, and was assured that what she had seen was better than the materializations at Paris. " Experiences like this make one feel how misleading the accounts of some completely honest witnesses may be; for the materializations in Paris were those which the Comte de Bullet had with Firman, where near relatives of the Count were believed constantly to appear, and which are among the most wonderful recorded in spiritualistic literature. And, after all, it appears that these marvelous séances were no better than this miserable personation by Haxby."

The Seybert Commission finds that " with every possible desire on the part of spiritualists to tell the truth,
the whole truth, and nothing but the truth, concerning
marvelous phenomena, it is extremely difficult to do so.
Be it distinctly understood that we do not for an instant impute willful perversion of the truth.   All that
we mean is that, for two reasons, it is likely that the
marvels of spiritualism will be, by believers in them,
incorrectly and insufficiently reported.   The first reason is to be found in the mental condition of the observer ; if he be excited or deeply moved, his account
cannot but be affected, and essential details will surely
be distorted.   For a second reason, note how hard it
is to give a truthful account of any common, everyday
occurrence.   The difficulty is increased a hundredfold
when what we would tell partakes of the wonderful.
Who can truthfully describe a juggler's trick?   Who
would hesitate to affirm that a watch, which never left
the eyesight for an instant, was broken by the juggler
on an anvil; or that a handkerchief was burned before
our eyes ?   We all know the juggler does not break
the watch, and does not burn the handkerchief.   We
watched most closely the juggler's right hand, while
the trick was done with his left.   The one minute circumstance has been omitted that would have converted
the trick into no-trick.   It is likely to be the same in
the accounts of the most wonderful phenomena of
spiritualism."

If we desire a concrete instance of this omission of
an important detail, we may turn once more to Dr.
Furness's narrative.   Certain highly intelligent observers had described to him the marvelous accomplish-

ments of a Boston medium ; and this is his own account: " There are two tables in the room of séance,
at one of which sits the medium, at the other, the
visitor.   The visitor at his table writes his question in
pencil at the top of a long slip of paper, and, after
folding over several times the portion of the slip on
which his question is written, gums it down with mucilage and hands it to the medium, who thereupon places
on the folded and gummed portion his left hand, and
in a few minutes with his right hand writes down answers to the concealed questions ; these answers are
marvels of pertinency, and prove beyond a cavil the
clairvoyant or spiritual powers of the medium." Dr.
Furness went to the medium, prepared his slip of
paper about as described, and thus continues : " As
soon as he took his seat, and laid the strip on his table
before him, I rose and approached the table so as to
keep my paper still in sight ; *the row of books entirely
intercepted my view of it.* The medium instantly
motioned to me to return to my seat, and, I think, told
me to do so.   I obeyed, and as I did so could not re-
press a profound sigh.   Why had no one ever told me
of that row of books ? "

III

I have thus passed in review a series of facts and
considerations in pursuance of the general inquiry as to
why the manifestations produced in evidence of spirit
agency deceive, and as to the origin of the vast testimony in favor of spiritualistic marvels.   It is not
necessary for the purposes of the psychological discussion to demonstrate that all such manifestations are

fraudulent; it is not even necessary — although with limitless time and energy it might be desirable — to examine all of the various kinds of manifestations which the ingenuity of mediums has devised, or which have been presented through mediumistic agency.[1] All that is necessary is to examine a sufficient number of manifestations of acknowledged standing and repute among spiritualists, — manifestations, be it clearly understood, which have actually brought hundreds and thousands of converts to its ranks, which have been persistently brought forward as indisputable evidence of supernatural agency — and to show that in reference to these, actual and extensive deception has taken place. It would not be proper to declare that at this point the psychologist's interest ends; for the centre of interest in such problems may shift from one point to another. The central point in the present discussion, however, is not what is the evidence in favor of the spiritualistic hypothesis logically worth, — although the considerations here presented have obvious and radical bearings upon that question. If that were our quest, we should put the

---

[1] I desire not to seem to overlook the fact that there are manifestations presented by Spiritualism of a different character from those above considered. There are, for example, the inspirational messages revealed through the medium when in a trance-like condition, and which are supposed to rest for their proof of supernatural origin on the testimony of the medium or upon their internal content. The psychological status of these and similar mediumistic phenomena must be interpreted in the light of our knowledge of hypnotic and allied conditions, of automatic writing, of modifications of conscious and subconscious personality. I do not consider that the evidence which these phenomena contribute towards the establishment of the probability of the truth of the spiritualistic hypothesis at all affects the estimate arrived at in the main discussion. That there are other than the physical phenomena of Spiritualism should, however, not be overlooked.

spiritualists upon the defensive; for the burden rests upon them to show the inadequacy of the natural explanation of the phenomena, and to present the special facts that point to the correctness of the spiritualistic as opposed to other explanations. We may recognize, in passing, to what sorry excuses they are driven in its defense: writing, they are driven to explain, is best produced in the dark, because dark is "negative," and light is "positive"; if the spirit that appears resembles the medium, that is an effect of the materializing process; if a piece of muslin is found in the medium's cabinet (and obviously used as drapery in the materializations), it is supposed to have been brought by the spirits to clothe their nakedness, or that the spirit which had brought the muslin "had to vanish so quickly that it had no time to dematerialize the muslin;" if writing does not appear when the slates are looked at, that is because the "magnetism" of the eye interferes with this spiritual process of writing; and did not Slade receive an express command from the spirits forbidding him, on penalty of cutting off all communication, to attempt to write on sealed slates? Some even claim that fraud and genuine manifestations go hand in hand, or that the former are the work of evil spirits counterfeiting conjuring tricks. A prominent spiritualist openly announces that Slade "now often cheats with an almost infantile audacity and naïveté, while at the same or the next séance, with the same investigators," genuine spiritualistic phenomena occur; while another disciple holds that the true spirit in which to approach the study is an "entire willingness to be deceived." Surely there is no duty resting upon scientific men to consider the claims of a system that resorts to such idle and extravagant hypotheses, and that fosters and prospers in such a moral atmosphere.

We may therefore profitably confine our attention to the psychological lessons to be drawn from the record of fraud and deception which the exploitation of Spiritualism has produced.[1] When the day comes when the manifestations above considered shall be definitely conceded to have a natural explanation along the general lines here presented, and the spiritualists shall have taken refuge in other and distinctively different manifestations, then it may become advisable to prepare a revised account of the psychology of Spiritualism.

There remains an important series of considerations that form an essential factor in the psychological comprehension of the phenomena of Spiritualism; this is the effect of bias and prepossession. When by one

[1] There is a minor problem of psychological interest in regard to the fraud apparent in these manifestations, that is worthy of consideration: namely, the motives for such fraud. That greed for gain and notoriety constitute two of the main inducements is obvious enough; that the latter is a far more widespread and variable mental inducement than we ordinarily realize, has been shown by the cases in which fraud has been detected. In addition we must recognize the existence of deception as the expression of a deep-seated instinct abnormally present in not a few persons. It is deception for the love of imposing upon humanity, mingled somewhat with a love of the conspicuousness and interest which the deceiver's position brings with it; and this often exists where the motives for it cannot be accurately determined. Cases of deception on the part of children, on the part of those who present suspicions of the hysterical temperament, and cases of so-called disinterested deception, have been collected in sufficient number to make the criticisms which are advanced against professional mediums quite as cogent in the case of unpaid and private mediums. I may refer to the discussion of the subject by Mr. Podmore. *Studies in Psychical Research*, p. 185, sqq.

means or another a strong faith in the reality of spiritualistic manifestations has been induced ; when the
critical attitude gives place to a state of extreme emotional tension ; when, perhaps, special griefs and trials
give undue fervor to the desire for a material proof of
life after death, of communion with the dear departed ;
when the convert becomes a defendant of the faith,
anxious to strengthen the proofs of his own conviction,
— then we have no longer mere unintentional lapses of
observation and memory to deal with, but actual mental blindness to obvious fraud and natural explanations ;
then caution is thrown to the winds and marvels are
reported that are the result of expectant attention and
imagination, or of real illusion and hallucination. The
blamelessness that may be conceded for one's mystifica-
tion by conjuring performances cannot be extended to the
present class of experiences ; here it is not unusualness
of external arrangements that forms the main factor in
the deception, but the abnormal condition of the observer's mind. The materialization séances offer a
sufficient example of this form of manifestation. To
recognize a departed friend in the thinly disguised form
of the medium is most naturally interpreted as a mark
of weak insight or of strong prejudice. " Again and
again," writes Dr. Furness, " men have led round the
circles the materialized spirits of their wives and introduced them to each visitor in turn ; fathers have taken
round their daughters, and I have seen widows sob in
the arms of their dead husbands. Testimony such as
this staggers me. Have I been smitten with color-
blindness ? Before me, as far as I can detect, stands
the very medium herself, in shape, size, form, and fea-

ture true to a line, and yet, one after another, honest men and women at my side, within ten minutes of each other, assert that she is the absolute counterpart of their nearest and dearest friend ; nay, that she *is* that friend. It is as incomprehensible to me as the assertion that the heavens are green, and the leaves of the trees deep blue. Can it be that the faculty of observation and comparison is rare, and that our features are really vague and misty to our best friends ? Is it that the medium exercises some mesmeric influence on her visitors, who are thus made to accept the faces which she wills them to see ? Or is it, after all, only the dim light and a fresh illustration of *la nuit tous les chats sont gris ?*" In the confessions of an exposed medium we read : "The first séance I held, after it became known to the Rochester people that I was a medium, a gentleman from Chicago recognized his daughter Lizzie in me after I had covered my small mustache with a piece of flesh-colored cloth, and reduced the size of my face with a shawl I had purposely hung up in the back of the cabinet." With such powerful magicians as an expectant interest and a strong prepossession, the realm of the marvelous is easily entered ; but the evidence thus accumulated may be said to have about the same scientific value as the far more interesting entertainments of the " Thousand and One Nights." " Sergeant Cox," Mr. Podmore tells us, "adduced the hallucinatory feeling of a missing limb in proof of a spiritual body ; and a writer in the ' Spiritualist,' ' not yet convinced of the spiritualistic theory,' could even pronounce the after-images produced by gazing at a straw hat to be ' independent of any known human agency.' From all of which it may be gathered that the conscientious spiritualist, when on marvels bent, did not display a frugal mind." Such opinions certainly justify Mr. Podmore's remark that there are spiritualists, " not a few, who would be capable of testifying, if their prepossessions happened to point that way, that they had seen the cow jump over the moon ; and would refer for corroborative evidence to the archives of the nursery."

It is natural to suppose that prepossession of such intensity could occur only amongst the less intelligent and less discerning portions of mankind ; but to a considerable extent, and certainly in sporadic instances, this is not the case. The distinguished naturalist who shares with Darwin the honor of contributing to modern thought the conceptions of evolution, in his ardent advocacy of Spiritualism, has recorded his assent to the belief that professional conjurers, performing at the Crystal Palace in London, could not accomplish their tricks without supernatural aid. With peculiar obliviousness to the double-edgedness of his remark, he writes : " If you think it all juggling, point out where the difference lies between it and mediumistic phenomena." The same prepossession renders him so impervious to the actual status of the evidence for Spiritualism as to permit him to record so preposterous a statement as the following : The physical phenomena of Spiritualism " have all, or nearly all, been before the world for twenty years ; the theories and explanations of reviewers and critics do not touch them, or in any way satisfy any sane man who has repeatedly witnessed them ; they have been tested and examined by skeptics of every grade of incredulity, men in every way qualified to detect imposture or to discover natural causes, — trained physicists, medical men, lawyers, and men of business, — but in every case the investigators have either retired baffled, or become converts." And in the latest utterances of the same authority the failure to credit the marvels of Spiritualism is put down along with the equal neglect of phrenology, as among the signal failures of our "wonderful century." If any further instances be required of the astounding effects of bias and prepossession in matters spiritualistic, the vast literature of the subject may be referred to as a sad but instructive monument of its influence.

IV

The consideration of the effects of a prepossession in favor of a belief in spirit-agency leads naturally to a consideration of the origin of the belief. This tendency to believe in the return to earth of the spirits of the departed, is probably to be viewed as a form of expression of the primitive animism that dominates savage philosophy, that pervades the historical development of religion and of science, and that crops out in various ways throughout all grades of civilization and all levels of society. Combined with it is an equally fundamental love for the marvelous, and a more or less suppressed belief in the significance of the obscure, the mysterious, the occult. These belief-tendencies, accordingly, have an anthropological significance and an historical continuity which Mr. Lang thus presents : " These instances prove that, from the Australian blacks in the Bush, who hear raps when the spirits come, to ancient Egypt, and thence to Greece, and last, in our own time, and in a London suburb, similar experiences real or imaginary are explained by the same hypothesis. No 'survival' can be more odd and striking, none more illustrative of the permanence, in human nature, of certain elements. To examine these psychological curiosities may, or may not, be 'useful,' but, at the lowest, the study may rank as a branch of mythology or folk-lore." Mr. Tylor fully concords with this view: "The received spiritualistic theory," he says, "belongs to the philosophy of savages. . . . Suppose a wild North American Indian looking on at a spirit-séance in London. As to the presence of disembodied spirits, manifesting themselves by raps, noises, voices, and other physical actions, the savage would be perfectly at home in the proceedings; for such things are part and parcel of his recognized system of nature." Mr. Podmore's comment upon the spiritualistic hypothesis expresses a kindred thought. "As the peasant referred the movement of the steam-engine to the only motive force with which he was acquainted, and supposed that there were horses inside, so the spiritualists, recognizing, as they thought, in the phenomena the manifestations of will and intelligence not apparently those of any person visibly present, invoked the agency of the spirits of the dead. We can hardly call this belief an hypothesis or an explanation; it seems indeed at its outset to have been little more than the instinctive utterance of primitive animism."

The strongly rooted, anti-logical tendencies of our nature, thus indicated, come to the surface in various and unexpected ways, and give rise to views and cults

that have much in common with the manifestations
and beliefs of Spiritualism. It is this very community that forms one of the recognizable stigmata of
such movements ; everywhere there is an appeal to the
yearning for the mysterious, for special signs and
omens that may reinforce the personal interpretation
of the events of the universe, and reveal the transcendence of the limitations of natural law. These
movements, too, seem at different epochs to flare up
and spread into true epidemics, utterly consuming all
inherent foundations of logic and common sense, in the
white heat of the emotional interest with which they
advance. It seems to matter little how trivial, how
absurd, how vulgar, how ignorant, or how improbable
the manifestations may be, the passion for belief in
their mysterious origin sets all aside. Why returning
spirits should devote their energies to playing tam-
bourines, and conjuring with slates, to Indian dances,
and vapid, bombastic, and ungrammatical " inspirational " speeches, seems not even to be considered. It
requires as little evidence and as ridiculous evidence
to prove a spirit to a spiritualist as it did to prove
a witch to a witch-finder. Those whose feelings are
not appealed to by the doctrines of Spiritualism will
assuredly never be attracted by its logic.

The psychologist who observes the natural history
of the belief in Spiritualism, — its origin, and mode of
propagation, its blossoming and fruitage, is naturally
led to consider the nature of its decline. That it
declines rapidly in the presence of newer rivals for
popular favor, appealing to much the same mental
and emotional traits, and therefore finding a similar

constituency, has been made evident in the vicissitudes of its career. It suffered considerably at the period when the meteoric showers of Theosophy passed over our planet; it is subject to the waning of interest that always accompanies familiarity, and that makes even the most exciting experiences pale with time. Such familiarity also gives opportunity for the return of a calm and critical investigative attitude, such as the last two decades, in particular, have brought about. That such investigation is destined seriously to influence opinion, and eventually to triumph over error and superstition, no one with confidence in the ultimate rationality of mankind will be inclined to doubt. In the case of Spiritualism, logic will find a worthy ally in the more discerning development of the moral sensibilities which true culture always brings with it. When it is realized that a system that aims to instruct men in regard to beliefs appealing most earnestly and deeply to the human heart appears in the light of exact investigation as a tottering framework, held together by gross fraud, covered over with innocent self-deception, but also with vulgar sham; when it is realized that under the shelter of such a system men and women all over our land are daily and hourly preying upon the credulity of simple-minded folk, and obtaining a livelihood by means for which the law provides punishment, — the moral indignation following upon this realization will impart vigor to the protest against such practices, which a mere sense of their irrationality would fail to incite. The moral and æsthetic aversion which many of the practices and tenets of Spiritualism arouses in those whose ideals are sound

and steadfast may prove to be a more serious menace
to the spread of the belief, a more potent source of its
decay, than even its inherent inconsistencies and im-
probabilities.

HYPNOTISM AND ITS ANTECEDENTS

IMPORTANT periods in the history of science are as likely to be characterized by changes in attitude towards the accepted body of knowledge, as by the extension of its realm through new discoveries. The contrast between the undeveloped and the advanced stages of a science is as well realized by noting the totally different mode in which facts are viewed, as by observing the vast increase in the range of recorded fact. The alchemist and the chemist have far more in common in the way of operations and material than in their conceptions of the purposes and the method of their pursuits. The astrologer and the astronomer are again most characteristically differentiated by their motives and point of view; both observe the positions of planet and star, and calculate orbits and phases and oppositions; but nothing is more absurdly irrelevant to the astronomer's purpose than the hope of predicting the fortunes of men. A more modern example of a similar relation is that between phrenology and the physiological doctrine of the localization of functions in the brain. And alchemist, astrologer, and phrenologist have this in common: that they aimed at immediately practical ends. The one hoped to create wealth, the other to foretell and control fate, and the third to insure success by discovering the earmarks of natural gifts. They distorted the facts of nature, and in the narrow pursuit of a practical goal, substituted for realities their own fanciful theories, or the elaborations of their defective logic. Science advances most favorably when the best energies are devoted to a comprehension of fundamental principles and to the accumulation of data under the guidance of the interests to which these principles give rise ; and when the work proceeds with the confidence that, more indirectly but more surely, will the richest practical benefits thus accrue. The marked contrast exemplified in the history of chemistry and astronomy, and in a more limited way of brain physiology, make it proper to speak of the very different pursuits with which they were associated as their antecedents and not as early stages of their own development. Intimate as may be the relations between the two historically, the one represents but the forerunner of the other ; it indicates in what direction interest guided thought before that changed interest appeared, which made possible the germination and growth of the true science. Only when the weeds had been rooted out did the flowers begin to thrive.

I

The history of hypnotism furnishes another and a varied illustration of a similar relation. If we accept as the essential fact of modern hypnotism the demonstration of an altered nervous and mental state, in which suggestibility is increased to a quite abnormal degree ; in which, accordingly, functions not ordinarily under the control of voluntary effort become so controllable, and there are induced simple and complex modifications of physiological and psychological activities, — then the condition of opinion that prevailed prior to the recognition of the true significance of the phenomena in question, the false and unfounded and mystical conceptions concerning them, may properly be grouped together as the antecedents of hypnotism. The entire aspect of the problem under the one régime is strikingly different from its appearance under the reign of the successor.

In the presentation, from the point of view of modern hypnotism, of the more important steps in the tortuous and laborious transition from unbridled speculation and fantastic practices to a rational and consistent body of truth, a twofold interest may be maintained; the one, in the fluctuation of opinion antecedent to the scientific recognition of hypnotism, and the other in the *dramatis personæ* concerned in this history and their contributions, great and small, for good or for ill, to that gradual and irregular change of attitude the tested residue of which modern hypnotism embodies. The latter interest will form a helpful guide for selection among the complex sequence of events with which we shall have to deal.   Accounts of the well-established phenomena of hypnotism are so readily accessible, that it seems sufficient to emphasize these two fundamental points — the ultimate recognition of an altered psychophysiological state, and of the dominant part which suggestion plays in the development of hypnotic phenomena — and to accept them as furnishing the principles according to which the survey of the antecedents of hypnotism is to be conducted.

It will appear that much of the conflict which the

present tale unfolds is the conflict between the rational investigation of intelligible facts and the unwarranted attempts at an explanation of alleged miracles, — a phase of the conflict between science and mysticism. The imperfectly understood is apt to be explained by the still more obscure ; totally imaginary forms of energy are called upon to account for poorly observed effects ; and so the mystery deepens, superstition spreads, and charlatanism finds a fertile field for its display. This conflict in the present instance is by no means confined to the past ; the mystical and the miraculous, or at least the unintelligible side of hypnotic phenomena still finds its exponents. Accounts of observations and experiments purporting to demonstrate that hypnotism not only presents hyperæsthesia and exaggerated forms of mental activity, but transcends all normal psychological processes and reveals a hidden world in which other forces and other modes of mental communication freely appear, are widely circulated and sometimes with the authority of names of repute. But the more discerning, the more exact, and the more logical students of hypnotism, cannot accept such observations, and have often been able to point out the unmistakable sources of error which gave rise to them. The shrewdness of hypnotized subjects, the unconscious suggestion of the operator, looseness of observation and theoretical bias, exercise the same influence for error to-day as they presented in the antecedents of hypnotism.

In reading the story of former opinion, it is of advantage to keep in mind the well-established facts regarding hypnotism, not alone for the sake of recognizing what is important and what unessential, what are the instructive and what the irrelevant facts and details, but also for the equal advantage of securing data for the interpretation of phenomena, which in the absence of present-day knowledge, and in the misleading accounts current at the time, naturally gave rise to extravagant forms of explanation. Our knowledge of insanity, hysteria, and trance-conditions, of the influence of the mind over the body, of the nature of illusion and hallucination, of prepossession and suggestion, shed a strong light upon religious ecstasy, upon demon-possession, upon cures by shrines and relics, or by the king's touch, upon the contagion of psychic epidemics, upon the action of magnetized tree or "mesmerized" water, upon the performances of "sensitives" and somnambulists, and the sensational scenes enacted about the "baquet." Our historical survey might accordingly include an account of the states of insensibility and of the potent power of suggestion, which occurred in connection with the religious observances in the practices of ancient civilizations, and have always formed, as they still form, a characteristic cult among primitive peoples. That such states, closely corresponding to the hypnotic trance, are induced for magical purposes among savages is more than probable; equally clear is it that interspersed through the venerable record of magic and witchcraft and ecstasy and exorcism and miraculous cures, are accounts of states, induced usually by religious fervor, which are strongly suggestive of some of the characteristics of the hypnotic condition. But in the interests of unity and brevity it will be best to limit attention to those ancestors of hypnotism, of whose methods and practices we have fairly definite information. More especially does the career of Mesmer supply the most favorable starting-point of the survey; yet some notice should be taken of those who preceded him in achieving reputation as healers of disease.

II

One of the best known of these healers was Valentine Greaterick (or Greatrakes), who was born in Ireland in 1628, and who came to England (about 1665) by invitation of Lord Conway, upon a mission thus quaintly expressed: to cure "that excellent lady of his, the pains of whose *head*, as great and as unparalleled as they are, have not made her more known and admired at home and abroad, than have her other endowments." Lady Conway seems to have been intensely devoted to mystical pursuits, and assembled at Ragley Castle such men as Greatrakes, Rev. Joseph Glanvill, F. R. S., author of *Sadducissimus Triumphatus*, Dr. Henry Moore, the Cambridge Platonist, and others of whom Mr. Lang speaks as "an unofficial but active society for psychical research, as that study existed in the seventeenth century." They told tales of "levitation" and witchcraft and the movements of bodies by unseen agencies, at all of which one or the other had been an eyewitness; and Greatrakes seems to have taken as prominent a part in these as in the healing proceedings. Greatrakes was called to his career by a special indication of providence — " he heard a voyce within him (audible to none else) encouraging to the tryals; and afterwards to correct his unbelief the voice aforesaid added this signe, that *his right hand should be dead, and that the stroaking of his left arme should recover it again*, the events whereof were fully verified by him three nights together by a successive infirmity and cure of his arme." While he failed to cure Lady Conway's headaches " he wrought a few miracles of healing among rural invalids," and seems to have been particularly successful with nervous complaints. "I saw him," writes a contemporary, "put his Finger into the Eares of a man who was very thick of Hearing, and immediately he heard me when I asked him very softly severall questions."

The status of the medical science of the day is well reflected in the comment of Henry Stubbe, physician at Stratford upon Avon, from whose contemporary account our knowledge of Greatrakes is obtained. For explanation of the cures, he suggests " that God had bestowed upon Mr. *Greatarick* a peculiar Temperament, or composed his Body of some particular Ferments, the *Effluvia* whereof, being introduced sometimes by a light, sometimes by a violent Friction, should restore the Temperament of the Debilitated parts, re-invigorate the Blood, and dissipate all heterogeneous Ferments out of the Bodies of the Diseased, by the Eyes, Nose, Mouth, Hand and Feet." However crude may seem this cure by the " Precipitation of the Morbifique Ferment," the theoretical position of Mesmer is not less hypothetical, dogmatic, and gratuitous. Indeed, to Greatrakes's and his biographer's credit, it should be noted that they recognized the distinction between functional and organic complaints ; that Mr. Greatarick "meddles" only with such diseases as " have their

Essence either in the masse of Blood and Spirit (or nervous liquors) or in the particular Temperament of the parts of the Body," that he cures no disease " wherein there is a decay of Nature." " This is a confessed truth by him, he refusing still to touch the Eyes of such as their sight has quite perished." None the less his cures were regarded as miraculous, and Dr. Stubbe tells us that " as there is but one Mr. Greataricks, so there is but one Sunne "; and to dispel incredulity in regard to these wonders, he adds: " We are all Indians and Salvages in what we have not accustomed our senses : What was conjuring in the last age is Mathematiques in this. And if we do but consider the sole effects of Gun-powder, as it is severally to be used, and revolve with ourselves what we would have thought if we had been told those Prodigies, and not seen them ; will we think it strange if men think the actions of extraordinary Ferments impossible ? " But to leave the " Ferments " for the recorded account of what was done, we can only note that Greatrakes's methods consisted mainly of strokings and passes and in driving the pains from one point to another until they went out at the fingers or toes. There is nothing recorded that definitely suggests the production of the hypnotic state ; but direct suggestion, reinforced by manipulations, obviously had much to do with the cures. They clearly approximate more closely to the faith-cure methods of to-day than to the phenomena of hypnotism.

The latter half of the eighteenth century seems to have offered social, intellectual, and political conditions peculiarly favorable to the success of fantastic schemers, of propagandists of strange philosophies, and advertisers of supernatural procedures for short-circuiting the road to health, wealth, knowledge, and immortality. In this period there appeared Swedenborg's inspired revelations and philosophic cult; Cagliostro's extravagant claims of personal power and bold-faced impostures; Schrepfer, who combined with Masonic mysteries a striking anticipation of the materializing séances of modern spiritualism; Gassner, the priest, exorcist, and healer; and finally Mesmer, the founder of animal magnetism, and through it the parent of an endless progeny of unproved and unprovable systems, and of equally irrational practices.

It is worth while to consider for a moment the career of Gassner, if for no other reason than that Mesmer witnessed Gassner's procedures, and that their methods have some points in common, — in particular the calling out of acute symptoms, or "a crisis," as a means of cure. Johann Joseph Gassner, a Suabian priest, appeared as a curer of disease about 1773; he regarded most maladies as of Satanic origin, and attempted cures by driving out the demon of disease by appeal to divine agency. After inquiry regarding the nature of the complaint and its symptoms, he would urge the patient to have faith, and perhaps would offer a prayer for his recovery; he would then call out the various symptoms of pain, stiffness, weakness, and the like, and at the word "*Cesset*" these symptoms would disappear. "*Cesset ista Debilitas*," — the patient becomes as strong and as active as though he had never been sick. "*Modo adsit Febris tantum in Manu et Brachio dextro*," — the right hand becomes cold and numb, and trembles, the pulse in this arm is rapid, feverish, and strong, but slow and normal in the left. "*Cesset in ista Manu et adeat sinistram*," — the left arm now becomes as the right had been, and the pulse of the right is now normal; and so the treatment proceeds, accompanied by the invocation, "*Præcipio hoc in nomine Jesu.*" This process of alternation of pain and its remission is continued, until at length the patient is dismissed as cured. The status of Gassner's cures, except for their more pronounced religious character, is much the same as those of Greatrakes; both exhibit the effects of suggestion, but neither recognized the process of suggestion, nor gives evidence of having produced an abnormal condition. This, however, is by no means excluded; and Greatrakes's account of the insensibility of his own arm, as well as the similar state induced in his patients by Gassner, indicate a high degree of suggestibility.

III

Friedrich Anton Mesmer was born in Iznang, on the Lake of Constance, May 23, 1734; destined by his parents for the church, he turned from the study of theology to that of law, and again changed to medicine. He graduated as a physician from the University of Vienna in 1776, and in his doctor's thesis upon "The Influence of the Planets on the Human Body," he attempted to revive the underlying doctrines of astrology from a medical point of view. He defined the "quality of animal bodies, rendering them susceptible to the influence of heaven and earth," as "animal magnetism;" and regarded the action involved as analogous to that of the moon upon the ebb and flow of the tide. The fluctuations and periodicities of disease he sought to produce artificially, and therefore called his theory the " imitative theory," the object being to imitate the ups and downs of nature. He records his first practical test on the 28th of July, 1774, when he placed magnets upon the chest and feet of his patient, a young lady, who was suffering from a variety of morbid symptoms. Shortly thereafter " she felt internally a painful streaming of a very fine substance going now here and now there, but finally settling in the lower part of her body, and freeing her from all further attacks for six hours." Somewhat later, when the same patient chanced to be suffering from one of her attacks, and was lying unconscious, she responded by violent movements to the slightest touch of Mesmer, but remained entirely unresponsive to the manipulations of a bystander. One of six cups was then chosen by Mesmer's visitor to be impressed with magnetic properties. Contact with this cup, which Mesmer had touched, produced in the patient movements of her hands and expressions of pain. Mesmer's influence made itself felt at a distance of eight steps, and even when a third person stood between the two. These simple observations were the humble beginnings of the practices of animal magnetism.

The details of Mesmer's early doings are of special value, for in them we may expect to discover the true nature of the man and his system; our knowledge of them is derived mainly from the account, written some thirty-five years after the events, by a not too discerning eyewitness. They give a sufficiently definite picture of his manner and methods. Magnets and electric machines, passes and strokings, fantastic dress and equally fantastic manipulations, he utilized even before he became well known. The method was always the same ; calling out pains and paroxysms and crises, and in turn allaying the symptoms thus aroused until the patient was pronounced cured. From the first, too, he was anxious to secure the recognition of authoritative bodies of scientific men. Early in 1775, Mesmer proposed his theory for acceptance to several learned societies, but received no encouragement. His use of magnets (which he probably derived from the astronomer, Hell) had aroused the opposition of his fellow-practitioners, and his professed cure of a protégé of Maria Theresa involved him in a somewhat unseemly dispute, ultimately necessitating his departure from Vienna. In February, 1778, he came to Paris, where he entered upon a remarkable but brief career, terminating somewhat abruptly in 1784.

Mesmer has left us a narrative of his doings during the first three of these years — a record devoted almost exclusively to a wearisome account of his controversies with the various learned societies of Paris. He appealed to the French Academy of Sciences and to the Royal Medical Society, announcing a most wonderful physical discovery, to describe which suitable words were as yet lacking. Mesmer wished these societies to sanction his discovery, not to act as judges of its truth, of which he says there can be no reasonable doubt. He offered them a series of dogmatic propositions, setting forth the nature of animal magnetism, and apparently desired the cures to be considered a subordinate part of the issue.   He was, however, continuously engaged in curing disease.   His most valuable convert was M. Deslon, a member of the Medical Faculty of Paris, a man of considerable influence, who at once espoused Mesmer's cause with unlimited enthusiasm. He invited a dozen of his colleagues to meet Mesmer at dinner, and had read to them an exposition of the system of animal magnetism.   The company seem not to have been very deeply impressed; for it was with difficulty that Deslon induced three of them to associate themselves with him in an investigation; and they soon deserted him, when their requests for simple, unambiguous tests and their explanation of the observed effect as due to an overstimulated imagination, were alike disregarded.   The point at issue in these tests seems to have been whether Mesmer in his own person possessed an influence or magnetic radiation, which brought him into rapport with his magnetically sensitive subjects; but Mesmer apparently regarded any test that reflected the skeptical attitude of the investigators as unbecomingly suspicious.   Deslon, however, remained a staunch believer in the new system, and defended its cause before the Faculty of Medicine, dwelling upon the honor of having it presented to them, and the eternal glory they would merit by accepting "the most important discovery at which the human mind had ever marveled."   But the Faculty voted to reject the propositions, and Deslon lost his seat in their body.

This adverse action, together with Mesmer's threat to leave France, seems to have swelled the enthusiasm in his behalf to enormous proportions.   He tells us that he received a letter from the queen urging him not to shirk his duty to mankind by leaving France at this juncture, that he was visited by a high official in behalf of the king offering him an annuity of 20,000 livres, with an additional 10,000 livres for the rental of an establishment for operating his cures. Mesmer insisted upon the formal and irrevocable admission of the existence and utility of his discovery as preliminary to all negotiations, and demanded, in addition to the annuity, the gift of an estate; but this was a step farther than royal protection would venture.

Our information regarding the latter portion of Mesmer's Parisian career is meagre. In 1781 Deslon published his work on " Animal Magnetism," in which he repeats with undiminished enthusiasm his praises of Mesmer, describes the marvelous cures he has witnessed and prophesies the eventual triumph of the system. Shortly thereafter Mesmer went to the Spa; Deslon remained in Paris and began to treat patients by animal magnetism and with great success. He formed a special private class of educated men and women, from each of whom he received ten louis d'or per month. Upon hearing of this, Mesmer hurried back to Paris and found his former adherents divided into Mesmerists and Deslonists. He then (October, 1782) denounced Deslon as one who had betrayed his secrets and was misrepresenting the system. Through the efforts of friends, an inner circle — the first of the " Loges d'Harmonie " — was formed, consisting of one hundred members, each of whom paid one hundred louis d'or for the privilege of hearing Mesmer's exposition of his whole secret. Dissensions and discussions continued to arise; one of his hearers said "that those who know the secret are in greater doubt than those who are ignorant of it;" and M. Berthellot, the chemist, who in paying his fee reserved the right of criticism, was so irritated at the pedantic and ridiculous treatment to which he was subjected, that he upset the "baquet" and left the room in a violent rage. Matters went on in this way, with frequent propositions of a scientific examination, and as frequent refusals on the part of Mesmer to have further dealings with scientific societies, until, in 1784, the famous commission was appointed by the throne.

This commission was composed of four members of the Faculty of Medicine, MM. Borie (who at his death was succeeded by M. Majault), Sallin, Darcet, Guillotin, to whom were added five members of the Academy of Sciences, MM. Franklin, Leroy, Bailly, Lavoisier, and de Bory. Their report describes in scrupulous and careful detail everything that they witnessed at the house of Deslon, who carefully and circumstantially assured them that Mesmer's procedures and his own were quite the same; and who allowed them the greatest freedom in examinations and tests. They tried the treatment themselves, but felt no effects. They emphasized the fact that public performances in which excitement and contagion have full play are more successful than private ones, and that the subjects most easily influenced are to be found among the ignorant rather than among the educated classes. They blindfolded one of their subjects, and pretended to perform the usual passes, while they really did nothing; yet the expected results ensued. It was believed that when the subject came in contact with a tree that had been magnetized, the symptoms of an approaching crisis would be manifested; accordingly they had a tree in Franklin's garden magnetized, but their subject went to four other trees and at each exhibited the usual phenomena. From such experiments, ingeniously devised and varied, the commissioners concluded that the effects witnessed were due to an overstimulated imagination, to an anticipation of the result, to excitement and contagion. " Let us represent to ourselves," they say, " the situation of a person of the lower class, and in consequence ignorant, attacked with a distemper and desirous of a cure, introduced with some degree of ceremony to a large company partly composed of physicians, where an operation is performed upon him, totally new, and from which he persuades himself beforehand that he is about to experience prodigious effects. Let us add to this that he is paid for his compliance, that he thinks he shall contribute more to our satisfaction by professing to experience sensations of some kind, and we shall have definite causes to which to attribute these effects."

There was presented at the same time a secret report by the same commission, dwelling upon the dangers to morality inherent in these practices. A commission appointed by the Royal Medical Society reported to the same effect. They found in all their experiments that an expectation of the result was necessary to its accomplishment, and they directed attention anew to the entire lack of proof of any of Mesmer's propositions regarding the magnetic fluid. To this second report there was one dissenting voice, that of Jussieu, the botanist, who, while rejecting all belief in animal magnetism, yet curiously regarded heat, as developed by friction, as an essential factor of the phenomena. Furthermore, M. Thouret reported, by request of the same society, upon the literature and history of the doctrine, and traced the notions which Mesmer advanced to older writers ; and showed the similarity of his practices to those of former astrologers and mystics. In opposition to these reports, of which more than twenty thousand copies were issued, Mesmer denounced the government, the scientific societies, the medical profession, and all who had opposed him. His attitude may be inferred from the closing words of a letter to Franklin. " I am like you, Sir, one of those whom one cannot oppress without danger, one of those men, who, because they have done great things, dispose of insult as other men dispose of authority. If any one like you, Sir, cares to try it, I have the world as my judge, and if the world can forget the good I have done, and prevent the good I wish to do, I have posterity as my avenger."

These adverse reports were most influential in terminating Mesmer's career in Paris ; but in this they were assisted by other events. Several deaths at the " baquet " alarmed his adherents, and were promptly turned to account by his opponents. The death of M. Court de Gébelin, an author and prominent man of the day, was the occasion of the characteristic comments of the period ; and especially so as he had recently and publicly announced his indebtedness for renewed health to Mesmer. One of the journals noted his death thus : " M. Court de Gébelin vient de mourir, guéri par le Magnetisme animale ; " another suggested for his epitaph : —

> " Ci gît ce pauvre Gébelin,
> Qui savait grec, hébreu, latin ;
> Admirez tous son héroïsme,
> Il fut martyr de magnetisme."

A comedy entitled " Docteurs Modernes " brought the " baquet" upon the stage, ridiculed Mesmer and his procedures, and hinted with no great delicacy at the abuses to which the popularity of his treatment might give rise. In England the system was thus satirized:

THE WONDERFUL MAGNETICAL ELIXIR

Take of the chymical oil of Fear, Dread,
    and Terror, each   4 ounces ;
    of the rectified Spirits of Imagination   2 pounds ;

Put all these ingredients into the bottle of fancy, digest for several days, and take forty drops at about nine in the morning, or a few minutes before you receive a portion of the Magnetic Effluvia. They will make the effluvia have a surprising effect, etc., etc.

In 1785 there appeared a mock funeral oration upon Mesmer, travestying with endless extravagance his pretensions and methods. Caricature was a favorite mode of attack ; and the examples that have escaped destruction vividly preserve the spirit and the local color of the times. Yet both learned and unlearned opinion was divided, and the press was the medium of eulogy as well as of denunciation. Of still greater importance were the discoveries of the Marquis de Puységur, one of Mesmer's disciples, which diverted the interest in animal magnetism into a new channel ; and,

finally, the turmoil of the French Revolution drove
Mesmerism into obscurity, and Mesmer to a retreat
in the town of Frauenfeld, near the lake of Constance.
Our last picture of Mesmer shows him living in simple
seclusion, complaining of the world's treatment of him,
performing cures among those about him, and cherish-
ing to the end his belief in animal magnetism. He
died March 5, 1815, at Meersburg, where he lies buried.

IV

The system of animal magnetism Mesmer summed
up in a series of twenty-seven propositions presented
entirely without proof, asserting the existence of an
" universally diffused subtle fluid, appearing in all portions of the celestial system, and affecting the animal
economy by insinuating itself into the nerves ; it has
properties analogous to that of the magnet, may be
reflected like light, propagated like sound, and may
be increased, opposed, accumulated, transmitted to
another object, and transported ; furthermore this principle, which is, in a way, a sixth sense artificially acquired, will cure nervous disease directly, and others
indirectly by provoking salutary crises, thus bringing
the art of healing to perfection." Mesmer's methods
varied at different stages of his career. The use of
magnets as the main or exclusive factor in his cures,
he seems to have abandoned before going to Paris ; at
first he made the passes with his hands, or with an
iron rod, directing his fingers toward his patient, and
emphasizing these movements by strokings and rub-
bings. The object of these manipulations was to concentrate and send out the magnetism with which his

body was saturated. This magnetism he could transfer to others or to inanimate objects. " I have magnetized paper, bread, wool, silk, leather, stone, glass, water, different metals, wood, men, dogs, — in one word, all that I have touched, so that these substances produced the same effects on the patients as the magnets." When his increasing success no longer allowed him to attend personally to all his patients, he employed a valet toucher, or imparted the curative properties to water, to a tree, etc. At the height of his career he devised the " baquet," which he describes as a " small open vessel on a three-legged support, from which emerged some bent iron rods, the points of which could be easily applied to the outer parts of the body, such as the head, breast, stomach, etc." The baquet and other paraphernalia served to concentrate and impart the fluid that issued abundantly from Mesmer's person. An eyewitness thus describes the results of the treatment: " Some patients experienced pains and fever; others fell into unusual and severe convulsions, frequently lasting for three hours; others became faint and dazed, and but few remained unaffected. There were manifested the most violent involuntary distortions of the limbs; partial suffocation, heaving of the abdomen, wild glances, were observed; one patient utters piercing cries, another has fits of laughter, while a third bursts into tears. Nothing can break this spell save the command of the magnetizer, and whether the patients be in the wildest frenzy or in the deepest stupor, a word, look, or nod of the master is sufficient to bring them to consciousness. This violent condition was technically termed a crisis, and deprived the patients of all consciousness so that none could at all remember what had been felt, heard, or done while in this condition; and yet they were so sensitive that one could not come in contact with them, not even touch the chair on which they sat, without causing fright and convulsions which only the master could pacify." As the cures progressed, the patients lost their sensitiveness to the magnetic fluid. The scenes about the baquet have come to be the most usual association with the name of Mesmer. The dimly lit room, the odor of incense, the mellow tones of the organ, the hushed silence and anxious expectancy; the entrance of Mesmer, wand in hand, clad in striking robes, to initiate the crises that then spread by the contagion of nervous disorder; all these reflect the intellectual and social conditions of the time, and are most naturally interpreted as the adaptation of a shrewd adventurer to his environment.

In the light of this account it becomes clear that while an altered condition of the nervous system and a state of increased suggestibility were constantly manifested in Mesmer's *salle des crises*, yet Mesmer did not at all appreciate the nature of the process by which the effects were produced, nor the condition which he brought about in his patients. In brief, Mesmerism in the hands of Mesmer was clearly only an antecedent of hypnotism. Yet certain of the more detailed descriptions of the scenes about the baquet unmistakably indicate that some of Mesmer's subjects went into a true hypnotic condition; that as many or more were the victims of more or less complex hysterical attacks is equally clear. But to this aspect

of the phenomena, Mesmer was entirely inattentive.
His attention was devoted to the elaboration of the
physical agencies which in his view were the cause of
the phenomena, and to the production of the rather
violent symptoms of the crisis which he always regarded
as an essential part of the curative procedure.   He
elaborated the baquet, filled it with bottles and glass
and iron filings and water arranged in fanciful ways,
and in some mystical sense suggestive of magnetic influences.   Mesmerism thus consisted of the induction
of crises by animal magnetism, as concentrated in
Mesmer's person and assisted by the baquet, by
passes and physical manipulations.   Farther than this
Mesmer never went in his comprehension of the phenomena that we now know as hypnotism.   Indeed,
when he was confronted with Puységur's subjects in
the somnambulic state, he regarded the production
of this true hypnotic condition as foolish, and considered it to be only a subordinate phase of the magnetic crisis.   Towards the close of his life, and when
the turmoil and the glory of his Parisian career were
memories of the past, when he had had abundant
opportunity for reflection and for the observation of
the altered condition which the status of Mesmerism
had assumed, Mesmer still maintained unaltered the
dogmas of animal magnetism.

In criticism of the attitude of the commission, it may
certainly be held that they underestimated the significance of what they saw and used the term " imagination " in a sense both vague and uncritical ; and yet
the tenor of their conclusions was as wholesome as it
was justifiable.   They were primarily concerned with

the correctness of the proposed explanation of the phenomena, and with the value of the curative procedures;
and on these points their verdict is logically reached
and forcibly stated. The psychic element in the guidance of conduct as in the treatment of diseases they
were prepared to acknowledge, but not as an indorse-
ment of animal magnetism. " In searching for an
imaginary cause for animal magnetism, the actual
power which man exercises over his fellow-beings without the immediate and evident intervention of a physical agent, is recognized." Their tests evidence their
appreciation of the efficacy of suggestion, a power
which they admit " can be elaborated to an art."
While it may properly be urged that the report contributed to the postponement of the scientific study of
this class of phenomena, its admirable logical qualities
entitle its authors to the gratitude and honorable remembrance of mankind. Indeed, in deference to the
excited state of public opinion of the time, they subjected themselves and others to most painstaking tests,
assuming the burden of disproof, and treating Mesmer's
arbitrary attitude with more than scientific fairness.
Their verdict not only destroyed Mesmer's pretensions,
but held out a rational, though in our present lights an
inadequate, interpretation of the phenomena, then so
sensationally presented to an excited and distraction-
loving public.

V

Before the commissioners had completed their examination, the aspect of animal magnetism was, in the
hands of a French nobleman, undergoing an entire

change.   The Marquis A. M. J. Chastenet de Puységur, born in 1752, came of a distinguished family, and
himself took an important part in the Revolution ;
his death was the result of a romantic but imprudent
act of devotion to the royalist cause, on the occasion of
the coronation of Charles X. in 1825.   He was one
of Mesmer's select pupils, and himself a good subject at
the baquet ; and likewise remained a firm supporter of
the doctrines of animal magnetism.   He had constructed
a baquet at his estate at Buzancy, and was applying the
" Mesmeric " practices among his dependents.   It happened on the fourth of May, 1784, that he had magnetized his subject, Victor, in the usual way, when (to
continue with his own words) " what was my surprise
to see at the end of a quarter of an hour this man
sleeping peaceably in my arms without convulsion or
pain. . . . He spoke and seemed occupied with his
own thoughts. . . . I perceived that these were affecting him unpleasantly, and I stopped them and suggested pleasanter ones, which indeed was not difficult.
Soon I saw that he was happy, imagining that he had
drawn a prize or was dancing at a fête, etc. ; these
ideas I fostered, and thus forced him to move about on
his chair as if dancing to a melody, which I made him
repeat aloud, by humming it myself."   Upon awakening, Victor remembered nothing of what had happened.
In this observation there are clearly recognizable an
altered mental condition, a sleep-like unconscious state,
loss of memory upon awakening, and suggestibility of
sensations, ideas, and movements, — all important
characteristics of a true hypnosis.   Indeed, this may
be considered as the first clearly recorded and uncom-

plicated production of the condition which made possible the study of hypnotism.

The phenomena thus presented might readily have
been the starting-point of a scientific investigation of
this peculiar state, had not a subsequent observation
unfortunately directed the experiments into a different
channel. When Victor was again thrown into this
"magnetic crisis" or sleep, — as Puységur at first
termed it, — he began to speak, describing his ailments,
directing what should be done to effect his cure, and
giving similar prescriptions, when questioned in regard
to the treatment of others. This strange condition,
which by its analogy to sleep-walking came to be termed
"artificial somnambulism," was destined to mark a
turning-point in the history of the topic. It was evident, almost from the outset, that the baquet and
the other paraphernalia, the crises, pain, and contortions were rendered quite unnecessary. The patients
had become their own physicians, prescribing such simple remedies as were familiar to them by use or hearsay,
and predicting the time of appearance and the nature of
the symptoms, such as they had witnessed about the
baquet or in everyday life. Within two months of
the first observation, 62 cures had been effected under
Puységur's direction, 300 patients were in attendance,
and 10 somnambulists had been discovered ; before the
close of the year (1784) Puységur published a volume
detailing his cures, his correspondence, and his theory
of animal magnetism.

From the point of view of modern hypnotism, Puységur's position is a most important one, more important,
indeed, than that of Mesmer. His literary productions

and his personal activity in the formation of the Loges d'Harmonie (organizations devoted to the study of animal magnetism) were the most influential factors in keeping alive the study of these phenomena after Mesmer's downfall, and in their revival after the long interruption of the Revolution. Puységur's views were at first identical with those of Mesmer; he believed in the magnetic fluid and the baquet and the crises; but his practices gradually dispensed with all these manipulations and regarded the action of the will upon the somnambules as the essential and sufficient method of effecting a cure. His conceptions were extremely fanciful, and the point of view of his later writings is considerably at variance with that of his earlier compositions. " Some day," he predicts, " after five or six thousand years of existence upon earth, mankind will admit that there is a fluid, or rather a conserving agent of their existence and their health, which they can utilize . . . and direct for the benefit of their fellow-men by the simple action of their wills." This universal magnetism is regarded as acting directly through the human will; " croyez et veuillez " is his motto. The tree likewise acts upon the patients connected with it, through the magnetic action imparted to it by the will of the magnetizer. Puységur regarded what he termed the instinctive electro-magnetism of man as analogous to the force by which the chick imparts movement and life to the germ upon which she broods. It was, however, his practical influence, and not that of his decidedly fantastic views, which guided the progress of the antecedents of hypnotism. The contributions of his successors, as of his predecessors, cannot deprive him of the credit of discovery of the hypnotic condition and of the first clear appreciation of its importance. But the progress which Puységur's discovery had brought about was almost at once lost by the extravagant claims which were soon made for the somnambules in their prediction and direction of the course of disease. They came to be regarded as possessed of supernormal powers by which they could perceive the anatomical conditions of their patients; they predicted the future, or rather they were impressed in advance with a sensation of what was to happen — "*presentiment*" or "*optique preliminaire*"; they traveled in spirit to distant times and places; they were *en rapport* with the magnetizer, hearing and obeying him alone, and interpreting his unexpressed thoughts and wishes; their remedies were declared infallible, and Puységur himself, after thirty years of experience, records that he had met with no case of a wrong prediction. The valuable discovery of an artificially induced condition, recognizable by definite physiological and psychological changes, was at once engulfed in a senseless search for the wonderful and the pursuit of fantastic theories.

Next in importance to the discoveries of Puységur were those of Dr. Pétetin, of Lyons. His general position is much the same as that of Puységur; for "animal magnetism," he substituted an "animal electricity," (such was the title of his posthumous volume, 1808); and he claimed to have found that the intervention of poor electric conductors opposed the appearance of certain of the phenomena of the somnambulic state. In a work published in 1787, he described a new condition characterized by a fixed rigidity of the limbs, to which he gave the name (still applied to it) of "catalepsy," and which continues to be one of the characteristic modifications artificially produced by hypnotization. Dr. Pétetin describes how his subject, when magnetized, became insensible to external stimuli, how her pulse slackened, her muscles became fixed, and how she would maintain any position in which she was placed with statue-like rigidity.   Dr. Pétetin was also the first to record the automatic repetition by the subject of the movements of the operator; the recollection when re-magnetized of what had happened in a previous somnambulic condition, but had been forgotten in the normal interval; and he also recorded the production of what is now known as a negative hallucination. When he had suggested to his subject that whoever would touch a certain candlestick would disappear from her sight, the subject no longer saw the individual thus spirited away.   But as in the case of Puységur, so also in that of Pétetin, he became known not for his most careful and significant observations, but for those which administered to the love of the marvelous, and which were in essence totally erroneous.   Pétetin's contribution to the aggregate of error in which this study was to be merged was the memorable " transposition of the senses."   The same subject who brought to his notice the cataleptic condition led him into this extravagance.   This subject while magnetized began to sing vociferously; while engaged in changing her position during her catalepsy, his chair slipped, and he fell toward her, exclaiming, " Oh, how unfortunate that I cannot stop this singing."   " Oh, doctor," she replied, "do not worry, I won't sing any more;" and she stopped at once. Presently the singing was resumed, and no words of the doctor could stop it, until he spoke to her in the attitude previously assumed by the accidental fall, with his head near her stomach. In this position she heard him and obeyed, but gave no heed to his commands when he shouted them into her ear. And thus was originated the transposition of the senses ; for Pétetin at once concluded, in accordance with the remarkable sensibilities attributed to somnambules, that his subject heard through her stomach. By further experiments he became convinced that tastes and odors could be similarly perceived, and that his subject could read what was written on a card applied to her stomach. He also credited the various other exalted and marvelous mental faculties of his subjects, and added to the prevailing mystery and supernatural tendency of the period. His historical influence was but slight ; he was regarded as a mesmerist, and was chiefly remembered by his introduction of the transposition of the senses into the traditional system of artificial somnambulism. It is interesting to note that the detection of error in another's work does not protect against a similar error in one's own ; Puységur, while accepting with implicit faith the extravagances of his own subjects, was able to recognize that unconscious suggestion lay at the basis of Pétetin's observations. If at first, he remarks, Pétetin had happened to suppose that his cataleptics could speak only during the wane of the moon in May, they would have been dumb for eleven and a half months.

VI

The early decades of the present century witnessed a revival of interest in animal magnetism. Those whom the Revolution had turned away from their favorite studies returned to them; new societies were organized; journals in the interest of the science were founded; it was recognized by various governments and scientific associations; the Berlin Academy in 1818 offered a prize of 3000 marks for the best memoir on the subject; Mesmer was brought forth from his obscurity, and many of the distinctive traits of his system were reintroduced and amplified. The movement was no longer confined to France, but spread all over Europe, and even reached America. Its most continuous connection was, however, still with Paris, and mainly with the learned societies to which Mesmer had appealed in vain.

In contrast to the dominant belief in the miraculous endowment of "somnambulic" subjects, there were a few who presented the subjective nature of the phenomena. The career of Faria, a priest of Portuguese extraction, who resided long in India, is regarded by some as occupying an important place in the history of hypnotism. The Abbe Faria came to Paris in 1814 and gave public exhibitions, in which he produced many of the typical hypnotic phenomena, and explained them as dependent not at all on his own powers, but entirely upon the susceptibility and the faith of his subjects. He rejected alike any belief in a personal influence or in a magnetic or other fluid. He simply asked his subjects to think determinedly of

sleep, or to look at the back of his hand; and then in
an authoritative voice he would call out "*dormez*,"
emphasizing the command by pressing his hand on the
subject's forehead. By such simple means he put to
sleep three or four of every five subjects, and that
within a minute or two. He demonstrated the production of forced movements, the deprivation of control of
simple movements, the false perceptions of sense, etc.,
all as products of suggestion, and indeed anticipated
many of the typical phenomena of modern hypnotism.
Faria's career was prematurely curtailed by an unfortunate incident; an actor succeeded in feigning sleep in
one of his performances, and forthwith branded him as
an impostor. If we may credit certain accounts, his
position practically anticipated that of Braid; but,
according to others, while impressed with the value of
verbal suggestion, he was not free from the prevailing
mysteries and dogmas of somnambulism.   In 1819
Bertrand delivered a course of public lectures on animal magnetism, notable for their appreciation of the
rôle of suggestion in their production. For example,
he sent a magnetized letter to his patient which, when
applied to the body, produced the desired symptoms;
but a second letter, not magnetized, but supposed to be
so, and a third letter, written by a friend in imitation
of Bertrand's handwriting, were equally efficacious.
These are, however, some of the exceptional exponents
of the doctrines, which in the main were concerned
with the miraculous element of somnambulism introduced by Puységur and his followers.

It is to be noted that in the revival of hypnotism the
scene of operation was transferred from the baquet

and *salle des crises* to the hospital; the subjects are no longer persons of fashion seeking release from ennui, but patients of the poorer classes, suffering mainly from one or other of the protean forms of nervous derangement. Some very remarkable subjects were discovered at the Salpêtrière by Georget and Rostan, and the former inserted a chapter on somnambulism in his textbook of physiology. In 1820 Husson authorized magnetism at the Hôtel Dieu; and within a brief time somnambules were to be found at almost all the hospitals of Paris. The phenomena presented were those introduced by Puységur; patients became somnambulic, prescribed for themselves and others, perceived by an internal sense the details of their own anatomy, foresaw the future, and developed a variety of abnormal sensibilities. Baron Du Potet, who experimented extensively at the Hôtel Dieu, was convinced that his subjects could perceive his silent wish and obey his unexpressed command. In Germany appeared eccentric systems of "Tellurism" and "Siderism," and the occult was rampant. The mysterious and extreme phenomena were accentuated, and the value and genuineness of the entire somnambulic condition were made to rest upon the demonstrability of miracles. Here and there a few of the simpler phenomena, such as insensibility to pain, were produced, but in the main these were neglected.

Of this type were the observations that, through the zeal of Dr. Foissac, the Academy of Medicine was called upon to consider in 1825. He offered to exhibit his subjects, claiming for them all the supernormal powers above indicated — that, indeed, "they were possessed of the genius that had inspired Hippocrates." The work of this commission was not free from dissensions; and five years elapsed before they were able to submit a report. The report was extremely favorable to the magnetists, and urged that, while some of the effects produced were too trivial to serve as evidence of a new system, and while others could be explained as due to the action of the imagination, "some results depend solely upon magnetism and cannot be produced without it." The commission corroborated the physiological and other effects that had been already recorded, — such as quickening of respiration and circulation, the induction of tremors and convulsive movements, insensibility to pain and to ordinary stimuli, the rapport between subject and operator, the continuity of memory in successive magnetic states; but the chief stress was laid upon the more wonderful operations. Of these they certified as genuine, reading with closed eyes, the prediction of the course of disease, clairvoyance, and general mental exaltation. They also testified to the value of the therapeutic effects, and conclude that the "academy should recognize and encourage researches into magnetism as an interesting branch of psychology and natural history." The report was read, but met with such decided disapproval that it was withheld from the public. Its fundamental error was the supposition that the demonstration of so unaccountable a phenomenon as reading without the use of the eyes was necessary to or could establish the existence of animal magnetism; they also erred through ignorance of the extreme rigidity of conditions necessary to exclude the endless possibilities of deception, conscious and unconscious, and of the remarkable subtlety and hyperæsthesia of hysterical and hypnotic subjects.

The next scene upon the stage of the Academy of Medicine was enacted in 1837. At this time, the painless extraction of a tooth from a patient in a somnambulic condition aroused considerable attention, especially as the operator, Dr. Oudet, was a member of the Academy. Other painless surgical operations upon magnetized patients were reported. At about this time, Dr. Berna directed the attention of the Academy to his subjects, for whom he claimed such powers as reading with closed eyes. To test these claims a commission of nine was appointed, and reported promptly, July 17, 1837. This report was negative in the extreme. It raised the objection that everything was made to rest upon the testimony of these somnambulists; it declared that even the proofs of insensibility were defective, and flatly denied the existence of the condition of somnambulism. The alleged interpretation of the will of the operator was referred to unconscious suggestion; the attempt at reading with the eyes closed and the recognition of objects applied to the occiput was either a total failure, or depended for its small measure of success upon the shrewd guesses of the subjects, whose honesty was regarded as not above suspicion. " We are at a loss what to think of a somnambulist who described the knave of clubs on a blank card, who transformed the ticket of an academician into a gold watch with a white dial plate inscribed with black figures, and who, if she had been pressed, would perhaps have gone on to tell us the hour marked by this watch." The commission of 1837, even more specifically than that of 1825, was called upon to consider alleged marvels ; and this circumstance should be taken into account in applying to them, as may properly be done, the same criticism as was directed against former commissions. They, too, have mistaken the real issue, and their justifiable skepticism regarding such facts as reading without the use of the eyes unduly biased their judgment in regard to the simpler and readily verifiable phenomena.

The next step was certainly a practicable one ; Burdin, a member of the Academy, offered a prize of three thousand francs to any one who could read without the use of the eyes. The offer was open for two years, and subsequently the time was extended. Considering the large number who had claimed this power, few offered themselves for examination ; and these either clearly failed to meet the test (being detected in the manipulation of the bandage, and the like), or those who had the somnambulists in charge refused to conform to the conditions required by the examiners ; and so the prize was never awarded. The Academy then voted, October 1, 1840, to refuse from that time on to give any consideration to questions relating to animal magnetism.

VII

Soon after the study of animal magnetism was thus denied academic recognition in France, it was in some measure divested of its mystifying and confusing accretions, by the independent observations of an English surgeon, James Braid. Braid's first experience with the phenomena of animal magnetism was at the séance given by Charles Lafontaine, a traveling mesmerist, at Manchester, on November 13, 1841. He came to this exhibition inclined to regard the phenomena as due to deception, trickery, and illusion, and saw nothing to disturb his belief. At a second attendance, he was impressed with the fact that the "magnetized" subjects were unable to open their eyes; this he attributed to a paralysis of the nervous centres by a too prolonged or too intense sensory strain. Braid at once initiated experiments at his home. He began by asking a friend to stare fixedly at the neck of a bottle, held close to and a little above his eyes; in a few minutes the subject's eyelids closed, his head dropped, and he went to sleep; the same process was repeated upon Mrs. Braid, with an equally successful result. These experiments were soon extended, and Braid was successful in sending to sleep nearly all who presented themselves. The regularity and simplicity of the process, as well as the unmistakable evidences of an altered mental condition, left no doubt of the genuineness of the induced sleep. "I now stated that I considered the experiments fully proved my theory, and expressed my entire conviction that the phenomena of mesmerism were to be accounted for on the principle of a derangement of the state of the cerebro-spinal centres, and of the circulatory, and respiratory, and muscular systems, induced, as I have explained, by a fixed stare, absolute repose of body, fixed attention, and suppressed respiration concomitant with that fixity of attention. That the whole depended upon the physical and psychical condition of the patient, arising from the causes referred to, and not at all on the volition, or passes of the operator, throwing out a magnetic fluid, or exciting into activity some mystical universal fluid or medium. I further added that having thus produced the primary phenomena, I had no doubt that the others would follow as a matter of course, time being allowed for their gradual and successive development." The practical importance of the change of view thus inaugurated was extreme; it combated the prevalent notion that to prove the reality of the magnetized condition, it was necessary to perform miracles; it recognized different degrees and stages of the induced condition; it emphasized the dependence of the condition upon the state of the nervous system, and supplied the physiologist with a rational interest in the phenomena; it discarded the vain hypothesis of an universal fluid; it simplified the methods of producing the state, and showed its analogy to ordinary sleep; it proved that the phenomena were independent of the will or any subtle power of the operator, but depended essentially upon the compliance and suggestibility of the subject.

The importance of Braid's position in the history of hypnotism is not easily overrated; it depends largely upon the fact that he was the first to recognize the physiological aspect of the phenomena and to abandon completely any relation with the fantastic theories and practices that grew up in the wake of animal magnetism. It cannot be said that Braid's discoveries, however original with him, had not been anticipated by others; indeed, it is clear that the Abbé Faria's method of inducing the condition and the phenomena that he exhibited were essentially the same as those to which Braid directed attention; while Bertrand, and even

Puységur and others, had recognized the rôle of suggestibility and imagination in producing many of the effects.   But Braid, far more clearly than any one else, presented the phenomena from a legitimate scientific view, correlated the various phenomena with one another, and laid the foundations of a true science of hypnotism.   Without disparaging the labors of others in this field, and without forgetting the unfortunate circumstances in Braid's career which detracted from his influence, the title may be justly claimed for him, of the founder of modern hypnotism, as he was also the inventor of the term.

It would take us too far into the details of the hypnotic condition to describe Braid's practices and experiments; attention will be directed only to those points which have a bearing upon the further history of the topic.   At the outset, Braid recognized that he was dealing with an altered nervous condition, in which were present hyperæsthesia, or exalted sensibility of several of the senses, together with a control over functions normally beyond the reach of the will ; that these powers could be used to neutralize pain, as well as for curative suggestions in the treatment of disease ; and that the phenomena had a distinct relation to ordinary sleep ; this last relation led him at first to speak of the topic as " Neurypnology," — the title of his first book, published in 1843.   It is quite intelligible that the confused and misleading form in which the phenomena were presented during Braid's time prevented him from grasping at once or completely the true subjective nature of the condition, in spite of the clearness with which he recognized the marks of its genuineness. Thus, he regarded that a physical influence had much to do with the result, and confessed that he was entirely at a loss to understand why a breath of air upon the skin, as by blowing upon it, should terminate the hypnotic condition; or make a rigid limb flexible, or restore the sight of one eye, and leave the other insensible; or change the condition from that of general inactivity to one of extreme mobility and excitability. Later, however, he recognized in all this, the action of suggestion combined with the imaginative ingenuity of the subject. But his most serious handicap was his connection with the doctrines of phrenology, then occupying a very conspicuous position in the public eye. It was brought into connection with mesmerism or hypnotism by the performances of professional exhibitors, who claimed that pressure upon different parts of the head of the magnetized subject induced the display of the corresponding "faculties." It seems quite clear that Braid was entirely misled by these curious experiments; and in spite of the fact that he later abandoned all belief in their reality, and explained them as due to suggestion and association; and further that he presented some grounds for believing that his former experiments were intended to disprove phrenology, — yet it is perfectly clear why the medical profession and the intelligent public should have discredited Braid's labors by reason of his notorious connection with the doctrines of phrenology. Surely a work which recorded such experiments as the following naturally excited a feeling of distrust. Patients, on being "pressed over the phrenologist's organ of time, always expressed a desire 'to write' — a letter

— to her mother or brother; over their organ of tune, ' to sing'; between this and wit, ' to be judicious'; the boundary between wit and causality, ' to be clever'; causality, ' to have knowledge'; in the centre of the forehead, to have 'a certain perception of learning'; and so on." And again: " I placed a cork endways over the organ of veneration and bound it in that position by a bandage passing under the chin. I now hypnotized the patient, and . . . after a minute and a half an altered expression of countenance took place, and a movement of the arms and hands, which latter became clasped as in adoration, and the patient now arose from the seat and knelt down as if engaged in prayer. On moving the cork forward, active benevolence was manifested, and, on being pushed back, veneration again manifested itself." We are then assured that the subjects knew nothing of phrenology, were perfectly honest, and that no indications were given of the expected results. Braid frankly records his belief in the possibility of calling out phrenological activities by pressure on definite points of the cranium; and the only loophole of explanation which he left open was the one to which he later resorted, claiming that the manifestations may be due to " a system of training during the sleep, so that they may come out subsequently as acts of memory, when corresponding points are touched, with which particular ideas have been associated through audible suggestion." In brief, in this explanation, given in 1854, Braid demonstrated the admitted possibility of arousing emotions in hypnotic subjects by inducing the expressions with which those emotions were associated. But in 1843 he wrote,

"If I am to believe the evidence of my senses, therefore, in anything, I cannot see how I can doubt the relation which consists between certain points of the cranium and the mental manifestations which are excited by acting on them during hypnotism. I believe there are few physiological phenomena which can be more clearly demonstrated, especially at such an early stage of their investigation."

Braid's later works did not attract the attention which they deserved, and perhaps it is proper to base an estimate of his insight into the phenomena of hypnotism upon his more mature but less influential writings. In these, Braid recognized the subjective nature of the phenomena as fully as they are recognized by the extreme representatives of the "suggestionist" school of to-day. Indeed, he spoke of the state as "Monoideism," to emphasize the fact that, while in this condition, the subject's mind was totally absorbed in one idea; and that this narrow concentration of consciousness, this influence of the dominant idea, completely controlled mental and physical action, and rendered the subject insensible to all other stimuli. Braid acquired a profound knowledge of the effects of suggestion, both directly, as verbal suggestion, and the indirect suggestion of manner and expectation. He tells of a physician in London who used "mesmerism" with his patients, and who produced catalepsy of the hands and arms and other wonderful effects by the application of magnets. Braid recognized that the subject, though asleep, was in a condition in which she could hear what was going on. He assured the physician (in the subject's hearing) that he had a little instrument in his pocket, which though not a magnet, would produce equally marked effects. Braid gave the patient the little instrument, with the remark to the physician that it would produce catalepsy in both hands and arms; and such was the result. Next, Braid declared that now she would be unable to hold it, which also was the case, the little instrument dropping out of her hands whenever it was given to her. When the patient was aroused, Braid next told the physician that when the little instrument was suspended on the third finger of the right hand of the patient, it would send her to sleep; to which the physician responded, "It never will." But Braid insisted that it would; and the event proved that he was correct. The little instrument, so variously potent in combination with a proper suggestion, was nothing more than his portmanteau key and ring. It illustrates the reverse of Voltaire's saying, that incantations, together with a sufficient amount of arsenic, will kill your neighbor's sheep. In the same way Braid proved that the experiments which seemed to show that certain persons were sensitive to metals were in reality due to unconscious suggestion, and that when, unknown to the subjects, wood was substituted for metals, the expected results ensued. The peculiar effects described by Reichenbach's sensitives he naturally referred to the same cause; as also the doctrine, then brought forward, that susceptible individuals could perceive the effects of drugs enclosed in sealed vials. All these alleged phenomena were correctly referred to unconscious suggestion and to hyperæsthesia. Homœopathic remedies, he argued, owed their efficiency to the same action of the expectant imagination; for the effect could hardly be ascribed to a quantity so minute that a patient would have to take a dose every second of the day and night for 30,000 years to get a single grain of the substance. He analyzed the possibilities of error in the interpretation of clairvoyance; and showed that perfectly natural and well-understood processes were sufficient to furnish an intelligible mode of accounting for so much of the success as could be verified. He recognized the dangers of hypnotism in inexperienced hands; although he believed that the moral sensibility of the subject was sufficiently retained in the hypnotic condition to prevent the abuse of the state for criminal purposes. He appreciated its field of applicability in the cure of disease, though he by no means regarded it as a panacea, and also its special use in surgical operations. In fine, Braid, in spite of certain shortcomings, which are characteristic only of his earlier writings, stands out preëminently as the first to appreciate at their true value the entire range of the complex factors of the hypnotic condition; to distinguish the genuine phenomena from those which owed their marvelous aspect to unconscious suggestion; and to show the relation of the whole topic to the recognized body of scientific knowledge.

VIII

In spite of these very great merits, Braid's influence was for a considerable time a slight and uncertain one; this was probably due not alone to the opposition which his methods and teachings aroused in the medical profession, but far more to the natural distrust of a topic which was exploited in the form of popular and vulgar exhibitions. The main association of hypnotism was still with the absurd notions of animal magnetism, and with attempts to demonstrate marvels, such as clairvoyance and the sensitiveness to magnets. It thus came about that, during the period subsequent to Braid's discoveries, hypnotism presented a varied aspect. On the one hand, unlimited skepticism and a determined repudiation of readily verifiable observations; on the other, uncritical enthusiasm without appreciation of science and its methods. But in addition to the conservatism of the man of science, and the groundless pretensions of the mesmerist, are found the contributions of a few discerning students aiding, though in a sporadic and uncertain way, the progress of the science. What had been repeatedly established was forgotten and had to be reëstablished; observations made by those who in some one direction had fallen into error were discredited, and had to be verified anew. The progress was thus tortuous and ill-defined, but none the less the essential and important phenomena were gaining wider and more authoritative recognition. The use of hypnotism as an anæsthetic was most influential in compelling the attention of the medical profession; for the frequent reports of surgical operations upon hypnotized patients by men of reputation could hardly be dismissed as illusory. As early as 1821 Recamier had utilized the magnetic insensibility for surgical purposes; in 1829 Clocquet performed a severe operation upon a magnetized woman; in 1837 Oudet extracted a tooth from a patient in this condition; from 1842 on a number of English surgeons

— Tupham, Ward, Elliotson, Purland — used hypnotism for various surgical operations, and a Mesmeric Infirmary for this purpose was successfully maintained. Many of the reports of such operations were received with extreme skepticism. The celebrated surgeon, Lisfranc, regarded Clocquet as a dupe; and Oudet met with a similar reception. Most extensive and remarkable were the series of operations performed in India upon natives by Dr. Esdaile, and reported in 1846. The most shocking and dangerous pathological growths were removed without pain and with the minimum of discomfort. Dr. Esdaile is entitled to high rank in the account of this period, because his work was done so largely in independence of others ; moreover, he developed a theory of the phenomena quite analogous to that of Braid ; and in days when anæsthetics were but little known naturally grew enthusiastic over the value of the practices which he had so successfully demonstrated.

A more detailed account of this period than is here possible would consider the physiological contributions of such as Carpenter and Bennett and Mayo, whose criticisms and explanations of the alleged marvels and false theories of mesmerism stemmed but could not stay the flow of extravagant practices and beliefs with which England was then deluged ; with the carefully detailed conclusions and experiments of Azam, of Demarquay, and Girard-Teulon, of Durand de Gros (who later assumed the name of Phillips, and through whom Braid's work was introduced into France) ; and of several other and often independent workers. There is one, however, whose position is worthy of separate notice, and who in a peculiar way forms the transition between the present status of hypnotism and that which prevailed a half century ago. I refer to Dr. A. A. Liebault, who, until within recent years, maintained at Nancy the hypnotic clinic founded by him forty years ago. In 1866, he published a valuable and original work describing his methods and practice. He put his subjects to sleep by verbal command, and suggested to them the relief of their pains and ailments, enforcing the suggestions with such prescriptions as were likely to be effective. He thus adopted the method of " suggestion " as the central point of the system, and may be regarded as the founder of the " suggestionist " school, also known, though not in the main by reason of his labors, as the school of Nancy. Living in retirement, out of touch with the medical profession, presenting his results in a form unattractive to the scientific mind, and encumbered by peculiar personal views, his work attracted no attention; and it remained for more influential investigators, particularly Charcot at Paris and Bernheim at Nancy, to establish the recognized doctrines of modern hypnotism.

IX

It will be instructive at this point to retrace our steps and complete the survey of the antecedents of hypnotism by some account of a series of contributions, which, while they may represent the backward steps in the zigzag line of progress from obscure speculations to science, are nevertheless important historical factors in the continuity of the movement, and in the maintenance of the interest in this branch of psychological study. The fanciful doctrines, which Mesmer revived, originated in mediæval mysticism and superstition; and at no time, from then till now, have such extravagant systems and notions failed to attract an all too extensive class of intellectual malcontents, to whom the progress of knowledge seems absurdly slow and laborious. Before the establishment of the scientific theory of the relation of body and mind, the opportunity in this field for such speculations was endless, and it is to the vast history of pseudo-science that an account of these properly belongs. It is for the purpose of gaining a proper understanding of the various conceptions which were and are associated with hypnotism that an excursion into this barren area is here made. The fantastic schemes of Mesmer, Puységur, and Pétetin, and even of Braid, have already been noticed, and the seed sown by them still bears undesirable fruit. To J. P. F. Deleuze (1785–1835), author of influential works on mesmerism, may be accorded the doubtful honor of ranking as leader in the movement which continued the mystic and eccentric elements of animal magnetism. He accepted the combined marvels of mesmerism and somnambulism. He directed his efforts towards the elaboration of the paraphernalia of the baquet, the wand and passes, and the inculcation of most detailed cautions and regulations for the guidance of the operator. Every movement of the hand, and eyes, and head assumed special significance. The poles of the human frame must be considered, and no departure made from the prescribed manipulation. The process of demagnetizing is thus described: —

" When you wish to put an end to the sitting, take

care to draw toward the extremity of the hands and toward the extremity of the feet, prolonging your passes beyond these extremities and shaking your finger each time. Finally, make several passes transversely before the face, and also before the breast, at the distance of three or four inches; these passes are made by presenting the two hands together, and briskly drawing them from each other, as if to carry off the superabundance of fluid with which the patient may be charged. You see that it is essential to magnetize, always descending from the head to the extremities, and never mounting from the extremities to the head." The magnetism is imparted to inanimate objects, and " one may magnetize a pitcher of water in two or three minutes, a glass of water in one minute. It is unnecessary to repeat here that processes pointed out for magnetizing water, like everything else, would be absolutely useless, if they were not employed with attention and with a determinate will." " The magnetizer who uses a wand ought to have one of his own, and not lend it to any person, lest it should be charged with different fluids — a precaution more important than it is commonly thought to be." It is this phase of the subject that found its way into Germany, and was most typically embodied in the writings of Wolfart, Kieser, and Ennemoser. For such mystics nothing seemed too absurd to find credence, nor too profound to find an explanation in animal magnetism.

It was through Deleuze's influence, also, that mesmerism was transplanted to America. As early as 1837, Charles Poyen lectured and wrote on animal magnetism in New England; he exhibited the usual phenomena, made the usual claims for supernatural faculties, and gave the usual fanciful expositions. It was, however, through Dods and Grimes, in 1850, that mesmerism became prominent in America, under the absurd name of "electro-biology." The popular interest which they aroused may be inferred from the fact that they were invited to exhibit before Congress, the signatures of Clay and Webster appearing in the letter of invitation. The absurdity of their writings is sufficiently evident in the following extracts: "Let two persons of equal brain, both in size and fluid, sit down. Let one of these individuals remain perfectly passive, and let the other exercise his mental and physical energies according to the true principles of mesmerizing, and he will displace some of the nervo-vital fluid from the passive brain and deposit it in his own instead. The next day let them sit another hour, and so on day after day, until the acting brain shall have displaced the major part of the nervo-vital fluid from the passive brain and filled up that space with its own nervous force, and the person will yield to the magnetic power and serenely slumber in its inexpressible quietude." "Your brain being magnetically subdued is worth hundreds of dollars to you. You are then ready for the day of distress." An ignorant young man is magnetized and forthwith converses with a "mental activity which put to blush men of superior education and intellectual endowments." An eminent lawyer is astonished at his learning and his quotations from legal authorities. He speaks Greek, Latin, French, Polish, all perfectly, and without accent; though when awake he knows no language but English. Grimes determined the function of parts of the brain from the answers of his somnambulist, and thus discovered that the corpus callosum is designed to equalize the flow of the nervous fluid. From the same source he received the assurance of the correctness of his phrenological views. "I then asked her concerning the location and uses of several new phreno-organs, which I supposed that I had discovered, and to my surprise she answered me without the least hesitation, and confirmed all my previous opinions, not even excepting those opinions which I had never mentioned to any one, and which she could only have known by clairvoyance."

"Electro-biology" made its way into England, and there found a place among the endless forms of absurdity and pseudo-science then prevalent. A few illustrations are powerless to give any adequate notion of the extent and variety of the extravagant pretensions with which animal magnetism was saturated in the years following Braid's observations. The diabolic origin of mesmerism was discussed by pulpit and press; a pamphlet, entitled "Dialogue between a Mesmerist and a Christian," maintained that the two faiths were incompatible. It was generally urged that mesmerism favored materialism, and in 1856 the Catholic Church issued an edict against the practice. The skepticism of the medical profession found expression in extreme and certainly unscientific statements. Dr. Buchanan (1851) of Glasgow, holding that the alleged condition was the result of acting and trickery, proposed the experiment of telling a hypnotized boy that he could not move, and then applying the birch; this, he felt confident, would satisfactorily refute the whole doctrine, and if, in ninety-nine cases out of one hundred, the boy did not scamper off, though his feet were mesmerized, he promised to recant " and to believe in mesmerism ever after." There is unfortunately no record of the acceptance of this test, which, in comparison with the hypnotic anæsthesia of surgical operations then performed, would have been easily met. From the following comment of a medical journal, in 1843, one may infer that the controversy did not always recognize the *politesses* of discussion. " The mesmero-mania has nearly dwindled in the metropolis into servile fatuity, but lingers in some of the provinces with the *gobe-mouches* and chaw-bacons, who, after gulping down a pound of fat pork, would, with well-greased gullets, swallow such a lot of mesmeric mummery as would choke an alligator or boa-constrictor."

The two writers to be presently cited are selected as illustrations of the truth that the possession of intellectual attainments in other directions does not insure against such gross errors as are about to be noticed, and the second, moreover, serves as a type of the compilations of the period, to which the reader may be referred for further instances. The reputation of Miss Harriet Martineau insured general attention to her " Letters on Mesmerism " (1845). Miss Martineau was cured of a long-standing illness by magnetic treatment, the operator being a noted mesmerist, Spencer T. Hall. The magnetizing-process gave rise to peculiar sensations which were attributed to the action of the magnetic fluid. " My head has often appeared to be drawn out, to change its form according to the traction of my mesmerist, and an indescribable but exceedingly agreeable sensation of transparency and lightness through a part or whole of the frame has followed." Miss Martineau was thus made a convert to mesmerism, and initiated experiments of her own, finding in her maid, J., a somnambule of unusual powers. She maintained her health by following the prescriptions given by the somnambule, and the latter exhibited the many varieties of marvels with which we have become familiar. The spontaneous or suggested utterances of the somnambule upon matters relating to her exalted condition were unquestioningly accepted. " Do the minds of the mesmerist and the patient become one ? " " Sometimes, but not often." — " Is it, then, that they taste, feel, etc., the same things, at the same moment ? " " Yes." — " Will our minds become one ? " " I think not." — " What are your chief powers ? " " I like to look up and see spiritual things ; I can see diseases, and I like to see visions." — " Can the mind hear otherwise than by the ear ? " " Not naturally ; but a deaf person can hear the mesmerist when in the sleep ; not anybody else, however."— " How is it that you can see without your eyes ! " " Ah ! that is a curious thing. I have not found it out yet."

From the " Letters to a Candid Inquirer on Animal Magnetism," by William Gregory, M. D., F. R. S. E., professor of chemistry in the University of Edinburgh, selections appropriate to our present purpose may be made almost at random. Some writing is placed in the hands of the somnambule, and from this she pictures the writer, tells of the lady's recent ailments, her surroundings, her travels, and her condition; and when the lady herself is presented she immediately recognizes her as the subject of her vision. A lost watch is recovered and the thief detected by the same means; the whereabouts of absent friends traveling in distant lands is determined by placing a sample of their handwriting or a lock of their hair in the somnambule's hands. The somnambule transports herself to past times, and details the events of the life of Mary, Queen of Scots, as she witnesses them. In her magnetic vision she follows, day by day, the adventures of Sir John Franklin, who was then in the Arctic regions. She frequently spoke of his occupations, and, when asked the time of day, found it either by looking at a timepiece in the cabin or by consulting Sir John's watch; and from the difference in time indicated by the somnambule the longitude of Sir John Franklin's location and the directions of his movements were calculated. "On a Sunday afternoon in February, 1850, she said it was about 10 A. M. there, and described the captain, Sir John, as reading prayers to the crew, who knelt in a circle with their faces upward, looking at him and appearing very sorrowful. She even named the chapter of St. Mark's gospel which he read on that occasion." Although we are naïvely told that, "as a general rule, we ought to verify the vision before admitting it as an instance of genuine clairvoyance," yet in this case the somnambule's assertions had been so uniformly verified that it seemed unnecessary to question the correctness of her mental Arctic explorations.

All the varieties of supernatural conditions — conscious lucidity, conscious clairvoyance, sympathetic clairvoyance, sympathetic retrovision, direct clairvoyance, mental traveling, introvision and prevision, spontaneous retrovision — were formulated and added their quota to the general mystery. The doctrine of cross-magnetism, or the disturbing influence of different magnetizers, was developed, and became a favorite mode of accounting for failures of all kinds. Extravagant doctrines originating in other fields of pseudo-science were incorporated into magnetism; the magic mirror or crystal was one of these. The notion is doubtless very ancient, — compare the shew-stone of Dr. Dee (1527–1608), — and was revived by Baron Du Potet, who drew a black magic circle on the floor with a piece of charcoal; this the subject approached, stared at it fixedly, and seemed fascinated by it; grew excited, breathed hard, moved to and fro, and then saw visions in the magic mirror. "It was no dream nor nightmare; the apparitions were actually present. A series of events were unrolled before him, represented by signs and figures which he could understand and gloat over, sometimes joyful, sometimes gloomy, just as these representations of the future passed before his eyes! Very soon he was overcome by delirium, he wished to seize the image, and darted a ferocious glance towards it; he finally started forward to trample on the charcoal circle, the dust from it arose, and the operator approached to put an end to a drama so full of emotion and terror."

"Darlingism" was a term brought forward by one Darling, who used a disc, said to be made of zinc and copper, to put his subjects to sleep. Like electro-biology, it was merely a new name for the same phenomena exhibited in connection with absurd theoretical notions. The phrenological manifestations, so unfortunately countenanced by Braid, continued to be exhibited by others in connection with the hypnotic state. Clairvoyance continued to be regarded as one of the most essential tests of the mesmeric condition, and took a prominent part in public exhibitions. Somewhat later it was incorporated into the equipment of spiritualism, and this movement probably exerted a mystic influence upon mesmerism.

The investigations of Baron Reichenbach added a new class of sensitives. Reichenbach announced the doctrine of an " odic " force or " odyle," streaming forth from magnets and from the human frame, and affecting the human system; certain sensitives could see these emanations, and magnetized subjects at once become " odic " sensitives. The doctrine that certain persons are sensitive to metals was an ancient one. It reappeared in the myths that were woven about Casper Hauser, the wild boy of Nuremberg (1828), who gave evidence of his unusual origin by shuddering in the presence of a needle, and evidencing intense agony in passing a hardware shop. Miss Martineau's J. holds a piece of steel so tightly that no one can wrench it from her, but touch the steel with gold and it falls from her hands at once. The following citation will show how this movement was utilized in mesmeric practices : " But to ascertain whether he (a Major Buckley, a mesmerist) can obtain conscious clairvoyance, he makes slow passes from his own forehead to his own chest. If this produces a blue light in his face, strongly visible, the subject will probably acquire conscious clairvoyance. If not, if the light be pale, the subject must first be rendered clairvoyant in the sleep. Taking those subjects who see a very deep blue light, he continues to make passes over his own face, and also over the object, a box or a nut, for example, in which written or printed words are inclosed, which the clairvoyant is to read. Some subjects require only a pass or two to be made clairvoyant, others require many. They describe the blue light as rendering the box or nut transparent, so that they can read what is inside. If too many passes be made by Major B., the blue light becomes so deep that they cannot read, and some reverse passes must be made to render the light less deep. Major Buckley has thus produced conscious clairvoyance in eighty-nine persons, of whom forty-four have been able to read mottoes contained in nut-shells, purchased by other parties for the experiment."

It must not be supposed that these practices have entirely disappeared. In a work published as late as 1869 we may read such sentences as, "the clairvoyance of an idiot in a state of somnambulism would inspire me with more confidence if I were sick than the greatest geniuses which grace modern medicine;" and again, "it never could be imagined with what tact, accuracy, and precision, somnambulists account for anything that takes place in them. They are literally present at the performance of all their organic functions; they detect in them the slightest disorder, the minutest change. Then of all this he forms a clear, exact, and mathematical idea. He could tell, for instance, how many drops of blood there are in his heart; he knows, almost to a gramme, how much it would require to satisfy his appetite at the moment;

how many drops of water would be necessary to satisfy his thirst, and his valuations are inconceivably exact. Time, space, forces of all kinds, the resistance and weight of objects, his thoughts, or rather his instinct measures, he calculates, appreciates all these matters by a single glance of the eye." In the lectures and cheap compendiums telling "How to Mesmerize," and giving "The Whole Art of Mesmerism," by which the traveling mesmerists of yesterday, if not of to-day, extend their fame, one may find these very same doctrines side by side with garbled accounts of recent discoveries in hypnotism. But we have already dwelt too long upon the aberrations of the human intellect, in which the ludicrous and the solemn are so curiously combined.

X

The transition from the antecedent to the present status of hypnotism was accomplished in the main by two factors; by the precise determination, according to rigidly scientific methods, of the physiological and psychological characteristics of the hypnotic state, and by the advocacy of its claims and the further development of its sphere of influence, on the part of professional men of ability and acknowledged standing. The mischievous and erratic associations of mesmerism, as also of hypnotism, were difficult to outgrow. Unjustifiable skepticism and neglect were the natural consequences of extravagance, perversion, and charlatanism. Even the repeated and verifiable production by hypnotic means of anæsthesia sufficient for serious surgical operations, was ignored; partly, perhaps, because of the discovery of ether, which turned the

interest in anæsthetics into new channels. The legitimate and progressive investigations of such as Braid,
Liebault, Azam, Durand de Gros, and others, were only
fitfully and sparsely recognized. As late as 1874 De-
chambre, in his Medical Encyclopedia, declares that
all the phenomena rest upon self-deception and delusion,
and that the condition does not exist. But beginning
with the third quarter of the century the attitude rapidly changed. Richet (1875) published an important
paper in an authoritative physiological journal, in
which he again established by scientific methods the
reality of the hypnotic condition. In this he wrote,
"It requires considerable courage to speak aloud the
word somnambulism. The stupid credulity of the
masses and the pretensions of certain charlatans have
brought the thing itself as well as the name into such
disfavor that there are but few men of science who do
not look disparagingly upon any communication on the
subject." The advocacy of Charcot (1878) and his
demonstrations at the Salpêtrière finally succeeded in
gaining the day; and in 1882 the ban placed upon
academic discussions of this subject was lifted by the
reception on the part of the Academy of Science of
a memoir by Charcot on hypnotism. The extensive
series of studies instigated by him at the Salpêtrière,
and carried on with marked ability and success by
those who in some measure drew their inspiration from
the field of inquiry which he inaugurated; the recognition which he secured for the presentation of studies
upon hypnotism before learned societies; the far-
reaching influence of his authority, — all contributed
to the acceptance of hypnotism as a scientific fact, and

the inclusion of its study within the circle of the sciences. It should be carefully noted, however, that the period (which, to connect it with the name of but one of its representatives, may be called the period of Charcot), though marked by important extensions of our knowledge of hypnotic phenomena, was in essence a period of reinstatement. All the essential and fundamental discoveries had been made and forgotten, and even had been rediscovered decades before; but not until this period were they extensively and authoritatively acknowledged. This reinstatement was naturally the result of coöperation of many workers; while hypnotism still remained a favorite study of French neurologists, other countries contributed extensively to its advance. In Germany the main impetus to its study seems to have been given by the striking demonstrations of hypnotic phenomena by a Danish hypnotist, Hansen (1879 and 1880), which led to their study by various physiologists. The earliest American contribution of this period (and which was somewhat independent in origin) was a study of trance-states by Dr. G. M. Beard, of New York, in 1881. But accounts of contributors and contributions belong no longer to the historical aspect which we are considering, but to modern hypnotism. Suffice it to say that the literature of the subject of the past two decades is almost alarmingly voluminous in its extent, and most cosmopolitan in its composition; that cognate departments of science — physiology, psychology, medicine —consider its bearings upon their special problems; that its therapeutic application to the cure of disease by the efficacy of the power of suggestion is recognized extensively by general practitioners, by neurologists, as well as in specific hypnotic clinics; that its utilization as a special method of psychology has been productive of interesting and valuable contributions; and that it illuminates many a dark recess in the story of the historical and sociological development of humanity. One phase of the matter, alone, seems destined to serve as an historical turning-point; the year of the new epoch is best marked by the appearance in 1886 of Dr. Bernheim's classic volume on "Suggestion and its Therapeutical Applications"; and the key-note of the newer doctrine lies in the term "suggestion." Charcot and his followers had, in different degrees and ways, emphasized the physical characteristics of the hypnosis; they held that in typical subjects there were objectively distinct hypnotic states, characterized and induced by physical manifestations. They recognized the importance of suggestion, but in addition to it also recognized the existence of objectively differentiated hypnotic phenomena. These and related doctrines are commonly referred to as those of the "school of Paris." In contrast with this is the "school of Nancy," of which Dr. Bernheim is the acknowledged leader, and which may be characterized as the "suggestionist" school. This school recognizes different degrees of suggestibility, and an endless variety of resulting phenomena, but regards suggestion, in its various forms, as furnishing a sufficient and comprehensive clue to the entire range of observations. It is compelled accordingly to regard the three distinctive states recognized by Charcot as themselves the product of unconscious suggestion and of a contagious *esprit de corps* of the Salpêtrière subjects. The school of Nancy to-day enjoys the most extensive following, and may be said to represent the dominant trend of present study. One may fairly say that the present psychological study in this domain is the study of suggestion, one form, though only one form, of which is hypnotic suggestion. With the complete realization of the psychological significance of the hypnotic state, the fierce and adventurous struggle for existence of hypnotism may be said to terminate in its undisturbed adaptation to a scientific environment.

XI

The history of the antecedents of hypnotism is rich in suggestiveness. For the historian of the inductive sciences it illustrates the influence of the circumstances accompanying a discovery upon the status of the discovery itself; that the acceptance of a discovery depends more upon its logical concordance with current scientific conceptions, upon the manner of its demonstration, than upon the intrinsic content of what is demonstrated. It is as difficult in science as in real life to escape the influences of unfortunate associates; the interesting state which we now recognize as hypnosis was naturally discredited when it consorted with animal magnetism and the marvels of somnambulism, but was recognized when its credentials were expressed in intelligible physiological and psychological terms. For the historian of human error the story is equally significant. It illustrates again that the mental attitude essentially influences truth and error alike; that with all due allowance for ignorance, for faulty observation, for defective organization of knowledge, error was due, more than to any of these, to the lack of suitable concepts for the proper absorption and appreciation of the phenomena in their true significance. For lack of these there was misconception and oversight, and in their stead prepossession by notions of a wholly irrelevant character. Such notions were fostered by what we retrospectively recognize as pseudo-science; such was the fictitious animal magnetism, an entity never demonstrated, but supported only by a superficial analogical plausibility. They were fostered also by the activity of the marvel-loving impulse, which is unresponsive to the uniformities of nature, and favors mystic fable, while overlooking sensible fact. " Wer unmögliches geglaubt, könnt unmögliches verrichten." The special form of belief, the name of the system, the nature of the explanatory theory, seem almost accidental. Throughout all times, the same intense craving to overthrow the limitations of the human mind has been present, and has been satisfied by much the same beliefs and theories. Mesmerism harks back to astrology; prophets and seers have always existed; the mystery of the attractive force of the magnet for long made magnetism a most popular explanation of any obscure phenomena; the same performances that convinced the mesmerist of the existence of the magnetic fluid are evidence to the electro-biologist of the electro-vital force, of the " od " to the followers of Reichenbach; and — more striking still — the outfit of the modern spiritualistic medium, the trance, the clairvoyant discovery of one's private affairs, the reading of messages in sealed envelopes, the conversation with

absent or departed friends, are all to be found in
the annals of somnambulism. Truly, history repeats
itself ; and the endless forms of mysticism, error, and
extravagance seem immortal ; they change in form and
accommodate themselves to the advance in knowledge
and civilization, and parody the forms of statement
and the methods of science in an age which has learned
to be impressed with scientific demonstrations.

For the special student of hypnotism no lesson of
the history of its antecedents is more practically significant than its illumination of the extent, variety, and
subtlety of unconscious suggestion. If Puységur's
subjects prescribe for their own ills and see without
their eyes ; if Pétetin's read what is placed on their
stomachs ; or the interposition of poor electric-conduc-
tors prevent manifestations ; if one of the subjects
examined by the commission of 1784 could not be
deprived of speech unless the magnetizing hand passed
below his mouth ; if one of the Salpêtrière subjects of
1829 could be cured only by immersion in the river ;
if Deleuze's subjects respond differently to the minute
differences in manipulations, which he believed to be
essential ; if the subjects whom Braid examined could
prove the truth of phrenology, and the mesmerist's
subjects feel the magnetic fluid streaming through
their systems ; if within recent times paralyses are
transferred from one arm to the other by the action
of a magnet, or Dr. Luys's subjects show the characteristic effects of a drug when a sealed vial containing it
is placed upon the subject's neck, or respond to the
puppets which he has manipulated, — surely it is as
obvious that some spontaneous caprice of the subject

or unconscious suggestions of the operator have originated these notions, and that unconscious imitation has further contributed to their dissemination, as it is obvious that all these in part mutually contradictory phenomena cannot be true, objective facts. The significance of more recent investigations in allied fields still turns upon the factor which unconscious suggestion plays in their production. The advocates of telepathy, whether occurring under hypnotic or more normal conditions, feel confident that unconscious suggestion as well as all other sources of error have been eliminated; the skeptical critics point out overlooked and novel modes of unconscious suggestion, and draw confidence from the history of the past, both of the unwarranted flight to improbable hypothesis on the basis of an alleged absence of a natural explanation, and of the solvent power which future investigation may hold in store.

The story of the conquest of a realm of fable by a campaign of enlightenment is always a tale of interest. The opening of a new vista directs one's gaze outward over unexplored areas. It may be, as our seventeenth-century chronicler tells us, that "we are all Indians and Salvages in what we have not accustomed our senses," and that, "what was Conjuring in the last age is Mathematiques in this"; but our more extensive acquaintance with the course of discovery and the demonstration of truth has given us a more logical sense of the probable and the improbable; and the evolution by which conjuring becomes mathematics is more intimately understood. The recent establishment of hypnotism in its scientific aspects furnishes the proper perspective for the comprehension of its antecedents; it gives confidence that its future development will incorporate the spirit of present research, as it will avoid the aberrations of the past; and it gives to the story of its vicissitudes a timely pertinence as well as a psychological significance.

THE NATURAL HISTORY OF ANALOGY

I

THE origin of human endowment lies hidden in an obscure and unrecorded past; the fact of development, of the gradual unfoldment of capacity, stands out conspicuously throughout the historical record of human achievement, and is equally recognizable in the extensive remains of prehistoric humanity. The story of the mental development of man is constructed from travelers' accounts of primitive peoples, from the records of early civilizations, from the sequences of thought and belief that are considered in the history of culture, from the study of the intellectual growth of childhood, from the observation of the less progressive elements of current civilizations. The present essay attempts to portray the status of one form of intellectual process, or of mental attitude, which characterizes undeveloped stages of human thought, and has played an important and variable part in the drama of mental evolution. I propose to present the "Natural History of Analogy," — meaning thereby the treatment, according to the methods of natural science, of a type of mental action, interesting at once as a psychological process, and again from its practical results as a factor in the anthropological history of the race.

An analogy is a type of reasoning, and as such is referred to the logician for more precise definition. His briefest explanation of the term may be stated as the inference of a further degree of resemblance from an observed degree of resemblance ; the argument that because the Earth and Mars agree in the common possession of a solid crust, an atmosphere, presence of water, changes of season, the possibilities of rain and snow, and other observed qualities, they will also agree in the further respect of being inhabited. This may serve as an exemplar of the analogical argument in its purest and most developed form; but in the survey of the varieties and distribution of this natural product of rationality, it will be necessary to include many forms of thought diverging more or less from, though always retaining, a recognizable relation to this type. The analogical inference, indeed, goes back to an inarticulate form, in which it merges into a feeling rather than an argument, a susceptibility to an influence supported by undefined plausibility, rather than a conclusion from tangible evidence. But however lacking in definiteness or formulation, however unconsciously realized and barely expressible, the tendency or disposition to believe is communicated to others and becomes an influential factor in the ultimate fixation of belief and in the guidance of conduct. Logically considered, analogy is always a weak argument ; and becomes weaker, as the range of observed resemblance is more and more limited, as the resemblances belong to accidental, unessential traits, and as the underlying basis of the inference is removed from direct verification. Psychologically, its power to influence belief may be very strong, and when this is not the case, there still may exist a disposition to be influenced by analogical considerations, even when these are successfully resisted or suppressed. The instinctive proclivity towards the use of analogies, whether it be logical or anti-logical in effect, forms an interesting psychological trait. Logic counsels how we may think most profitably and correctly ; psychology describes how we actually do think or tend to think. The logician is the gardener bent upon training certain selected flowers according to an ideal standard, and eradicating all others as weeds ; while the psychologist is the botanist to whom all plants, weeds, and flowers alike are worthy objects of study, and who, indeed, traces significant resemblances between the despised weed and the choice flower.

The natural history account of analogy will consider the status in less advanced stages of human development, and the evolution of this form of thought, which scientists to-day use only with the greatest caution, and to which they at best assign but a limited and corroborative value. It will appear that analogy is dominant in primitive types of thought ; that it has an important cultural history ; and has left an unmistakable impress upon many beliefs of our civilization, marked as obsolete, perhaps, in the dictionary of the cultured, but current still in the parlance of average and untutored humanity.

II

The great law of apperception, teaching that we observe according to our inherited capacities and our

acquired experience, that we in a very real sense create
the world in which we live, explains the difficulty of
realizing modes of thought strikingly different from
our own, either as more primitive, or more complex, or
as based upon other perspectives of the social, intellectual, and ethical rules that guide thought and conduct.
To the supremely civilized citizen of the nineteenth
century, the mental life of one who has hardly a firm
hold on the first round of the ladder of civilization is
naturally somewhat incomprehensible. An illustration
of the conspicuous contrast, though doubtless amidst an
inherent community, of the thought-habits of untutored
and of cultured man, may suggest the direction and
the nature of the evolutionary development that separates, yet binds, the one and the other. Prominent
among such contrasts is the different standing assumed
by the facts and reasonings of science in primitive and
in highly civilized life ; and an important part of this
difference may be viewed as the shifting of the position occupied by the argument by analogy. Deeper
than the language of words, and underlying their use
and formation, is the habit of comparing object with
object, of tracing resemblances and noting contrasts.
It would seem that in the primitive use of this process
there is lacking the distinction between the resemblances
more strictly inherent in the objects and those originating in the mode of viewing them ; subject and object
are still merged in a vaguer realm of perception where
myth and science, poetical fiction and evident fact, are
as yet undifferentiated and mingle without let or hin-
drance. The savage frames his world by the realization
of simple fancies suggested by slight analogies, where

the man of culture examines the objective causes of phenomena under the guidance of scientifically established principles and accurate logic. Fortunately, however, for our power of realizing bygone mental traits, these forms of belief still find currency as survivals, in Mr. Tylor's apt words, "of the lower culture which they are of to the higher culture which they are in." We thus can understand the belief we no longer share; we can appreciate as suggestive myth or far-fetched analogy what to our ancestors may have been a plausible belief or a satisfactory explanation.

The prominence of analogy among undeveloped peoples supplies unlimited illustrations of the rôle which it plays in primitive circles, the essential influence which it exerts over thoughts and customs in the early history of mankind. Consider first that widespread class of customs and observances by which the savage regards himself as influencing for good or ill the fate of friend or foe. The Zulu chewing a bit of wood to soften the heart of the man he wishes to buy oxen from, or of the woman he is wooing (Tylor); the Illinois Indians making figures of those whose days they desire to shorten, and stabbing these images to the heart, or by performing incantations upon a stone trying to form a stone in the hearts of their enemies (Dorman); the Peruvian sorcerer, making rag dolls and piercing them with cactus-thorns, and hiding them about the beds to cripple people; or the native of Borneo, making a wax figure of his enemy in the belief that as the image melts, the enemy's body will waste away (Tylor); the Zulu sorcerer who secures a portion of a desired victim's dress and buries it secretly, so that, as it rots away, his life may decay (Clodd) ; the confession recorded in a seventeenth-century trial for witchcraft, that the accused had " buried a glove of the said Lord Henry in the ground, so that as the glove did rot and waste, the liver of the said lord might rot and waste " (Brand) ; the New Britain sorcerer of to-day who burns a castaway banana skin, so that he who carelessly left it unburied may die a tormenting death (Clodd) ; bewitching by operating upon a lock of hair or the parings of the finger-nails, and the consequent widespread custom of religiously preventing such personal scraps from falling into others' possession ; — all these varied forms of primitive witchcraft rest upon the notion that one kind of connection, one link of resemblance, will bring with it others. The argument, if explicitly stated, as can hardly be done without doing violence to its instinctive force, may be put thus : this bit of wood or stone or lock of hair or scrap of clothing resembles this man or woman in that the one represents the other or that the one had a personal connection with the other ; therefore they will further resemble one another in that whatever will make the one soft and yielding or the other hard and unfeeling will have the same effect on the other, or in that whatever is done to the one will happen to the other. Other considerations combine with this underlying analogical factor to impart cogency and plausibility to a belief or custom ; but the type of the logic, crooked though it be, is recognizable throughout.

Another significant group of primitive beliefs, involving a similarly indirect argument by analogy, relates to the partaking of an animal for the sake of thus absorbing its typical qualities. The Malays eat tiger to acquire the sagacity as well as the cunning of that animal; the Dyaks refuse to eat deer for fear of becoming faint-hearted; the Caribs eschew pigs and tortoises for fear of having their eyes grow small (Lubbock); even cannibalism may be indulged in, in the hopes of absorbing the courage of a brave man, as in the case of Captain Wells, who was killed near Chicago in 1812, and whose body was cut up and distributed among the Indians, "so that all might have the opportunity of getting a taste of the courageous soldier" (Clodd); and in an ancient Mexican rite, called the eating of the god, there occurs an elaborated and symbolical form of the same belief.

The use of omens, the interpretation of signs and coincidences, forms another rich field for illustration of arguments by analogy. "Magical arts," says Mr. Tylor, "in which the connection is that of mere analogy or symbolism, are endlessly numerous throughout the course of civilization. Their common theory may be readily made out from a few typical cases, and thence applied confidently to the general mass. The Australian will observe the track of an insect near a grave to ascertain the direction where the sorcerer is to be found by whose craft the man died. . . . The Khondi sets up the iron arrow of the war god in a basket of rice, and judges from its standing upright that war must be kept up also, or from its falling that the quarrel may be let fall too; and when he tortures human victims sacrificed to the earth goddess he rejoices to see them shed plentiful tears, which betoken copious showers to fall upon his land." "In the burial ceremonies of the natives of Alaska, if too many tears were shed they said that the road of the dead would be muddy, but a few tears just laid the dust " (Dorman). " The Zapotecs had a very curious manner of selecting a manitou for a child at its birth. When a woman was about to be delivered, the relatives assembled in the hut and commenced to draw on the floor figures of different animals, rubbing out each one as fast as completed. The one that remained at the time of the birth was called the child's second self, and as soon as grown up he procured the animal, and believed his health and existence bound up with it " (Dorman). The taking of omens by the flight of birds or the tracks of animals, by the sky, by the inspection of sacrifices, by the trivial happenings of daily life, abound in savage ceremonials, and in a fair proportion of cases carry with them the rationale of their origin, that saves them from being mere caprice. And in all those endless appeals to chance or lot for the detection of crime, the unfoldment of the future, the prediction of the issue of disease or of important tribal events, there is always some underlying link of connection between the kind of omen or the nature of its interpretation and the issue it signifies ; and this connection it is, however slight or fanciful, that maintains the belief in the further bond of omen and issue.

III

That such connections may travel still farther along the path of analogy without losing force, is well illustrated in the observances regarding the use of names. The connection seems to pass from thing to image, to name, much as picture-writing passes into word-writing. The use of idols is abundant evidence of the extent of this mental operation; what is done to or for the idol is analogically transferred to the god, and the confusion may become so gross that when the oracles of two gods disagree, their idols are knocked against each other, and the one that breaks is declared in the wrong. A drawing or other rough resemblance may do service for the thing, especially in sacrifices of objects of value. By similar steps the name becomes an essential portion of the object or person named, and analogies formed through the name are applied to the thing. Accordingly, a man may be bewitched through his name; hence there arise the most elaborate and rigid observances prohibiting the use of the name, which are grouped together in the complex code of the Taboo, — that "dread tyrant of savage life, . . . the Inquisition of the lower culture, only more terrible and effective than the infamous 'Holy Office'" (Clodd). For uncomplicated illustrations of name analogies, however, we must go to other customs than the Taboo. It is related that in the British war with Nepaul, Goree Sah had sent orders to "find out the name of the commander of the British army; write it upon a piece of paper; take it some rice and turmeric; say the great incantation three times; having said it, send for some plum-tree wood, and therewith burn it;" thus was the life of the commander to be destroyed. Similarly it was suspected that the King of Dahomey refused to sign a letter, written in his name to the President of the French Republic, for fear that M. Carnot might bewitch him through it (cited by Clodd). "Barbaric man believes that his name is a vital part of himself, and therefore that the names of other men and of superhuman beings are also vital parts of themselves. He further believes that to know the name is to put its owner, whether he be deity, ghost, or mortal, in the power of another, involving risk of harm or destruction to the named. He therefore takes all kinds of precautions to conceal his name, often from his friend, and always from his foe " (Clodd). In Borneo the name of a sickly child is changed to deceive the evil spirits that torment it. " When the life of a Kwapa Indian is supposed to be in danger from illness, he at once seeks to get rid of his name, and sends to another member of the tribe, who goes to the chief and buys a new name, which is given to the patient. With the abandonment of the old name it is believed that the sickness is thrown off. ' On the reception of the new name the patient becomes related to the Kwapa who purchased it. Any Kwapa can change or abandon his personal name four times, but it is considered bad luck to attempt such a thing for the fifth time ' " (Clodd). The Mohawk chief can confer no higher honor on his visitor than by giving him his name, with which goes the right of regarding the chief's fame and deeds of valor as his own. A Tahitian chief became so smitten with Stevenson's charms that he assumed Stevenson's name; in exchange Stevenson took the name of the chief, and in one of his letters signs himself, " Teritera, which he was previously known as Robert Louis Stevenson." When totem and tribal names are assumed to obtain the qualities of the animal namesake, or the reverence due to the person is transferred to the name, and when incantations and the utterances of mystic formulæ are granted like efficacy as the manipulation of the things themselves, we see the operation of the mental law under discussion ; though it is still more saliently illustrated in the more artificialized practices of the Chinese physician, who, for lack of a desired drug, will " write the prescription on a piece of paper and let the sick man swallow its ashes or an infusion of the writing in water ; " or of the Moslem who expects relief from a decoction in which a verse of the Koran written on paper has been washed (Tylor).

What is true of names is also regarded as true of other representatives or embodiments of personality — the footprint, the drawing, the image, the shadow. "Broken bottle ends or sharp stones are put, in Russia and in Austria, in the footprints of a foe, for the purpose of laming him (Lang) ; or a nail may be driven into a horse's footprint to make him go lame " (Grimm). The Ojibways practice magic " by drawing the figure of any person in sand or clay, or by considering any object as the figure of a person, and then pricking it with a sharp stick or other weapon; . . . the person thus represented will suffer likewise " (Dorman). The same idea appears in King James's " Demonology," in which he speaks of " the devil teaching how to make pictures of wax or clay, that by roasting thereof the persons that they bear the name of may be continually melted or dried away by sickness ; " and even now Highland crofters perforate the image of an enemy with pins. The same idea finds a tangible illustration in the collection of objects in the Pitt Rivers Museum at Oxford (such as a pig's heart from Devonshire, with pins stuck into it), which were used for a like purpose. And Catlin's story of the accusation brought against him by the Yukons, that he had made buffaloes scarce by putting so many pictures of them in his book, may be paralleled by the stories gathered from Scotland to Somerset, of "ill health or ill luck which followed the camera, of folks who 'took bad and died' after being 'a-tookt'" (Clodd). "The Basuto avoids the river-bank, lest, as his shadow falls on the water, a crocodile may seize it and harm the owner. In Wetar Island, near Celebes, the magicians profess to make a man ill by spearing or stabbing his shadow; the Arabs believe that if a hyæna treads on a shadow, it deprives the man of the power of speech; and in modern Roumania the ancient custom of burying a victim as sacrifice to the earth-spirit under any new structure has a survival in the builder enticing some passer-by to draw near, so that his shadow is thrown on the foundation-stone, the belief being that he will die within the year" (Clodd).

To the underlying notions thus variously embodied may be applied Mr. Clodd's characterization: they form "a part of that general confusion between the objective and the subjective — in other words, between names and things, or between symbols and realities — which is a universal feature of barbaric modes of thought. This confusion attributes the qualities of living things to things not living; it lies at the root of all fetichism and idolatry; of all witchcraft, Shaman-ism, and other instruments which are as keys to the invisible kingdom of the dreaded." It is in such an atmosphere that the philosophy of analogy rules with undisputed sway.

"Ideas are universal, incidents are local," says Mr. Clodd, in speaking of the diffusion of folk-lore tales. The same is true of thought tendencies. We may realize more intimately the analogical potency of names by recalling their survivals from the solemn uses of curses and excommunications, to the charms carried about the person consisting of magic or cabalistic writing, to the playful or the serious German usage of saying *unberufen* and rapping three times under the table if a word or thought "tempting Providence" has fallen from the lips. Clearly, if we follow analogy as a guide, there is much in a name.

IV

We may next proceed to more general uses of the analogical trait, — more general because the special analogical appropriateness of thought or custom is no longer so apparent, but requires to be viewed more as a special and, it may be, a somewhat arbitrary application of a principle, itself supported or believed in on analogical grounds. Metaphor and simile and symbolism may be based upon the same types of resemblances that underlie analogy, but it is desirable, so far as may be possible, to hold these distinct; yet what is metaphor to us may still be analogy to others.

When we speak of a head of cabbage, the trunk of a tree, or the legs of a table, we understand that we have applied these names on the basis of resemblances to objects to which the names more strictly belong, and there is no thought that the name carries with it any further connection; but when the Chinese doctor administers the heads, middle parts, and roots of plants, for the heads, bodies, and legs of his patients respectively, he is clearly led to do so by a vague sense of analogical fitness, by a feeling that the bodily similarities are indicative of further connection of a quasi-causal type. This kind of reasoning abounds in primitive ceremonials, in which the appropriateness of the observances and of the elements of the ritual depend upon resemblances or symbolical suggestiveness. It is difficult to find instances of this trait in which a more or less conscious symbolism is excluded, for we know how readily the savage mind, in its somewhat more developed stages, uses this mode of thought, as is evidenced by the ingenuity of their picture-writing, gesture-language, and tribal systems. But apart from symbolical procedures, in which the unreality of the underlying resemblances is half acknowledged, we may note the application of such general principles as that unusual phenomena have unusual significance, and that to accomplish important objects drastic means and rare substances must be employed; that operations and remedies will be effective according to their divergence from the usual and the common experience of mankind. The influence of this principle is traceable in the bizarre fancies and grotesque performances of savages, as also in the reverence shown to the belongings of the white man and the curious uses to which they are put. In their ritual observances, as well as in medical practice, the same principle is involved; a single illustration will suffice to recall this well-known form of thought. Dorman cites the fate of an Indian warrior brought to camp after a most disastrous encounter with a grizzly bear. To repair his very serious injuries " the doctor compounded a medicine that really ought to have worked wonders. It was made by boiling together a collection of miscellaneous weeds, a handful of chewing tobacco, the heads of four rattlesnakes, and a select assortment of worn-out moccasins. The decoction thus obtained was seasoned with a little crude petroleum and a large quantity of red pepper, and the patient was directed to take a pint of the mixture every half hour. He was a brave man, conspicuous for his fortitude under suffering, but after taking his first dose he turned over and died with the utmost expedition."

Another one of these general principles may have been suggested by the failure of the ordinary omens ; and thus the conclusion was reached that the analogy proceeds not according to resemblance but by contrast. For example, the Zulus, when dreaming "of a sick man that he is dead, . . . say, ' because we have dreamt of his death he will not die.' But if they dream of a wedding dance it is the sign of a funeral. So the Maoris hold that a kinsman dreamt of as dying will recover, but to see him well is a sign of death. Both races thus worked out, by the same crooked logic that guided our own ancestors, the axiom that dreams go by contraries " (Tylor). It will be seen in later portions of our exposition that these and other general principles of an analogical type have lost none of their potency in their more modern or more erudite phases.

V

The parallelism between the mental development of the individual and of the race, though necessarily incomplete, is yet deeply suggestive and significant. In a very true sense the unfoldment of mental faculty from childhood to maturity reflects the allied course of evolution from savagery to civilization; yet the reflection is distorted and is traceable only in general outlines. Undeveloped forms of thought and instinctive tendencies, of a related though by no means of an identical character, should be traceable in each; and among them the natural proclivity for dependence upon analogies. That children are fond of reasoning by analogy there can be no doubt; their confusion of fact with fancy, their lack of extensive knowledge and the ability to refer effects to proper causes, their great love for sound effects and play of words, the earnestness of their play convictions — all these furnish a rich soil for the growth of such habits of thought as we are now considering. On the other hand, the influence of their adult companions, of their conventional surroundings, of the growth of the make-believe sentiment by which the laws of the real world are differentiated from those of fairy-land, make it difficult to pronounce as an argument by analogy what may really be a half-conscious play of fancy or jugglery of words and ideas. There is, further, considerable difficulty in collecting characteristic and unimpeachable illustrations of arguments by analogy in children, owing to the general lack of suitable collections of children's spontaneous and original mental reactions. What fond parents are apt to observe and newspaper paragraphers to record are sayings that amuse by a quaintness or the assumption of a worldly wisdom beyond their years, while the truly suggestive traits pass unrecorded for lack of psycho-

logically informed observers. There is thus a gap
to be supplied by valuable and suggestive study of
analogy in childhood. However, not to pass by the
topic without illustration, I may cite the reply of the
little boy who, when asked his age, said he was nine
when he stood on his feet but six when he stood on his
head, because an inverted 9 makes a 6; he was certainly reasoning by a far-fetched analogy, however
little faith he may have had in the correctness of his
reasoning. The children who believed that butter
comes from butterflies, and grass from grasshoppers,
beans from bees, and kittens from pussy-willows (Stanley Hall), may have been simply misled by sound
analogies; but when Sir John Lubbock tells us of a
little girl saying to her brother, " If you eat so much
goose you will be quite silly," and adds that, " there
are perhaps few children to whom the induction would
not seem perfectly legitimate," we appreciate that such
arguments, so closely paralleling the superstitions of
savages, may be more real to children than we suspect.

VI

We may now enter in the search for reasonings by
analogy into a field of greatest interest to the student
of the history of culture; namely, the household traditions, the superstitions, and the pseudo-scientific systems, that originated among our ancestors, remote or
immediate, and are still far from obsolete in all but
the upper strata of our civilization. This portion of
the theme indeed presents an *embarras de richesses*,
and the illustrations to be cited form but an insignificant share of those that could readily be collected.

Certainly more than one chapter of the history of human error could be profitably devoted to those due to an unwarranted use of the argument by analogy.

We may begin by taking a flying excursion into that body of superstitions and folk-lore customs which no nation, however high or low in the scale of civilization, is without. The widespread custom of carrying baby upstairs before being taken to the lower floors of the house, so that he may be successful in life and participate in its ups rather than its downs, rests upon baby-logic indeed. The belief that if baby keeps his fists tightly closed he will be stingy, but if he holds an open palm he will be generous, likewise requires no interpretation. It is forbidden, too, to measure a child, for measuring it is measuring it for its coffin. To the German peasant, if a dog howls looking downward it means death, if upward recovery from sickness. "The Hessian lad thinks that he may escape the conscription by carrying a baby-girl's cap in his pocket — a symbolic way of repudiating manhood." "Fish," says the Cornishman, "should be eaten from the tail to the head, to bring other fishes' heads towards the shore, for eating them the wrong way turns them from the coast." "It is still plain," says Mr. Tylor, from whom I have cited some of these examples, "why the omen of the crow should be different on the right or left hand, why a vulture should mean rapacity; a stork, concord; a pelican, piety; an ass, labor; why the fierce, conquering wolf should be a good omen, and the timid hare a bad one; why bees, types of an obedient nation, should be lucky to a king, while flies returning, however often they are driven off, should be signs of importunity and

impudence." And as parallels to these signs, in the
vegetable world, one may cite the amaranth as signify-
ing immortality; ivy, strength; cypress, woe; helio-
trope, attachment; aspen, fear; aloes, bitterness; while
through more artificial associations the laurel becomes
the sign of renown; the rose, of love; the olive, of
peace; and the palm, of victory.

Less directly analogical are the customs of a semi-
symbolic character, depending upon a mysterious or
potent sympathy. Thus, in "Bavaria, flax will not
thrive unless it is sown by women, and this has to be
done with strange ceremonies, including the scattering
over the field of the ashes of a fire made of wood con-
secrated during matins. As high as the maids jump
over the fires on the hilltops on Midsummer Night, so
high will the flax grow; but we find also that as high
as the bride springs from the table on her marriage
night, so high will the flax grow in that year." This
is paralleled by the custom, recorded by Mr. Frazer,
current in the interior of Sumatra. There "the rice is
sown by women who, in sowing, let the hair hang loose
down their backs, in order that the rice may grow
luxuriantly and have long stalks." It is hardly necessary to continue these illustrations, which will at once
suggest others, with which the wealth of superstitious lore
overflows; nor do they require elaborate interpretation.
The resemblances involved may be fanciful or symbolic,
obvious or obscure, superficial or intrinsic, natural or
artificial, but the subtle and protean bases of analogy
become recognizable as soon as the mind is directed
towards their detection.

It will be more profitable to limit the inquiry to a

few groups of beliefs, which have been more or less fully elaborated into systems. Of these the interpretation of dreams offers a promising harvest of analogies. This practice has a venerable history, the study of which would constitute an interesting task for the patient student of the by-paths of human culture. I shall draw only from the contemporaneous survivals of this ancient lore, the dream-books purchasable in every city and village.

My selections from this literature have been made with a view of presenting the typical kinds of analogy through which modern dream omens are believed in and through which this kind of reading finds a sale. "To dream of using glue," an authority tells us, "foretells imprisonment for yourself or friend ; " and this because a prison and glue are alike in that it is difficult to be released from the hold of either. Similarly, because the pineapple has a rough and forbidding appearance it becomes in dreams the omen of " crosses and troubles." This seems hardly more than a play of words ; indeed, we have here touched one of the many points where metaphor and analogy meet. For instance, we commonly speak of the ladder of success and the ups and downs of fortune ; the dream-book tells us that " to dream of going up a ladder foretells the possession of wealth ; coming down, of poverty." The common phrase of " mud-slinging " is thus interpreted by the dream-books, " to dream of dirty dirt or mud signifies that some one will speak ill of you. If some one throws dirt on you it foretells that you will be abused." To the same category belong the dream-book maxims, that " to dream of being mounted on

stilts denotes that you are puffed up with vain pride;"
"to dream that you gather fruit from a very old tree
is generally supposed to prognosticate that you will
succeed to the wealth of some ancient person; if you
dream of a clock and the hands stop it means death;
if the hands keep moving, recovery;" "to dream of a
concert means a life of harmony with one you love."
So, too, various objects become significant of their
striking characteristics: the earthworm, from its habits
of underground and secret destruction, denotes "secret
enemies that endeavor to ruin and destroy us;" and
all strongly redolent food, such as onions, garlic, and
leek, easily betraying the one who has partaken of
them, becomes indicative of the betrayal of secrets and
the like.   Mr. Dyer cites some apt lines in which the
logic is about as meritorious as the verse: —

> " To dream of eating onions means
> Much strife in thy domestic scenes;
> Secrets found out or else betrayed,
> And many falsehoods made and said."

From Mr. Tylor's collection of dream omens of
similar character I cull the following: "to wash the
hands denotes release from anxieties;" "to have one's
feet cut off prevents a journey;" "he who dreams he
has lost a tooth shall lose a friend;" "he that dreams
that a rib is taken out of his side shall ere long see the
death of his wife;" to dream of swimming and wading
in the water is good, so that the head be kept above
water.   A good share of the omens depend upon contrasts and not upon resemblances: "to be married denotes some of your kinsfolk are dead;" "to dream of
death denotes happiness and long life;" and so on.

Others of these dream-book analogies depend rather upon verbal resemblance, and still others involve resemblances too subtle and peculiar to be readily explained. There is perhaps nothing more underlying the dictum that "dreaming about Quakers means that you will meet a friend soon" than the fact that the Quakers are a "Society of Friends;" a little more elaborate punning underlies the prediction that "to dream of a dairy showeth the dreamer to be of a milk-sop nature;" and finally what a curious mixture of perverted analogy is reflected in the notion that to dream of "a zebra indicates a checkered life"!

The great parts that names and numbers play in superstitions of all kinds is so familiar that a few instances will be sufficient. It is well to bear in mind that these number and name predictions, in the course of their venerable and eventful lives, have been systematized, and the gaps in the system supplied by arbitrary associations. Thus the modern fortune-telling books have an omen for each one of a pack of cards, or a set of dominoes, in which we find, among what seems little more than an arbitrary assignment of the ordinary events of life, good and bad, pleasant and unpleasant, important and trivial, — among the several cards or dominoes, here and there some underlying basis of analogy ; hearts relate to love affairs, diamonds to wealth ; kings and queens play important rôles ; the jack is about as often a lover as a knave ; threes and sevens have special significance ; and double throws in dice, especially the two sixes, have important consequences. So in folk-lore, operations, to be effective, must be done just three times, or thrice

three, or seven. The seventh child of a seventh child
has special powers, as we all know. The twelfth hour
that divides night from day is a momentous instant,
as is also the time of the cock's crow. "Against a
warty eruption the leeches advised the patient to take
seven wafers and write on each wafer, Maximianus,
Malchus, Johannes, Martinianus, Dionysius, Constan-
tinus, Serafion ; then a charm was to be sung to the
man, and a maiden was afterwards to hang it about his
neck " (Black). In a similar strain the dream-book
informs us that if a number of young women, not less
than three nor more than seven, assemble on a certain
night, and if, as the hour strikes eleven, they each take
a sprig of myrtle and throw it, together with nine hairs
from the head, upon a live coal, and if they go to bed
at exactly twelve o'clock, they will dream of their future
husbands as a reward of their pains and their mathematical accuracy. Not a few of number and name
ceremonials are invested with their power by religious
associations ; the ill luck of thirteen and of Friday is
commonly regarded as due to this source. In the
northern English countries, witches are said to dislike
the bracken fern, because it bears on its roots the initial C (indicating Christ), which may be seen on cutting the root horizontally (Dyer). The clover, on
account of its trefoil form, suggesting trinity, is likewise good against witches (Dyer). A like explanation seems applicable to the efficacy of the cross and
the cross-roads, both of which enter, in a variety of
ways, into folk-lore beliefs and customs. While numbers and names and definite associations seldom form
the whole basis of analogy by which the belief becomes

plausible, they very frequently enter to emphasize and give point to practices suggested on other grounds. The argument involved in the number analogy is extremely simple; it is nothing more than because two phenomena have in common the association with the same number, therefore they will be connected in further respects. This slender line of connection affects the minute code of superstitious action, and forms the thread whereon are strung momentous omens, powerful recipes, dire predictions, and wise precautions against various imaginary dangers.

The logic by which the treatments current in folk-medicine acquire their efficacy is passing strange; at first acquaintance with this wonderland we are apt to imagine ourselves in some weird topsy-turvydom, where everything uncanny and incongruous is greedily collected, and the most bizarre and trivial doings become endowed with marvelous efficacy. Upon closer acquaintance we discover some little order in the medley, and, in spite of much that remains arbitrary and capricious, we begin to trace the analogies according to which the various treatments are composed and the potions concocted. The common connection of toads with warts, both as giving and curing them, is due to nothing more than the warty appearance of the toad's skin; similarly, in Gloucestershire, against ear-ache a snail is pricked and the froth that exudes dropped into the patient's ear (Black) ; and this by reason of the snail-like passages in the ear. Fevers being connected with heat and blood, and both these closely associated with red, red things become efficacious in diseases characterized by fever. That this should be especially in vogue against scarlet fever is no more than natural; and it is related that when the son of Edward II. was sick of the small-pox, the physician directed that the bed-furniture should be red (Black). Other forms of such associations will be met with in the discussion of the doctrines of signatures and sympathies.

Folk-medicine forms a particularly apt field for the application of the two general forms of analogy indicated as prevalent among savages : analogies by contrast and the assignment of unusual effects to uncommon causes. If something is done with the right hand, doing it with the left reverses the action ; one set of directions applies to men and contrary ones to women ; saying a thing backwards is particularly efficacious. The prescription against hiccough, that you should " cross the front of the left shoe with the forefinger of the right hand while you repeat the Lord's prayer backwards " (Black) may serve to illustrate the one crooked type of argument, while for the other we have only to recall the Shakespearean witches, with their —

> " Round about the cauldron go ;
>   In the poison'd entrails throw.
>   Toad, that under coldest stone,
>   Days and nights has thirty-one
>   Swelter'd venom sleeping got,
>   Boil thou first i' the charmed pot !
>   Fillet of a fenny snake,
>   In the cauldron boil and bake ;
>   Eye of newt and toe of frog,
>   Wool of bat and tongue of dog,
>   Adder's fork, and blind-worm's sting,
>   Lizard's leg, and owlet's wing,
>   For a charm of powerful trouble,
>   Like a hell-broth boil and bubble.

> Scale of dragon, tooth of wolf ;
> Witches' mummy ; maw and gulf,
> Of the ravin'd salt-sea shark ;
> Root of hemlock digg'd i' the dark ;
> Liver of blaspheming Jew ;
> Gall of goat, and slips of yew,
> Silvered in the moon's eclipse ;
> Nose of Turk, and Tartar's lips ;
> Finger of birth-strangled babe,
> Ditch deliver'd by a drab, —
> Make the gruel thick and slab ;
> Add thereto a tiger's chaudron,
> For the ingredients of our cauldron.
> Cool it with the baboon's blood,
> Then the charm is firm and good."

VII

From folk-medicine to false and absurd forms of reme-
dial systems, the transition is slight. For present purposes the most instructive of such systematized beliefs
is the doctrine of sympathy, of which the most familiar
survival is the phrase, " to take a hair of the dog that
bit you." The system appeared in various phases and
at various times. We find Paracelsus a believer in it
in the form of a " weapon salve," which is to be applied
to the weapon that caused the wound and thereby to
heal the wound ; weapon and wound having once been
related as cause and effect, this relation is supposed
to insure further connection. The system found wide
circulation through the efforts of Sir Kenelm Digby.
While Sir Kenelm's practices involved bad observation
and ignorance of medicine, what gave the method its
plausibility and induced the faulty observation was an
underlying belief in the argument by analogy. His
treatment may be gathered from a story he tells of a

Mr. Howell, whose hand was cut in an attempt to stop a duel between friends.   Sir Kenelm arrives on the scene and asks for anything that had the blood upon it; he is given the garter wherewith the hand was first bound; this he places in a basin of water, when suddenly Mr. Howell, who is unaware of what is going on, experiences a cooling effect and a relief from pain.   When the garter is placed before a great fire, Mr. Howell experiences an intense burning in the wound.   Still another form of this idea appears in the " sympathetic alphabet," in which each of two friends cuts out a piece of his skin and has it transferred to the other; on this grafted skin an alphabet is tattooed, and when a letter is pricked on the skin of the one friend, the other feels the pain at the corresponding point; and thus intercourse is established.   A still more curious form of the doctrine appears in an out-of-the-way pamphlet; its title (a German translation from the French) is " The Thought Telegraph: or the instantaneous communication of thought at any distance, even from one end of the world to the other, by means of a portable machine.   The most wonderful invention of our age." The true basis of the method, we are told, depends upon a " sympathetic-galvano, magnetic, mineral, animal, adamitic fluid ; " the practice depends upon the alleged discovery of a species of snails, placed in a sympathetic relation, so that ever after their movements are in harmony.   Accordingly each operator takes one of the snails and places it upon the alphabet chart; the snail crawls over the chart resting upon certain letters, and the other snail, however far removed, will do just the same, and thus the thought-telegraph will be established. Like Charles the Second's famous fish, that would not add to the weight of a dish of water in which it was placed, it lacks nothing but truth to be a great invention. Practices of the same general nature are still current; in the Netherlands, the knife that cut one is rubbed with fat in the belief that as the fat dries the wound will heal. The relation may become more remotely analogical and more arbitrary, as when, to cure ague, as many notches are cut in a stick as there have been fits; as the stick dries the ague is to disappear; ruptured children are passed through a split tree, and thus a sympathy is produced between child and tree, so that as the tree heals the child will be cured. A like sympathy is supposed to exist between celestial objects and human events; this is particularly applied to the moon, the moon's growth and wane indicating the fortunate times for growth and decay of earthly things. One must sow grain, cut the hair, and perform sundry other operations with the increase of the moon, to insure increase of growth. The tides are similarly significant, as the ever-pathetic Barkis "going out with the tide" sufficiently illustrates.

While in the doctrine of sympathy, the resemblance basal to the analogy is one of relation, — such as the relation of cause and effect, of owner and the object owned, of implement and the action performed by its use, — in the doctrine of seals or signatures, the resemblance is an outward, usually a visible one, of form, color, or the possession of marked peculiarities. Underlying this doctrine seems to be the belief that no object or event is without profound significance for

man's welfare. The key to this significance is to be
found in a resemblance obvious or remote, actual or
ideal. Hence the uses of things are suggested by their
appearance. The euphrasia or eyebright is useful in
case of sore eyes on account of the bright eye-like spot
in its corolla ; special virtues are ascribed to the gin-
seng on account of the resemblance of its roots to a
human shape. The granulated roots of the white
meadow saxifrage were regarded as efficacious against
calculous complaints. The Solomon's-seal is so called
on account of the marks in the cross-section of its
roots, and is used to seal wounds. Water-soldier, on
account of its sword-shaped leaves, was regarded as
useful for gunshot wounds. The red rose suggests its
use in blood diseases ; and yellow flowers were used in
jaundice and liver complaints. The walnut was clearly
defined for use in mental diseases : for its shape was
that of the head, the outer green covering being the
pericranium, the hard shell the skull, and the kernel
the brain. Old ladies' thistle was for stitches in the
side, nettle tea for nettle-rash, hearts'-ease for heart
troubles. Plants whose parts resembled teeth were
prescribed for toothache, quaking grass against shakes,
and so on with consistent illogicality (Dyer). The
resemblances here involved are obvious enough ; they
are just such as underlie popular names of plants and
the metaphorical use of terms. They form another
illustration of how metaphor and analogy overlap ;
what we accept as a sufficient suggestion for an appropriate name was by pseudo-science, by folk-lore, or by
superstition regarded as sufficiently significant to support a cause-and-effect-like or a teleological relation.

This, furthermore, is a line of practice in which modern superstition and savage belief stand on an equal footing; the prescriptions just cited are matched by the operations of the Cherokee, who make "a decoction of the cone-flower for weak eyes because of the fancied resemblance of that plant to the strong-sighted eye of the deer" (Clodd); who carry out the notion more elaborately when they "drink an infusion of the tenacious burrs of the common beggars'-lice, an American species of the genus Desmodium, to strengthen the memory," or to "insure a fine voice, boil crickets and drink the liquor" (Clodd). The "Zulu medicine-man, who takes the bones of the oldest bull or dog of the tribe, giving scrapings of these to the sick, so that their lives may be prolonged to old age," in turn finds a parallel in the seventeenth-century doctors, "who, with less logic, but perchance unconscious humor, gave their patients pulverized mummy to prolong their years" (cited by Clodd). Analogy in savagery, in pseudo-science, and in undeveloped science, in superstition and in survival, are of a nature all compact.

The transition from magic to science was made possible by, and itself illustrates the supplanting of, loose and false reasoning by close and logical thought; the pseudo-sciences represent weak and erroneous inference even more than they embody defective observation or mere ignorance. An over-dependence upon analogy characterizes some portions of them all, and finds its fullest development in astrology, as also in the various forms of alchemy and magic with which it is historically connected. Although this body of thought engaged the energies of many able and famous scholars, we can look upon it only as a system of resemblances and coincidences, elaborate and complex indeed, but requiring little more than a vivid imagination and a somewhat keen sense for far-fetched analogies. " This investigation," says the astrologer in Rydberg's " Magic of the Middle Ages," " relies on the resemblances of things, for this similarity is derived from a correspondence, and causality is interwoven with correspondence. Thus, for instance, we judge from the resemblance between the splendor of gold and that of the sun, that gold has its celestial correspondence in that luminary and sustains to it a causal relation." Again, " the two-horned beetle bears a causal relation to the moon, which at its increase and wane is also two-horned ; and if there were any doubt of this intimate relation between them, it must vanish when we learn that the beetle hides its eggs in the earth for the space of twenty-eight days, or just so long a time as is required for the moon to pass through the zodiac, but digs them up again on the twenty-ninth, when the moon is in conjunction with the sun." (Agrippa, " De Occulta Philosophiæ," i. 24.)

It will readily be seen how limitless are the results obtainable with such a system. Each planet becomes associated with a definite part of the body, and an argument such as the following becomes possible : " Since Capricornus, which presided over the knees in the house of Saturn, and all crawling animals are connected with the planet, the fat of snakes is an effective remedy against gout in the knees, especially on Saturday, the day of Saturn " (Rydberg). Tables of correspondences were freely devised showing the representatives of the sun, moon, and five planets among the elements, the microcosm, animals, plants, metals, and stones. Thus Mars was represented in these spheres respectively, by fire, acid juices, beasts of prey, burning, poisonous and stinging plants, iron or sulphuric metals, diamond, jasper, amethyst, and magnet; the vein of analogy lying in the fierce character of the god, whose name the planet bears. This idea of correspondence dominates the queer collection of odds and ends by which the old-time magician worked his charms. "Here," for instance, he would say, " is a plate of lead on which is engraved the symbol of a planet; and beside it a leaden flask containing gall. If I now take a piece of fine onyx marked with the same planet symbol and this dried cypress branch, and add to them the skin of a snake and the feather of an owl, you will need but to look into one of the tables given you to find that I have only collected various things in the elementary world which bear a relation of mutual activity to Saturn, and if rightly combined can attract both the powers of that planet and of the angels with which it is connected " (Rydberg). Mr. Tylor thus ably characterizes the analogies on which such systems are built and the uses to which they are put. " But most of his pseudo-science seems to rest on even weaker and more arbitrary analogies, not of things but of names. Names of stars and constellations, of signs denoting regions of the sky and periods of days and years, no matter how arbitrarily given, are materials which the astrologer can work upon and bring into ideal connection with mundane events. That astrono-mers should have divided the sun's course into imaginary signs of the zodiac, was enough to originate astrological rules, that these celestial signs have an actual effect on real earthly rams, bulls, crabs, lions, virgins. A child born under the sign of the lion will be courageous, but one under the crab will not go forward in life; one born under the waterman will be drowned, and so forth. . . . Again, simply because astronomers chose to distribute among the planets the names of certain deities, the planets thereby acquired the characters of their divine namesakes. Thus it was that the planet Venus became connected with love, Mars with war, Jupiter (whose ♃ in altered shape still heads our physicians' prescriptions) with power and joviality." The various positions of the heavenly bodies at one's birth, interpreted by such wild analogies, readily yield material for the prediction of future careers, vague enough to defy close denial, and bold enough to claim readily foreseeable consequences as striking verifications. Astrology represents the climax of the argument by analogy, fully systematized and calling into play many of the resources of modern learning. What is so clearly represented in astrology appears to a less extent in other pseudo-scientific systems; notably in palmistry and phrenology. It captivates the well-informed as well as the ignorant, it appeals to minds that are strong as well as those that are weak, and emphasizes the pricelessness of our scientific inheritance and the necessity of guarding it by the cultivation of sound logical habits of thought.

It would be pleasant, but unwarranted, to think of these forms of thought as obsolete; human nature is more deep-seated than learning. "In every department of human thought," says Mr. Clodd, "evidence of the non-persistence of primitive ideas is the exception rather than the rule. Scratch the epiderm of the civilized man, and the barbarian is found in the derm. In proof of which, there are more people who believe in Zadkiel's 'Vox Stellarum' than in the Nautical Almanac; and rare are the households where the 'Book of Dreams' and 'Fortune-Teller' are not to be found in the kitchen. The Singhalese caster of nativities has many representatives in the West, and there may lie profit in the reminder of the shallow depth to which knowledge of the orderly sequence of things has yet penetrated in the many. Societies and serials for the promulgation of astrology exist and flourish among us; Zadkiel boasts his circulation of a hundred thousand, and vaunts the fulfillment of his Delphic prophecies; while the late Astronomer Royal, Sir George Airy, was pestered, as his successor probably is, with requests to work the planets, accompanied by silver wherewith to cross his expert palm." The old astrology finds its descendants in modern fatuous volumes on Heliocentric Astrology, or Kabalistic Astrology, abounding in absurd pseudo-philosophic jargon and science-aping demonstrations, but in reality only the "vulgarest travesty of the old."

VIII

By way of conclusion it may be helpful to consider certain general truths in the field of anthropology and mental evolution, upon which the illustrations we have been considering have a bearing. We have seen what a widely extended genus the analogical argument compasses; and yet, if we were to include under this head certain closely allied and yet distinguishable forms of thought, it would be much wider still. I refer particularly to the use of metaphor and symbolism, which, like the children's make-believe with their dolls or fairies, is none the less on the boundary line between the real and the fictitious. Myth equally readily passes from the unconscious to the conscious stage, and much of what is plausibly interpreted as an argument by analogy, seems equally well an intentional use of symbolism and myth. That savages, at least in all but the lower stages, appreciate the use of myth is beyond all doubt. Primitive ceremonials, as also primitive explanations of the changes of nature, are full of symbolisms, which involve the same mental habit, whose products in the domain of analogy have been portrayed. This mythological instinct, Mr. Tylor well says, "belongs to that great doctrine of analogy from which we have gained so much of our apprehension of the world around us. Distrusted as it now is by severer science for its misleading results, analogy is to us still a chief means of discovery and illustration, while in earlier grades of education its influence was all but paramount. Analogies which are but fancies to us were to men of past ages reality. They could see the flame licking its yet undevoured prey with tongues of fire, or the serpent gliding along the sword from hilt to point; they could see a live creature gnawing within their bodies in the pangs of hunger; they heard the voices of the hill-dwarfs answering in the echo, and the chariot of the heaven god rattling in thunder over the solid firmament. Men to whom these were living thoughts had no need of the schoolmaster and his rules of composition, his injunctions to use metaphor cautiously and to take care to make all similes consistent."

The principle that what was once the serious occupation of men becomes in more advanced stages of culture the play of children, or is reduced from seriousness to mere amusement, finds illustrations in the mental as in the material world. The drum, once the serious terrifying instrument of the savage warrior, and the rattle, once the powerful emblem of the medicine man, have become the common toys of children. The bow and arrow are used for skill and sport only. In a similar way the formidable and trusted argument by analogy finds its proper field in riddles and puns. When we put the question, " Why is this object like the other ? " we understand that some out-of-the-way and accidental resemblance is asked for, some not very close analogy, that provokes amusement but not belief ; in many cases the resemblance is in the name only and degenerates into a pun. In such exercises of fancy we are employing the same faculties that our ancestors used in arriving at the customs and beliefs that we have been considering. The laws governing the progress of industrial arts, of mechanical inventions and social institutions seem thus to find equally ready application to the evolution of habits and customs in the mental world.

From another, and that also a comparative anthropological point of view, the natural history of analogy illustrates, though imperfectly, the evolutionary bond that unites the development of the race from primitive culture to civilization, from infantile helplessness to adult power, and again the dissolution of these processes in disease or their atavistic retention in less progressive strata of society. Significant, even though sporadic, parallelisms have been pointed out in the use of analogy by savages and by children; and far more completely can it be shown that superstitions and pseudo-sciences, folk-lore traditions and popular beliefs show the survival of these same analogical habits of mind, which may be viewed in part as reversions to outgrown conditions of thought, in part as the cropping out, in pathological form, of retarding tendencies which the course of evolution may have repressed but not wholly destroyed. For there is hardly a form of modern superstition, there is hardly a custom sanctioned by the unwritten tradition of the people, but what can be closely duplicated among the customs and beliefs of the untutored savage.

All this impresses us with the enduring qualities of man's barbaric past, the permanent though latent effect of his complete adaptation for thousands of years to a low intellectual environment. " The intrusion of the scientific method," Mr. Clodd aptly comments, "in its application to man's whole nature, disturbed that equilibrium. But this, as yet, only within the narrow area of the highest culture." The earlier and more fundamental psychological factor of humanity is feeling and not thought, or more accurately an incipient rationality, thoroughly suffused with emotional motives; and primitive analogies proceed by a feeling of analogical fitness, and not by an intellectual justification. " The exercise of feeling has been active from the beginning of his history, while thought, speaking

comparatively, has but recently had free play. . . .
Man wondered long chiliads before he reasoned, because feeling travels along the line of least resistance,
while thought, or the challenge by inquiry, with its
assumption that there may be two sides to a question,
must pursue a path obstructed by the dominance of
taboo and custom, by the force of imitation, and by
the strength of prejudice, passion, and fear."

The survey of the argument by analogy brings home
the conviction that there are forms of mental action,
psychological tendencies or thought-habits, characteristic of undeveloped stages of human mentality; that
these appear in versatile and instructive variety; and,
more important still, that they furnish glimpses of the
workings of a great progressive law, visible in the
shifting of importance attached to the argument by
analogy, and in its gradual subordination to, and ultimate retirement in favor of the sturdy principles of
inductive logic.   We are thus led to appreciate the
means by which error is converted into truth, the slow
and painful steps by which the logic of the sciences is
unfolded and mastered.   When Lord Chesterfield relates that the people expected a fatal issue of the
king's illness, because the oldest lion in the tower, of
about the same age as the king, had just died, he cannot help commenting upon the wildness and caprice of
the human mind; but Mr. Tylor more judiciously remarks, "Indeed the thought was neither wild nor
capricious; it was simply such an argument by analogy
as the educated world has at length painfully learned
to be worthless, but which it is not too much to declare
would to this day carry considerable weight to the

minds of four-fifths of the human race." Analogy
has doubtless lost the prestige of olden time; but the
remains of effete and misleading forms of thought,
upheld by a feeling of their analogical plausibility, continue to survive, and may at any time, when cloaked
in a modern garb, regain their former efficiency, and
feed the contagion of some new fad or pseudo-science;
while superstition, like poverty, we shall always have
with us, so long as there are social and intellectual
distinctions amongst men. In the light of the natural
history survey of analogy, these phenomena appear in
their true significance, testifying at once to the inherent progress, despite reversions, and to the underlying
unity of constitution and purpose, through which these
phenomena acquire their deeper and more human interest.

THE MIND'S EYE

Hamlet. My father, — methinks, I see my father.
Horatio. O, where, my lord ?
Hamlet. In my mind's eye, Horatio.

I

It is a commonplace taught from nursery to university that we see with our eyes, hear with our ears, and feel with our fingers. This is the truth, but not the whole truth. Indispensable as are the sense organs in gaining an acquaintance with the world in which we live, yet they alone do not determine how extensive or how accurate that acquaintance shall be. There is a mind behind the eye and the ear and the finger-tips which guides them in gathering information, and gives value and order to the exercise of the senses. This is particularly true of vision, — the most intellectual of all the senses, the one in which mere acuteness of the sense organ counts least and the training in observation counts most. The eagle's eye sees farther, but our eyes tell us vastly more of what is seen.

The eye may be compared to a photographic camera, with its eyelid cap, its iris shutter, its lens, and its sensitive plate, — the retina; when properly adjusted for distance and light, the image is formed on the retina as on the glass plate, and the picture is taken. So far the comparison is helpful; but while the camera takes a picture whenever and wherever the plate happens to be exposed, the complete act of seeing requires some coöperation on the part of the mind. The retina may be exposed a thousand times and take but few pictures; or perhaps it is better to say that the pictures may be taken, but remain undeveloped and evanescent. The pictures that are developed are stacked up, like the negatives in the photographer's shop, in the pigeon-holes of our mental storerooms, — some faded and blurred, some poorly arranged or mislaid, some often referred to and fresh prints made therefrom, and some quite neglected.

In order to see, it is at once necessary that the retina be suitably exposed toward the object to be seen, and that the mind be favorably disposed to the assimilation of the impression. True seeing, observing, is a double process, partly objective or outward — the thing seen and the retina, — and partly subjective or inward — the picture mysteriously transferred to the mind's representative, the brain, and there received and affiliated with other images. Illustrations of such seeing with the " mind's eye " are not far to seek. Wherever the beauties and conformations of natural scenery invite the eye of man, does he discover familiar forms and faces; the forces of nature have rough-hewn the rocks, but the human eye detects and often creates the resemblances. The stranger to whom such curiosities of form are first pointed out often finds it difficult to discover the resemblance, but once seen, the face or form obtrudes itself in every view, and seems the most conspicuous feature in the outlook. The flickering fire furnishes a fine background for the activity of the mind's eye, and against this it projects the forms and fancies which the leaping flames and the burning embers from time to time suggest. Not all see these fire-pictures readily, for our mental eyes differ more from one another than the physical ones, and perhaps no two persons see the same picture in quite the same way. It is not quite true, however, as many have held, that in waking hours we all have a world in common, but in dreams each has a world of his own; for our waking worlds are made different by the differences in what engages our interest and our attention. It is true that our eyes when open are opened very largely to the same views, but by no one observer are all these views, though visible, really seen.

This characteristic of vision often serves as a source of amusement. The puzzle picture with its tantalizing face, or animal, or what not, hidden in the trees, or fantastically constructed out of heterogeneous elements that make up the composition, is to many quite irresistible. We turn it about in all directions, wondering where the hidden form can be, scanning every detail of the picture, until suddenly a chance glimpse reveals it, plainly staring us in the face. When several persons are engaged in this occupation, it is amusing to observe how blind each is to what the others see; their physical eyes see alike, but their mental eyes reflect their own individualities.

Of the many thousands of persons who handle our silver dollar, but few happen to observe the lion's head which lies concealed in the representation of the familiar head of Liberty; frequently even a careful examination fails to detect this hidden emblem of British rule; but, as before, when once found, it is quite

obvious (Fig. 1).[1] For similar reasons it is a great
aid in looking for an object to know what to look for;
to be readily found, the object, though lost to sight,
should be to memory clear. Searching is a mental
process similar to the matching of a piece of fabric in
texture or color, when one has forgotten the sample
and must rely upon the remembrance of its appearance. If the recollection is clear and distinct, recognition takes place when the judgment decides that what
the physical eye sees corresponds to the image in the
mind's eye; with an indistinct mental image the recognition becomes doubtful or faulty. The novice in the
use of the microscope experiences considerable difficulty in observing the appearance which his instructor
sees and describes, and this because his conception of
the object to be seen is lacking in precision. Hence
his training in the use of the microscope is distinctly
aided by consulting the illustrations in the text-
book, for they enable his mental eye to realize the
pictures which it should entertain. He may be altogether too much influenced by the pictures thus suggested to his mental vision, and draw what is really
not under his microscope at all; much as the young
arithmetician will manage to obtain the answer which
the book requires even at the cost of a resort to very

---

[1] In order to obtain the effects described in the various illustrations
it is necessary in several cases to regard the figures for a considerable
time and with close attention. The reader is requested not to give up
in case the first attempt to secure the effect is not successful, but to
continue the effort for a reasonable period. Individuals differ considerably in the readiness with which they obtain such effects; in some
cases, such devices as holding the diagrams inverted, or at an angle, or
viewing them with the eyes half closed, are helpful.

unmathematical processes. For training in correct and accurate vision it is necessary to acquire an alert mental eye, that observes all that is objectively visible, but does not permit the subjective to add to or modify what is really present.

II

The importance of the mind's eye in ordinary vision is also well illustrated in cases in which we see or seem to see what is not really present, but what for one cause

Fig. 1. — In order to see the lion's head, look at the above cut upside down, and the head will be discovered facing the left, as above outlined. It is clearer on the coin itself than in this representation.

or another it is natural to suppose is present. A very familiar instance of this process is the constant overlooking of misprints — false letters, transposed letters, and missing letters — unless these happen to be particularly striking. We see only the general physiognomy of the word, and the detailed features are supplied from within ; in this case it is the expected that happens. In a series of experiments by Professor

Münsterberg a word was briefly shown, while just before a certain idea or train of thought was suggested. Under these circumstances the word shown was often misread in accordance with the suggested idea; if the idea of future is suggested, part may be read as past; if vegetable is the suggested line of thought, fright may be read as fruit, and so on. Reading is thus done largely by the mental eye; and entire words, obviously suggested by the context, are sometimes read in, when they have been accidentally omitted. This is more apt to occur with the irregular characters used in manuscript than in the more distinct forms of the printed alphabet, and is particularly frequent in reading over what one has himself written. In reading proof, however, we are eager to detect misprints, and this change in attitude helps to make them visible. It is very difficult to illustrate this process intentionally, because the knowledge that one's powers of observation are about to be tested places one on one's guard, and thus suppresses the natural activity of the mind's eye and draws unusual attention to objective details. Let the reader at this point hold the page at some distance off — say, eight or twelve feet — and draw an exact reproduction of the letters shown in Fig. 2. He should not look at Fig. 2 at close range nor read further in the text until this has been done; and *perhaps* he may find that he has introduced strokes which were not present in the original. If this is not the case, let him try the test upon those who are ignorant of its nature, and he will find that most persons will supply light lines to complete the contours of the letters, which in the original are suggested but not really present; the original outline, Fig. 2a, becomes something like Fig. 2b, and so on for the rest of the letters. The physical

FIG. 2. — These letters should not be seen at all until they have been observed at a distance of eight to twelve feet. An interesting method of testing the activity of the mind's eye with these letters is described in the text.

eye sees the former, but the mental eye sees the latter.

FIG. 2a.   FIG. 2b.

I tried this experiment with a class of some thirty Uni-

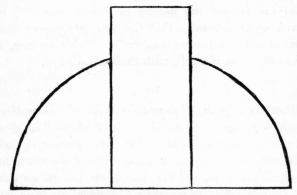

FIG. 3. — For description, see text, page 282.

versity students of Psychology, and, although they were disposed to be quite critical and suspected some kind of an illusion, only three or four drew the letters correctly; all the rest filled in the imaginary light contours; some even drew them as heavily as the real strokes. I followed this by an experiment of a similar character. I placed upon a table a figure (Fig. 3) made of light cardboard, fastened to blocks of wood at the base, so that the pieces would easily stand upright. The middle piece, which is rectangular and higher than the rest, was placed a little in front of the rest of the figure. The students were asked to describe precisely what they saw; and with one exception they all described, in different words, a semicircular piece of cardboard with a rectangular piece in front of it. In reality there was no half-circle of cardboard, but only portions of two quarter-circles with the portion back of the middle piece omitted. The students, of course, were well aware that their physical eyes could not see what was behind the middle cardboard, but they inferred, quite naturally, that the two side pieces were parts of one continuous semicircle. This they saw, so far as they saw it at all, with their mind's eye.

III

There is a further interesting class of illustrations in which a single outward impression changes its character according as it is viewed as representing one thing or another. In a general way we see the same thing all the time, and the image on the retina does not change. But as we shift the attention from one portion of the view to another, or as we view it with a different mental conception of what the figure represents, it assumes a different aspect, and to our mental eye becomes quite a different thing. A slight but interesting change takes place if we view Fig. 4 first with the conception that the black is the pattern to be seen and the white the background, and again try to see the white as the pattern against a black back-

FIG. 4. — The black and white portions of this design are precisely alike; but the effect of looking at the figure as a pattern in black upon a white background, or as a pattern in white upon a black background is quite different, although the difference is not easily described.

ground. I give a further illustration of such a change in Fig. 5. In our first and natural view of this we focus the attention upon the black lines and observe the familiar illusion, that the four vertical black bands seem far from parallel. That they are parallel can be verified by measurement, or by covering up all of the diagram except the four main bands. But if the white part of the diagram be conceived as the design against a black background, then the design is no longer the same, and with this change the illusion disappears, and

the four bands seem parallel, as they really are. It
may require a little effort to bring about this change,
but it is marked when once realized.

A curious optical effect, which in part illustrates
the change in appearance under different aspects, is

Fig. 5. — When this figure is viewed as a black pattern on a white background, the four main vertical black bands seem far from parallel; when
it is viewed as a white pattern on a black background the pattern is different and the illusion disappears (or nearly so), and the four black bands as
well as the five white ones seem more nearly parallel.

reproduced in Fig. 6. In this case the enchantment
of distance is necessary to produce the transformation.
Viewed at the usual reading distance, we see nothing
but an irregular and meaningless assemblage of black
and white blotches. At a distance of not less than
fifteen to eighteen feet, however, a man's head appears

quite clearly. Also observe that after the head has once been realized it becomes possible to obtain suggestions of it at nearer distances.

A much larger class of ambiguous diagrams consists of those which represent by simple outlines familiar

FIG. 6. — This is a highly enlarged reproduction taken from a half-tone process print of Lord Kelvin. It appeared in the *Photographic Times*.

geometrical forms or objects. We cultivate such a use of our eyes, as indeed of all our faculties, as will on the whole lead to the most profitable results. As a rule, the particular impression is not so important as what it represents. Sense-impressions are simply the symbols or signs of things or ideas, and the thing or the idea is more important than the sign. Accordingly, we are accustomed to interpret lines, whenever we can, as the representations of objects. We are well aware that the canvas or the etching or the photograph before us is a flat surface in two dimensions,

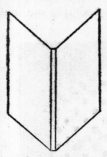

FIG. 7. — This drawing may be viewed as the representation of a book standing on its half-opened covers as seen from the back of the book; or as the inside view of an open book showing the pages.

FIG. 8. — When this figure is viewed as an arrow, the upper or feathered end is apt to seem flat; when the rest of the arrow is covered, the feathered end may be made to project or recede like the book-cover in Fig. 7.

but we see the picture as the representation of solid objects in three dimensions. This is the illusion of pictorial art. So strong is this tendency to view lines as the symbols of things, that if there is the slightest chance of so viewing them, we invariably do so; for we have a great deal of experience with things that present their contours as lines, and very little with mere lines or surfaces. If we view outlines only, without shading or perspective or anything to definitely suggest what is foreground and what background, it becomes possible for the mind to supply these details and see foreground as background, and *vice versa*.

A good example to begin with is Fig. 7. These outlines will probably suggest at first view a book, or better a book-cover, seen with its back toward you and its sides sloping away from you; but it may also be viewed as a book opened out towards you and presenting to you an inside view of its contents. Should the change not come readily, it may be facilitated by thinking persistently of the appearance of an open book in this position. The upper portion of Fig. 8 is practically the same as Fig. 7, and if the rest of the figure be covered up, it will change as did the book cover; when, however, the whole figure is viewed as an arrow, a new conception enters, and the apparently solid book cover becomes the *flat* feathered part of the

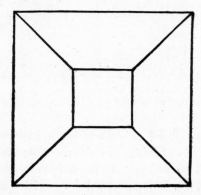

FIG. 9. — The smaller square may be regarded as either the nearer face of a projecting figure or as the more distant face of a hollow figure.

arrow. Look at the next figure (Fig. 9), which represents in outline a truncated pyramid with a square base.

Is the smaller square nearer to you, and are the sides of the pyramid sloping away from you toward the larger square in the rear? Or are you looking into the hollow of a truncated pyramid with the smaller square in the background? Or is it now one and now the other, according as you decide to see it? Here

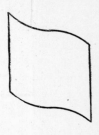

FIG. 10. — This represents an ordinary table-glass, — the bottom of the glass and the entire rear side, except the upper portion, being seen through the transparent nearer side, and the rear apparently projecting above the front. But it fluctuates in appearance between this and a view of the glass in which the bottom is seen directly, partly from underneath, the *whole* of the rear side is seen through the transparent front, and the front projects above the back.

FIG. 11. — In this scroll the left half may at first seem concave and the right convex; it then seems to roll or advance like a wave, and the left seems convex and the right concave, as though the trough of the wave had become the crest, and *vice versa*.

(Fig. 12) is a skeleton box which you may conceive as made of wires outlining the sides. Now the front, or side nearest to me, seems directed downward and to the left; again, it has shifted its position and is no longer the front, and the side which appears to be the front seems directed upward and to the right. The presence of the diagonal line makes the change more striking: in one position it runs from the left-hand *rear* upper corner to the right-hand *front* lower corner ; while in the other it connects the left-hand *front* upper corner with the right-hand *rear* lower corner.

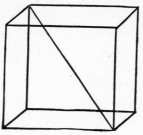

FIG. 12.

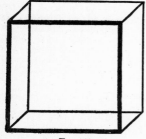

FIG. 12a.

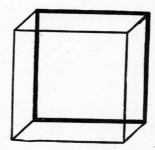

FIG. 12b.

FIGS. 12, 12a, 12b. — The two methods of viewing Fig. 12 are described in the text. Figs. 12a and 12b are added to make clearer the two methods of viewing Fig. 12. The heavier lines seem to represent the nearer surface. Fig. 12a more naturally suggests the nearer surface of the box in a position downward and to the left, and Fig.12b makes the nearer side seem to be upward and to the right. But in spite of the heavier outlines of the one surface, it may be made to shift positions from foreground to background, although not so readily as in Fig. 12.

Fig. 14 will probably seem at first glimpse to be the view of a flight of steps which one is about to ascend from right to left. Imagine it, however, to be a

view of the under side of a series of steps; the view
representing the structure of overhanging solid mason-
work seen from underneath.   At first it may be difficult to see it thus, because the view of steps which we
are about to mount is a more natural and frequent
experience than the other ; but by staring at it with
the intention of seeing it differently the transition will
come, and often quite unexpectedly.

The blocks in Fig. 15 are subject to a marked fluctuation.   Now the black surfaces represent the bottoms of the blocks, all pointing downward and to the

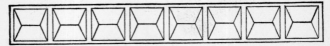

Fig. 13. — Each member of this frieze represents a relief ornament, applied upon the background, which in cross-section would be an isosceles
triangle with a large obtuse angle, or a space of similar shape hollowed
out of the solid wood or stone.   In running the eye along the pattern, it
is interesting to observe how variously the patterns fluctuate from one of
these aspects to the other.

left, and now the black surfaces have changed and
have become the tops, pointing upward and to the
right.   For some the changes come at will ; for others
they seem to come unexpectedly, but all are aided by
anticipating mentally the nature of the transformation.
The effect here is quite striking, the blocks seeming
almost animated and moving through space.   In Fig.
16 a similar arrangement serves to create an illusion as
to the real number of blocks present.   If viewed in
one way — the black surface forming the tops of the
blocks — there seem to be six, arranged as in Fig. 17 ;
but when the transformation has taken place and the
black surfaces have become the overhanging bottoms

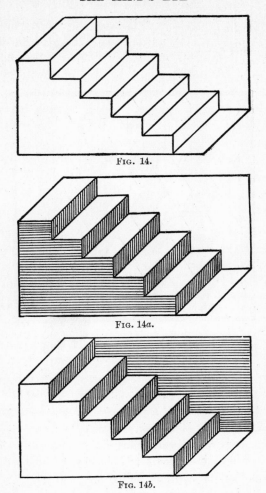

Fig. 14.

Fig. 14a.

Fig. 14b.

Figs. 14, 14a, and 14b. — The two views of Fig. 14 described in the text are brought out more clearly in Figs. 14a and 14b. The shaded portion tends to be regarded as the nearer face. Fig. 14a is more apt to suggest the steps seen as we ascend them. Fig. 14b seems to represent the hollowed-out structure underneath the steps. But even with the shading the dual interpretation is possible, though less obvious.

of the boxes, there are seven, arranged as in Fig. 18. Somewhat different, but still belonging to the group of ambiguous figures, is the ingenious conceit of the duck-rabbit shown in Fig. 19. When it is a rabbit, the face

FIG. 15. — This interesting figure (which is reproduced with modifications from *Scripture: The New Psychology*) is subject in a striking way to interchanges between foreground and background. Most persons find it difficult to maintain for any considerable time either aspect of the blocks (these aspects are described in the text); some can change them at will, others must accept the changes as they happen to come.

looks to the right and a pair of ears are conspicuous behind; when it is a duck, the face looks to the left and the ears have been changed into the bill. Most observers find it difficult to hold either interpretation steadily, the fluctuations being frequent, and coming as a surprise.

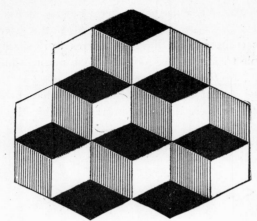

FIG. 16.

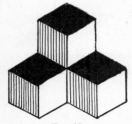

FIG. 16a

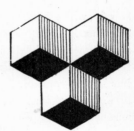

FIG. 16b.

FIGS. 16, 16a, and 16b. — How many blocks are there in this pile? Six or seven? Note the change in arrangement of the blocks as they change in number from six to seven. This change is described in the text. Figs. 16a and 16b show the two phases of a group of any three of the blocks. The arrangement of a pyramid of six blocks seems the more stable and is usually first suggested; but hold the page inverted, and you will probably see the alternate arrangement (with, however, the black surfaces still forming the tops). And once knowing what to look for, you will very likely be able to see either arrangement, whether the diagram be held inverted or not. This method of viewing the figures upside down and in other positions is also suggested to bring out the changes indicated in Figs. 12, 12a, 12b, and in Figs. 14, 14a, 14b.

IV

This collection of diagrams serves to illustrate the
principle that when the objective features are ambiguous, we see one thing or another according to the
impression that is in the mind's eye; what the objective factors lack in definiteness the subjective ones

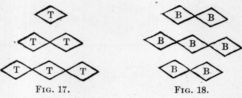

Fig. 17.   Fig. 18.

T indicates that the shaded portion of Fig. 16 in this view represents
the top of a block; B that in the other view it represents the bottom.

supply, while familiarity, prepossession, as well as other
circumstances influence the result.   These illustrations
show conclusively that seeing is not wholly an objective matter depending upon what there is to be seen,
but is very considerably a subjective matter, depending
upon the eye that sees.   To the same observer a given
arrangement of lines now appears as the representation of one object and now of another; and from the
same objective experience, especially in instances that
demand a somewhat complicated exercise of the senses,
different observers derive very different impressions.

Not only when the sense-impressions are ambiguous
or defective, but when they are vague — when the light
is dim or the forms obscure — does the mind's eye eke
out the imperfections of physical vision.   The vague
conformations of drapery and make-up that are identified and recognized in spiritualistic *séances* illustrate

extreme instances of this process. The whitewashed tree or post that momentarily startles us in a dark country lane takes on the guise that expectancy gives it. The mental predisposition here becomes the dominant factor, and the timid see as ghosts what their more sturdy companions recognize as whitewashed posts. Such experiences we ascribe to the action of suggestion and imagination — the cloud " that's almost in shape like a camel," or " like a weasel," or " like a whale."

FIG. 19. — Do you see a duck or a rabbit, or either ? (From *Harper's Weekly*, originally in *Fliegende Blätter*.)

But throughout our visual experiences there runs this double strain, now mainly outward and now mainly inward, from the simplest excitements of the retina up to the realms where fancy soars free from the confines of sense, and the objective finds its occupation gone.

MENTAL PREPOSSESSION AND INERTIA

I

THOSE who are actively engaged in educational pursuits are called upon from time to time to consider the
nature of the difficulties in the imparting of knowledge,
the psychological impediments that stand in the way
of successful instruction.   These are many and various;
and pertain as well to the givers as to the receivers of
learning.   This large and well threshed field I have
no intention of gleaning once more; I desire simply to
draw attention to one form of difficulty on the part
of the learner, which has been brought home to me so
frequently and at times so forcibly, that I should be
inclined to select it as the most salient stumbling-block
in the successful acquisition of those branches of study
which it falls to my lot to expound.

This characteristic, which may be called mental prepossession, is well illustrated in the following narrative,
the truth of which, however, is not guaranteed.   The
story dates from the exciting days when the American
public was completely fascinated by the mental gymnastics of the "spelling bee;" and relates that towards
the close of a very fierce contest with the alphabet,
when only a few stalwart champions remained to
encounter the erratic eccentricities of English ortho-
graphy, the conductor of the "bee" announced with
an air of grave importance a word that he felt quite

certain would retire not a few of the spelling virtuosi. He then asked their closest attention to his precise pronunciation, and solemnly gave utterance to what for all the world sounded like *cat*. Each hearer attempted to spell this extraordinarily difficult word with a suitably unusual rearrangement of the letters suggested by the sound, and when each effort had in turn been pronounced a failure, the information was given that the correct spelling was *c-a-t*. *Haec fabula docet* that when one expects a difficulty he is apt to find it or to make it. Believing the problem to be unusual, he applies unusual methods to its solution; believing it to be complex, he overlooks the simple means by which its mysteries may be unlocked. It matters little how this reputation has come about, whether as the result of personal prejudice or of inherited tradition, whether suggested by the technicality of the subject or the awkwardness of the treatment, whether by the use of a few unusual terms or operations, or by any one of the countless methods, conscious and unconscious, by which such impressions are formed, — the result will be much the same.

Many a student approaches a study such as psychology or logic with an unshakable conviction that he is about to consider matters abstruse and difficult; things totally unrelated to what he has studied elsewhere or experienced before, and accordingly requiring an exercise of the mental faculties as different as possible from that to which he has been accustomed. It is not altogether strange that such notions should be current, because the tradition to that effect is ancient and strong, and originated in times when scholars generally, and philosophers perhaps more than others, took pride in exclusive erudition, in the possession of a more or less esoteric wisdom quite unrelated to the knowing and the thinking of οἱ πολλοί. It requires the combined operation of long periods of time and of persistent effort to weaken such beliefs; and it is only within recent times that the notion has been successfully disseminated that the processes considered in psychology and logic derive their validity from our daily experience, and require for their comprehension no mental gymnastics or intellectual contortions; that in brief these sciences simply aim to systematize and improve, to interpret and explain the every-day processes by which knowledge is gained. This, at all events, is one of their functions, and one profitably emphasized in the introductory study of their scope and content.

When one has once formed the impression, or has had it produced or suggested for him, that the study or the task he is about to attack is a difficult one, his mental powers are at once sufficiently reduced to make it really difficult; the signal is given of an approaching intricate turn in the road, the brakes are turned on, and the train of thought creeps along slowly. Mental prepossession leads to mental inertia. The same question which the student would answer readily and fully when asked by a friend as an item of general information, becomes utterly beyond his comprehension when it appears in the text-book, the title-page of which bears the ominous name of one or other of the studies reputed as difficult. The mind is not properly set; there is little receptiveness, little alertness. When we are asked in a conundrum-like tone, why one thing is like another, we ignore obvious and simple resemblances, and look about for obscure ones.   The student who labors under the illusion that psychology is a maze of conundrums, employs mental processes appropriate to such a pursuit.   The schoolboy finds it impossible to answer a question in arithmetic during the geography lesson, and the same lack of adaptability is shown by his older counterpart when he greets the answer to a very simple question (which, however, he himself failed to answer) with the all too familiar, " Oh, of course I knew *that*."   Perhaps the most extreme instance of the many that I could cite is that of a student so irresponsive and apparently at sea regarding the topic under discussion — the senses — as to force me to ask him, "With what do you hear ? " and who answered with perfect sincerity, " I don't know."   This was a psychological question, and as such became as difficult as the spelling of *cat* at the end of a " spelling bee."

When the student has been made to feel that the questions he is asked can be answered from his everyday experience, and that common sense is often quite as serviceable a guide as special knowledge, a progress ensues in every way satisfactory.   Such a conviction, however, is not a matter of verbal acknowledgment ; it yields slowly to explanation and proceeds somewhat unconsciously and inwardly.   Moreover, it is a trait very sensitive to the power of contagion, so that a comparatively small proportion of the class may successfully spread this mental attitude to the whole number. A question which two or three have failed to answer becomes invested with a spurious difficulty which makes it a deep mystery to all the others.

This mental prepossession may at times have quite different and curious results. When, for instance, the goal to be reached is given, when the answer may be looked up in the back of the book, it is surprising what peculiar and irrational steps will be taken to secure and justify the answer so given. This is all the more striking when the answer happens to be wrong; however simply such error may be discovered, the prepossessed mind will work away until by a more or less roundabout procedure the desired answer is reached. A noted professor of chemistry has an apt illustration of such a case. In a chemical test his assistant by mistake referred the class to the wrong bottle, so that the substance which the correct liquid would have dissolved could not be at all dissolved in the liquid actually used. However, on the professor's next round in his laboratory nearly every student assured him that the substance had dissolved, and a few went so far as to describe the precise manner of its dissolution.

It is quite clear that illustrations of mental prepossession, as also of inertia, may be found in many of the industries and occupations of life. The bicycle has added a very characteristic one. At a certain stage in the acquisition of the art of cycling, there comes a time when every obstacle and irregularity in the road absorbs the attention of the rider with a fascination that is quite irresistible. The rider is so possessed with the idea that he or she is going to run into the post or the curb or a rut or another vehicle, that the dreaded calamity may actually ensue. When the attention can be directed to the clear pathway, and the obstacles driven out from the focus of attention, the difficulty is surmounted. So in jumping or running and in other athletic trials, the entertainment of the notion of a possible failure to reach the mark lessens the intensity of one's effort, and prevents the accomplishment of one's best. He who hesitates is lost, because the hesitation makes possible the suggestion of a failure, the prepossession by a sense of difficulty.

II

Some of the illustrations of prepossession are somewhat trivial ; others more important, but perhaps not so definite as might be desired. It is seldom that an instance of this propensity can be pointed out in which an accurate and quantitative comparison may be made between the possessed and the unpossessed mind. One such illustration, which seems to me comprehensive and significant, is worthy of more detailed record.[1] It is derived from the experience of the United States Census office in 1890, in tabulating the returns of the enumeration by means of machines specially devised for this purpose. I give an account of the manipulation of these machines in the words of one who had an intimate acquaintance with their use, and add italics to emphasize the points of special psychological significance.

" The adoption of Mr. Hollerith's tabulating machine for counting the population of the country according, at one and the same time, to sex, color, age, marital condition, nationality, occupation or profession, language and school attendance presented an entirely novel problem to the office. The machines having

[1] This account I owe to Mrs. May Cole Baker, of Washington, D. C.

never been used for any purpose, there was no previous experience by which to act or on which to predicate results. The necessity was upon the office of employing for a very limited time (ninety days) at least five hundred people for this work alone, in addition to the one thousand who could be taken from other branches of the work and placed on this one. Every one, including Mr. Hollerith himself, felt that the rapid and accurate use of the punching machines called for a degree of cultivated intelligence not possessed by every clerk. So much for the mental attitude.

" The clerks (an instructor for every twenty) were taught to edit the family schedules from which the count was to be made, thus learning thoroughly how to read and classify the returns. In order to accommodate the returns to the capacity of a punching machine, a great variety of symbols were adopted for occupations and professions : thus Ad was used for farmer : Ac for farm hands : Kd for merchants : Gd for agents, etc., through twenty-four two-columned octavo pages of ordinary type. Some one symbol must be used for each occupation recorded, and the use of the symbols must be learned, and, for rapid work, they must be committed to memory.[1] *After five weeks of editing*, one by one, the most reliable and intelligent workers were set to use the punching machines. The task is much like that of using a typewriter, substituting for keys a movable punch which passes through

[1] It should be noted that it is only the classification of occupations that requires so extremely elaborate and artificial a system ; the returns for nationality, age, sex, marital condition, etc., are far simpler to record. The editing consists in writing the symbols on the returns, so that they need not be memorized.

lettered holes, and in place of the forty keys of an ordinary typewriter, about two hundred and fifty holes are to be learned.

" Mr. Hollerith set the number of cards for a day's work at 550. (Each finished card contained, on the average, 10 holes.) *It was two weeks before that number of cards was reached by any clerk*, and that only in exceptional cases. Then the entire force of the division was set to work. In two weeks most of them had reached five hundred, and the average was daily increasing. These clerks worked at first from edited schedules; that is, those on which had been written the symbols to be punched on the machine. A roll of honor was made out daily showing the highest records, *and in a week* the clerks were doing from *six hundred to fifteen hundred a day*, but at a great cost of nervous force. So severe was the nervous strain that complaints were made to the Secretary of the Interior, who forbade any further posting of daily reports, and instead an order was posted that no clerk was required to do more than such a day's work as he or she could readily perform, and that no arbitrary number was required of any one.

" *After the work was well under way about two hundred new clerks were put into one room and scattered through the force already at work. They had no experience with schedules, knew nothing of the symbols, had never seen the machines. They saw those around them working easily and rapidly, and in* THREE DAYS SEVERAL OF THEM HAD DONE FIVE HUNDRED, IN A WEEK NEARLY EVERY ONE, *while the general average was rising.* There was no longer any question of nervous strain, and one of these temporary clerks the day before she left beat the record by doing 2,230. I think the influence of the mental attitude quite as remarkable in the matter of their doing the work easily as in that of doing it rapidly. During the first month many were actually sick from overwork when doing seven hundred, while after that time the idea that the work was unusually trying was never referred to. Another significant fact is that after the posting of the daily record was abolished there was no falling off in the daily average, as had been anticipated, while complaints of overwork necessarily ceased."

It is thus demonstrated that an unskilled clerk, with an environment proving the possibility of a task and suggesting its easy accomplishment, can in *three days* succeed in doing what a skilled clerk, with a preliminary acquaintance of five weeks with the symbols to be used, could do only after *two weeks'* practice ; and this because the latter, doubtless not a whit inferior in ability, had been led to regard his task as difficult.

III

If we consider the psychological relations of the processes involved in the above illustrations, we are led to the conviction that we seldom exert our powers to their full capacity. Instances in which, under the influence of some stirring, perhaps dangerous circumstance, persons exert physical energies ordinarily beyond their resources, are quite familiar ; and the same is true though less readily demonstrated of mental effort. The success of the various methods of " mind cure," in which the conviction of the possibility of a cure so markedly aids its realization, adds another class of illustrations; and among the experiments with hypnotized persons occur countless instances of the performance of actions, both physical and mental, quite surpassing what is regarded as normal. The powers which are here called upon through somewhat extreme and drastic means, can doubtless be drawn upon to a less extent by the use of more moderate agencies; and this at once suggests the educational utilization of the mental attitude in question. Perhaps the ideal aim is to impress the student indirectly rather than directly, by manner rather than by instruction, with the conviction that what is required of him is well within his powers; and to do this without in the least impugning the necessity of honest, hard work for the accomplishment of serious results. The complaint is often made that the American boy takes longer by several years to reach a given grade of scholarship than his foreign brother; and the reason of this difference is usually assigned to the extremely slow progress made in the elementary public schools. The machinery is started at too slow a rate, and seems to leave the impress of its inertia upon all succeeding periods.

It is not possible to devise any readily formulated and easily applied cure for this mental prepossession; our aim must be to sterilize the mental atmosphere, so that the germs of the disease may not gain a foothold; to set a healthy normal step and take it for granted that it can be followed by all but the laggards. But in spite of all effort, the failing is quite certain to crop out, and will always continue to demand for its treatment much educational tact and insight.

When we come to a a slippery place in the road, we involuntarily take short steps and become extremely conscious of our locomotion. It is important to prevent the growth of the habit of imagining slippery places in the paths about to be trodden ; and even when they are actually to be encountered, it is well to meet them with the bracing effort that comes from the use of a reserve energy, to proceed without too much consciousness of the path, and with as nearly a normal gait as possible. There are sufficient difficulties in the various walks of life without adding to them those that arise from mental prepossession, and that lead to mental inertia.

A STUDY OF INVOLUNTARY MOVEMENTS

I

QUITE a number of delusions find a common point of origin in the natural tendency to view our mental life — the aggregate of our thoughts and doings — as coextensive with the experiences of which our consciousness gives information and which our will directs. The significance of the unconscious and the involuntary is apt to be underestimated or disregarded. We are more ready to acknowledge that in certain unusual and semi-morbid conditions persons will exhibit these peculiar expressions of the subterranean strata of our mental structure — that some have the habit of walking or talking in their sleep, that others occasionally fall into an automatic, trance-like condition, that hypnotism and hysteria and obscure lapses of consciousness and alterations of personality bring to the surface curious specimens of the mysteries of this underworld, — but we are slow to appreciate that the sub-conscious and the involuntary find a common and a natural place amidst the soundly reasoned and aptly directed activities of our own intelligence. While it is reasonable and proper to have faith in the testimony of consciousness, it is desirable that this confidence should be accompanied by an understanding of the conditions under which such testimony is presumably valid, and when presumably defective or misleading. Sense-deceptions, faulty observation, distraction, exaggeration, illusion, fallacy, and error are not idle abstract fancies of the psychologist, but stern realities ; and their existence emphasizes the need in the determination of truth and the maintenance of a sound rationality, of a calm, unprejudiced judgment, of an experienced and balanced intelligence, of a discerning sense for nice distinctions, of an appreciation of the circumstances under which it is peculiarly human to err. A demonstration of the readiness with which perfectly normal individuals may be induced to yield visible evidence of unconscious and involuntary processes, thus possesses a special interest ; for when the naturalness of a few definite types of involuntary movements is made clear, the application of the experience to more complex and more indefinite circumstances will easily and logically follow. While the circumstances under which involuntary indications of mental activity are ordinarily given, are too various to enable one to say *ab uno disce omnes*, yet the principle demonstrated in one case is capable of a considerable generalization, which will go far to prevent misconception of apparently mysterious and exceptional phenomena.

II

When some years ago, the American public was confronted with the striking exhibitions of muscle-reading, the wildest speculations were indulged in regarding its true *modus operandi ;* and the suggestion that all that was done was explicable by the skillful interpretation of the unconscious indications given by the subjects, was scouted or even ridiculed. It was not supposed that such indications were sufficiently definite for the purposes of the "mind-reader," or were obtainable under the conditions of his tests. Again, it was urged that this explanation was hardly applicable to certain striking performances, which in reality involved other and subtler modes of thought-interpretation, and the accounts of which were also exaggerated and distorted. And furthermore, it was argued, too many worthy and learned persons were absolutely certain that they had given no indications whatever. For a time the view that mind-reading was muscle-reading rested upon rather indirect evidence, and upon a form of argument that carries more weight with those familiar with the nature of scientific problems than with the public at large. But the development of experimental research in the domain of psychology has made possible a variety of demonstrations of the truth and adequacy of this explanation. It was with the purpose of securing a visible record of certain types of involuntary movements, that the investigation, the results of which are here presented, was undertaken.

Inasmuch as the movements in question are often very slight, somewhat delicate apparatus is required to secure their record ; the apparatus must in a measure exaggerate the tendency to motion though without altering its nature. The form of apparatus which I devised for this study, and which may be appropriately called an automatograph, is illustrated in the accompanying figure (p. 310). It consists of a wooden frame, enclosing a heavy piece of plate glass (fifteen inches square), and mounted upon three legs which are pro-

vided with screw adjustments for bringing the plate
into a perfect level. Upon the plate of glass are
placed in the form of a triangle three well turned and
polished steel or brass balls; and upon the balls rests
a thin crystal-plate glass set in a light wooden frame.
The finger-tips of one hand rest upon the upper plate
in the position indicated. When all is properly ad-

FIG. 1. — THE AUTOMATOGRAPH. When in use a screen
(not shown in the illustration) cuts off the view of the apparatus from the subject. The recording device, which may also
be used separately, is shown in outline in half its full size.
R is a glass rod which moves freely up and down in the
glass tube T, which is set into the cork C. A rubber band B
is provided to prevent the rod from falling through the tube,
when not resting upon the recording-plate.

justed and glass and balls are rubbed smooth
with oil, it is quite impossible to hold the
apparatus perfectly still for more than a few
seconds ; the slightest unsteadiness or movement of the hand at once sets the plate rolling with an irregular motion. If one closes the eyes
and fixes the attention upon a definite mental image or
train of thought, it is easy to form the conviction that
the plate remains quiet, but the record proves that this

is not the case. The other parts of the apparatus are designed to give a record of the movements of the plate. Fastened to the light frame containing the upper glass plate is a slender rod some ten inches long, bearing at its end a cork ; and piercing the cork is a small glass tube within which a snugly fitting glass rod has room to move. The rod is drawn to a smooth, round point ; and when in position rests upon a piece of glazed paper that has been blackened over a flame and then smoothly stretched over a small glass plate. The point of the rod thus records easily and accurately every movement of the hand that is imparted to the upper plate, and by the manner of its adjustment accommodates itself to all irregularities of movement or recording surface. This recording device is shown in greater detail in the illustration, and was used to good advantage as a simple automatograph in independence of the balls and plates. In that case the recording part is held in the hand as though it were a pencil, but in a vertical position, and the record-plate may be placed upon a table ; or for special purposes the plate may be held in the other hand or fastened to the top of one's head. When not otherwise stated, the records here reproduced were obtained by use of the automatograph. Some of the records are noted as having been secured with the simpler device just described.

The process of securing a record is as follows : the subject, standing, places his hand upon the automatograph, with the arm nearly horizontal and not quite fully extended, and the elbow bent in a fairly comfortable posture ; his attention is engaged by asking him to listen to and count the strokes of a metronome ; to look at and count the oscillations of a pendulum ; to read from a book ; to call out the names of colors ; to think of a given direction or locality, or the position of an object ; and so on. He is instructed to think as little as possible of his hand, making a reasonable effort to keep it from moving. To cut off the apparatus from the subject's field of vision and attention, a large screen is interposed between him and the record, a curtain with a suitable opening for the arm forming part of the screen. The operator holds the glass pencil in his hand, and when all is in readiness allows it to slip through the glass tube and begin to write, removing it again after a definite interval or when the record seems completed.

III

We may now consider a few typical results. Fig. 2, an ordinary average result, was obtained while the sub-

FIG. 2. — READING COLORS. Time of record, 95 seconds. Position of colors ≫——→. Subject facing ≫——→. In all the figures A represents the beginning of the record, and Z the end. The arrows are used to indicate the direction in which the object attended to was situated, and also the direction in which the subject was facing. The tracings are permanently fixed by coating them with a weak solution of shellac in alcohol.

ject was calling out the names of a series of small patches of color, displayed on the wall facing him, about eight feet distant. It will be observed that the move-

instances, such as Fig. 5, this pervades the whole record. Here the hand moves to and fro, keeping time — not accurately at all, but in a general way — with the strokes of the metronome.

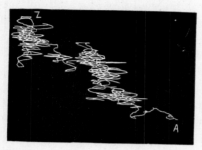

FIG. 5. — COUNTING THE STROKES OF A METRONOME. Shows the oscillations of the movements with the strokes of the metronome.

To obtain similar results for a visual impression a silently swinging pendulum is used, the subject following the oscillations with his eyes and counting them. The result is more frequently simply a move-

FIG. 6. — COUNTING THE OSCILLATIONS OF A PENDULUM. Time of record, 45 seconds. Direction of the attention ⟫⟶. Subject facing ⟫⟶. The points 1, 2, 3, show the positions of the writing-point, 15, 30, and 45 seconds after the record was started.

ment towards the pendulum, Fig. 6; but occasionally there appear periodic movements induced by those of the pendulum. A very excellent instance of the latter appears in Fig. 7 (p. 318).

We may more closely approximate the ordinary
experiment of the muscle-reader by giving the subject
some object to hide, say a knife, and then asking him

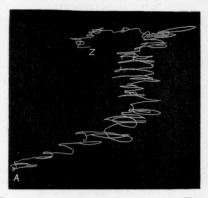

Fig. 7. — Counting pendulum oscillations.   Time of record, 80
seconds. Shows movement at first toward the pendulum, and then
synchronous with its oscillations.

to place his hand upon the automatograph, and to
think intently of the place of concealment.   As before
there is a movement of the hand ; and on the basis of

Fig. 8. — Thinking of a hidden object.   Time of record, 30
seconds.   Direction of the attention ⟫——➤.

the general direction of this movement one may venture a prediction of the direction in which the knife
lies.   The results will show all grades of success, from

complete failure to an accurate localizing of the object;
but as good a record as Fig. 8 is not infrequent. As
indicated by the letters and the arrow, the hand moved

FIG. 9. — READING FROM PRINTED PAGE. The page
was moved about the sub-   ject in the direction of the
arrows.

irregularly toward the hidden knife. In this case the
eyes are closed, and the concentration of the attention
is maintained by a mental effort without the aid of the

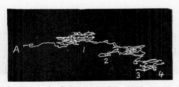

FIG. 10. — COUNTING PENDULUM OSCILLATIONS. Time of record,
120 seconds. Direction of the attention ⫸⟶. Subject facing ⫸⟶.
Illustrates slow and indirect movement. The points, 1, 2, 3, 4, indi‑
cate the position of the writing-point, 30, 60, 90, and 120 seconds after
the record was started.

senses. The peculiar line of Fig. 9 was obtained in an
experiment in which a book was slowly carried about
the room, the subject being required to read continu-

ously from the page. It is evident that the hand followed the movement of the attention, not in a circle but in an irregular outline closing in upon itself; the

Fig. 11. — Counting the strokes of a metronome. Time of record, 70 seconds. The points, 1, 2, 3, 4, indicate the positions of the writing point at 15, 30, 45, and 60 seconds after the record was begun. Direction of the attention >>>———>. Subject facing >>>———>. Illustrates slight hesitation at first and then a rapid movement toward the object of attention. Reduced to ¾ size.

change in posture which this process involved has an undoubted influence upon the result.

Before passing to a more specific interpretation of the data, it may be interesting to illustrate more fully the scope of individual variations; for the great dif-

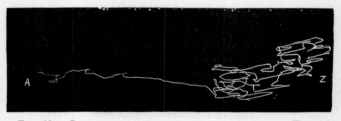

Fig. 12. — Counting the strokes of a metronome. Time of record, 90 seconds. Direction of attention >>>———>. Subject facing >>>———> Illustrates initial directness of movement followed by hesitancy.

ference in availability of subjects to the muscle-reader is equally prominent in tests with the automatograph. Some movements are direct and extensive, others are circuitous and brief. Fig. 10 is a good type of a small movement, but of one quite constantly toward the object of the attention. This may be contrasted with an extreme record, not here reproduced, in which there is a movement of six and a half inches in forty-five seconds; or with a fairly extensive movement as in Fig. 11. In some cases the first impulse carries the hand toward the object of thought, and is followed by considerable hesitation and uncertainty; a marked example of this tendency may be seen in Fig. 12. There

FIG. 13. — THINKING OF A LOCALITY. Time record 120 seconds. Direction of the attention ←——≪. Subject facing ←——≪. Illustrates initial hesitancy followed by a steady movement toward the object thought of.

is, too, an opposite type, in which the initial movements are variable, and the significant movement toward the object of thought comes later, when perhaps there is some fatigue. This tendency appears somewhat in Figs. 11 and 13.

IV

What is the origin of the movements involved in these records? To what extent are they movements of the hand, of the arm, or of the entire body? Casual observation is sufficient to show that with a given position of the arm, certain movements are much more readily made than others; and the involuntary tendencies will naturally follow the lines of least resistance. If, for instance, you hold your arm nearly on a level with the shoulders and in line with them, you perceive at once that movements of the hand to the front are much more readily made than to the rear, and movements toward the body more readily than those away from the body ; the tendency of the hand is to move forward in a circle of which the shoulder is the centre.   What we require is a position in which movements in any one direction are as readily made as in any other; and this may be approximated, though only approximated, by holding the hand at an angle of about 45° with the line joining the shoulders, and with the elbow bent at an angle of about 120°.   This was the position in most of the tests, and the usual result was a movement toward the object of attention ; but when the object attended to lies in back of the subject, this tendency is sometimes outweighed by the natural tendency for the arm to move forward, and the result may be a movement *forward*, but a less direct movement forward than when the object of attention is to the front.   In a good subject, however, the involuntary tendency is strong enough to prevail, and a movement *backward* results.   An instance of this, obtained under other but comparable circumstances, appears in Fig. 14.   It is to be noted that in this figure the tracing marked I. was obtained with the subject seated, and the metronome beating behind him ; the hand after some hesitation moves backward slowly towards the metronome to a moderate extent.   In tracing II., with the subject also seated, the metronome is to the front, and the hand moves directly and quickly towards it.

We conclude that the position of the body is an important factor in the resultant movements, but that it does not interfere with their accepted psychological interpretation.

When observing the subject during a test, we may note the movements of the body as a whole, and of the arm or hand. The movement of the body is an irregular swaying with the feet as the centre of the movement; this swaying is most readily recorded by fixing the recording-plate upon the subject's head, and hav-

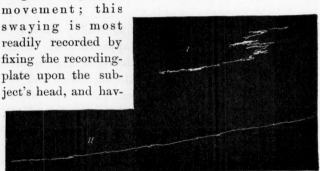

FIG. 14. — COUNTING THE STROKES OF A METRONOME. Subject seated. In tracing I. the metronome is at the rear. Time of record, 105 seconds. Direction of the attention ◄——◄◄. Subject facing ≫≫——≫. In tracing II. the metronome was to the front. Time of record 45 seconds. Direction of the attention ≫≫——≫. Subject facing ≫≫——≫. ⅘ size.

ing the recording-rod held in a suitable position above it. It was found that in connection with the swaying movements there were general movements towards the object of attention; and such movements were as readily made when the object was to the front, to the rear, or to either side. To determine how far this movement is the same in head and hand, it is necessary to record both simultaneously. Fig. 15 illustrates the correspondence of the two movements. It thus becomes clear that the swaying of the body as a whole constitutes an important factor of these automatograph records; that the movements of the head (being farther

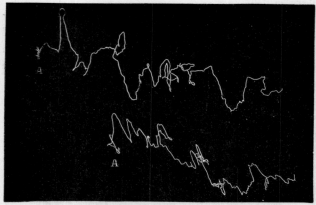

FIG. 15. — COUNTING THE STROKES OF A METRONOME. Time of record, 45 seconds. The upper tracing shows the movements of the head recorded upon a plate resting on the head. The lower tracing shows the usual record of the hand upon the automatograph. Direction of the attention ≫≫——➤. Subject facing ≫≫——➤.

away from the centre of motion) are more extensive than those of the hand; and that both head and hand are sensitive organs for the expression of involuntary movements. That the muscle-reader is aware of this fact is obvious from the usual positions which he maintains towards his subject in reading the direction of the hidden object.

To eliminate the record of the swaying of the body, we may experiment with the subject seated; we obtain a distinctive record in which certain phases of the fluctuations have almost disappeared, and in which the record approximates to a straight line (tracing II. of

Fig. 14). One may also eliminate the record of the swaying by dispensing with the automatograph, and simply holding the recording plate in one hand and the recording device or pencil in the other ; for then the plate and pencil sway together, and naturally no record of it is made. The relatively fine movements thus obtained are shown in Fig. 16 ; the contrast between this record and such records as Figs. 4, 5, 6, is mainly the contrast between a record in which the general swaying of the body is registered, and one from which it has been eliminated. It is interesting to note that in records thus taken, there is but a slight difference in the result when the subject is standing and when he is sitting; which is a further proof that the swaying of the body has been eliminated. (Compare these with

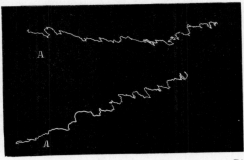

FIG. 16. — COUNTING THE STROKES OF A METRONOME. Right hand holds the pencil, and left hand holds the record plate. Direction of metronome ➤➤➤➤. Subject facing ➤➤➤➤. In the upper tracing the subject was standing; time of record, 90 seconds. In the lower tracing the subject was sitting; time of record, 90 seconds.

Fig. 14.) Traces of periodic oscillations are noticeable in Fig. 16 ; these are due to movements of respiration, and in tracing II. of Fig. 17, they are unusually

distinct and regular, about twenty to the minute. In
this case the forearm of the hand holding the record-
plate was braced against the body, while the recording

FIG. 17. — THINKING OF A
BUILDING. Right hand holds pencil, and left hand holds record plate.
Subject facing ↑ . In tracing I.,
direction of the attention ↑;
in tracing II., direction of
the attention ↓ . Time of each
record, 60 sec- onds. II.
shows respira- tion records.

FIG. 18. — COUNTING THE STROKES
OF A METRONOME. Right hand
holds pencil, left hand holds record
plate. Direction of the attention
from A to B ↑, from B to C ⟫⟶,
from C to D ↓, from D to E ⟵⟪.
Time of each portion, 45 seconds.

hand was held free from it; and thus the abdominal
movements were registered. The movements toward
the object of attention appear throughout. Fig. 17
shows a movement towards the rear of the subject, as
well as towards the front; which again shows that
under suitable conditions, involuntary movements may
be recorded in one direction as readily as in another.
Fig. 18 presents a most beautifully regular movement
in all four directions. As the metronome, the strokes
of which the subject was counting, was carried from
one corner of the room to another and so on around

the room, the hand involuntarily followed it and recorded an almost perfect square. So striking and regular and so varied an involuntary movement, in conformity with changes in the direction of attention, one can expect to secure but seldom, and then only with a good subject.

The outline presented in Fig. 19 was obtained in a test in which the movements of the hands were separately recorded, in order to determine the degree of correspondence between them. The result shows a marked general resemblance, indicating in part a com-

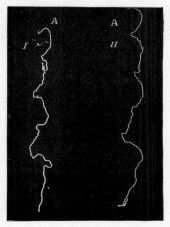

FIG. 19. — THINKING OF A BUILDING. Both hands hold record plates, the pencils being held fixed above them. Time of record 35 seconds. Direction of the attention ↓ . Subject facing ↓ . I., left hand; II., right hand.

mon origin of the two movements. The next figure, Fig. 20, shows that this correspondence is dependent in part upon the similarity of the positions of the two

hands.   The hand that is held away from the body
moves more extensively ; but the form of the movements remain similar.   The records reproduced in
Figs. 14–22 and 26 were obtained upon the same subject, though with slightly varying conditions, and are
fairly comparable with one another, and thus illustrate
the analysis of the resultant movements into their component factors.

Fig. 20. — Thinking of a building.   Each hand holds record
plate.   Time of record, 35 seconds.   Direction of the attention ↯.   Subject facing ↯.   I., left hand held extended far out.   II., right   hand
held close ↑ to body. ↓

Involuntary movements are not limited to the horizontal plane ; vertical movements may be recorded by
holding the recording device in a slanting position,
and fixing the record plate upon the wall.   The main
characteristic of such a record is the sinking of the
arm through fatigue ; the movement is rapid and

coarse (tracing I. of Fig. 20). If the attention be
directed to the front, we obtain a resultant of the ten-

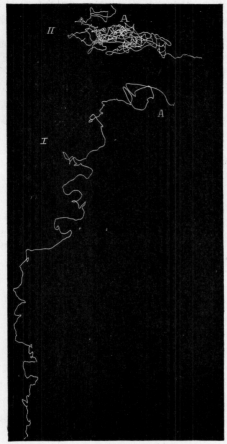

Fig. 21. — THINKING OF ONE'S FEET. Record plate vertical. Time
of record, 45 seconds. Direction of the attention ↓. II., thinking of a
point overhead. Time of record, ↑ 45 seconds. ↓ Recording plate
vertical. Direction of the attention ↟.

dency to move towards the object of attention, and of
the sinking of the arm, as appears in the diagonal line
of Fig. 22. Fig. 21 illustrates an interesting point
similar to that illustrated in Fig. 14. When the attention is directed downward, the hand
falls rapidly (tracing I.); but
when the attention is di-
rected upward, very lit-
tle movement at all
takes place,

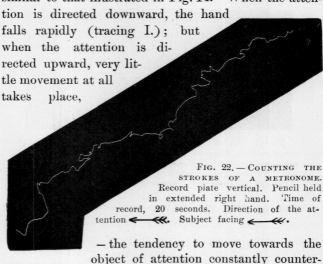

FIG. 22. — COUNTING THE
STROKES OF A METRONOME.
Record plate vertical. Pencil held
in extended right hand. Time of
record, 20 seconds. Direction of the attention ←— ←←. Subject facing ←— ←←.

— the tendency to move towards the
object of attention constantly counter-
acting the tendency for the arm to fall (tracing II.).

V

While I have not been altogether successful in determining by this method the relative efficiency of different sense-impressions in holding the attention, the
successful results are especially interesting. In Fig.
23 the tracing marked I. shows the movement of the
hand during the thirty-five seconds that the subject
was counting the strokes of a metronome; tracing
II. shows the movement while counting for twenty-
five seconds the oscillations of a pendulum. The latter

movement is in this case much more extensive than
the former, thus indicating that the visual impression
held the attention much better than the auditory. The

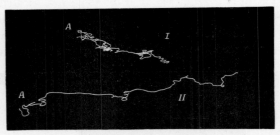

Fig. 23.—I. Counting the strokes of a metronome. Automatograph record. Time of record, 35 seconds. Direction of the attention ⋙⟶. Subject facing ⟋⟶. II. Counting pendulum oscillations. Automatograph record. Time of record, 25 seconds. Direction of the attention ⟋⟶. Subject facing ⋙⟶.

subject of this record is a well-known writer and
novelist ; and his description of his own mental processes entirely accords with this result ; he is a good

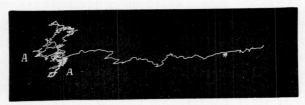

Fig. 24. — From A to A′, reading colors; from A′ on, counting
pendulum oscillations. Automatograph record. Time of record,
from A to A′, 35 seconds: from A′ on, 25 seconds. Direction of the
attention ⋙⟶. Subject facing ⋙⟶.

visualizer, and visual impressions and memory-images
dominate his mental habits.

We may next turn to Fig. 24. The subject was
asked to call the names of a series of small patches of

color hanging upon the wall in front of him. He did
this with some uncertainty for thirty-five seconds, and
during this time his hand on the automatograph moved
from A to A'. At the latter point he was asked to
count the oscillations of a pendulum; this entirely
changed the movement, the hand at once moving
rapidly toward the pendulum. The pendulum was a

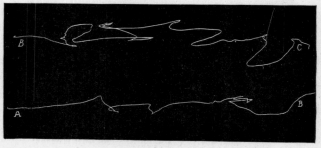

Fig. 25. — Counting pendulum oscillations. Time of record, 35
seconds. The record from B to C is continuous with that of A to B.
Direction of the attention ⫸—→. Subject facing ⫸—→. The subject, a child of eleven years. Record reduced to ⅔ of original size.

more attractive sense-impression than the colors. The
special point of interest in this record is, that upon
examination the subject's color-vision proved to be defective, and thus accounted for the failure of the colors
to hold his attention.

An important problem relates to the possible corre-
lation of types of involuntary movements with age,
sex, temperament, disease, and the like. A few observations upon children are interesting in this respect.
They reveal the limited control that children have
over their muscles, and their difficulty to fix the attention when and where desired. Their involuntary move-

ments are large, with great fluctuations, and irregularly
towards the object of attention. Fig. 25 illustrates
some of these points ; in thirty-five seconds the child's
hand moved by large steps seven inches toward the
pendulum, and the entire appearance of the outline is
different from those obtained upon adults.

Much attention has recently been paid to automatic
writing, or the unconscious indication of the *nature*,
not merely the *direction* of one's thoughts, while the
attention is elsewhere engaged. I attempted this upon
the automatograph by asking the subject to view or
think of some letter or geometric figure, and then
searching the record for some trace of the letter or
figure ; but always with a negative result. While un-
successful in this sense, the records prove of value in

FIG. 26. — THINKING OF LETTER O. Pencil held in hand; record on
table. I., subject standing; II., subject seated.

furnishing a salient contrast to the experiments in
which the attention was fixed in a definite direction.
For example, the subject is thinking of the letter O ;
he does not think of it as in any special place, and the
record (Fig. 26) likewise reveals no movement in any
one direction. Two records are shown quite similar in
significance, and illustrating as well the difference between the movements while standing and while sitting.

VI

There have thus been passed in review a variety of involuntary movements obtained in different ways, and with bearings upon many points of importance to the psychologist. They by no means exhaust the possibilities of research, or the deduction of conclusions in this field of study ; but they may serve to illustrate how subtle and intricate are the expressions of the thoughts that lie within. That involuntary movements are by no means limited to the type here illustrated is easily shown. In the exhibitions of muscle-reading, the changes in breathing, the flushing, the tremor of the subject when the reader approaches the hiding-place, and the relative relaxation when he is on the wrong scent, serve as valuable clues ; to borrow the apt expression of " hide and seek," the performer grows " hot " and " cold " with his subject. Then, too, the tentative excursions in one direction and another, to determine in which the subject follows with least resistance, present another variation of the same process. The hushed calm of the audience when success is near, the restlessness and whispering during a false scent, are equally welcome suggestions which a clever performer freely utilizes, thereby adding to the éclat of his exhibition. When a combination of numbers or of letters in a word is to be guessed, the operator passes over with the subject the several digits or the alphabet, and notes at which the tell-tale tremor or mark of excitement occurs, and so again performs the feat on the basis of the involuntary contractions that express the slight changes of attention or interest when the correct number or letter is indicated. In much the same way we unwittingly betray our feelings and emotions, our interest or distraction or ennui ; the correct interpretation of these in others and their suppression in one's self form part of the artificial complexity of social intercourse. But in the line of experimental demonstration also, another form of involuntary movement has been brought forward in recent years by the investigation of Hansen and Lehmann upon " involuntary whispering." This investigation brings out the fact that many of us, when we think intently of a number, tend to innervate the mechanism appropriate to its utterance. We do not actually speak or whisper the word or sound, but we initiate the process. If one person thinks of a number, — say from one to ten, or from one to one hundred, — and the other records any number which at the same moment suggests itself to him, it may result that the proportion of correct or partially correct guesses exceeds that which chance would produce ; and arguments for telepathy have been based on such results. In the series of experiments in question these "involuntary whisperings" were not severely suppressed, — much as in the automatograph tests one might determine to let the glass move if it would. It must be understood that there was no true whispering nor any movement of the speaking mechanism which a bystander could detect ; and yet it seems likely that the one participant was influenced in his guessing by the vague but yet real, subconscious, embryonic articulation of the other. The proof of this lies mainly in the analysis of the successes and errors ; for the confusions are strikingly between numerals of somewhat similar sound, — as between fourteen and forty, or sixty and thirty, or six and seven.

If the two persons are seated in the respective foci of two concave surfaces which collect the sound (thus in a measure paralleling the exalted sensibility of specially gifted or hypnotized subjects), the chances of success seem to be increased. While the investigation is both complex and incomplete, yet the general trend of it is sufficiently clear to make it probable that "involuntary whispering" serves more or less frequently as a sub-conscious and involuntary indication of thought. It shows again that below the threshold of conscious acquisition and intentional expression lie a consider-able range of activities, which though they blossom unseen do not quite waste their fragrance, but come wafted over in vague and subtle essence. The falling of a drop of water is unheard, but the sound of the roaring torrent is but the sound of myriads of drops. The boundary between the conscious and the uncon-scious is broad and indefinite; and vague influences, if not direct messages, pass from one side to the other.

The general bearing of the study of involuntary movements I have indicated at the outset; and no elaborate comment on the practical significance of the results described seems necessary. They certainly facilitate the appreciation of the reality of the subcon-scious and the involuntary; and in connection with explanations of muscle-reading or telepathy, they illus-trate how naturally a neglect of this realm of psycho-logical activity may lead to false conclusions. They bring a striking corroboration of the view that thought is but more or less successfully suppressed action, and as a well-known muscle-reader expresses it, all willing is either pushing or pulling.

THE DREAMS OF THE BLIND

I

MAN is predominantly a visual animal. To him seeing is believing, — a saying which in canine parlance might readily become smelling is believing. We teach by illustrations, models, and object-lessons, and reduce complex relations to the curves of the graphic method, to bring home and impress our statements. Our every-day language, as well as the imagery of poetry, abounds in metaphors and similes appealing to images which the eye has taught us to appreciate. The eye is also the medium of impressions of æsthetic as well as of intellectual value; and one grand division of art is lost to those who cannot see. The eye, too, forms the centre of emotional expression, and reveals to our fellow-men the subtile variations in mood and passion, as it is to the physician a delicate index of our well-being. There are reasons for believing that it was the function of sight as a distance-sense that led to its supremacy in the lives of our primitive ancestors. Whatever its origin, the growth of civilization has served to develop this eye-mindedness of the race, and to increase and diversify the modes of its cultivation.

The eye, thus constantly stimulated in waking life, and attracting to its sensations the focus of attention, possessing, as it does, in the retinal fovea a special and unique aid to concentrative attention, does not yield up its supremacy in the world of dreams. The visual centres subside but slowly from their day's stimulation; and the rich stock of images which these centres have stored up is completely at the service of the fancy that guides our dreams. Indeed, the dream itself is spoken of as a vision.

Though, as a race, we are eye-minded, individually we differ much with regard to the rôle that sight plays in our psychic life. In one direction a good index of its importance is to be found in the perfection of the visualizing faculty, of which Mr. Galton has given an interesting account. He asked various persons to describe, amongst other things, the vividness of their mental picture when calling to mind the morning's breakfast-table. To some the mental scene was as clear and as natural as reality, lacking none of the details of form or color; to others the resulting mental image was tolerably distinct, with the conspicuous features well brought out, but the rest dim and ill-defined; while a third group could only piece together a very vague, fragmentary, and unreliable series of images, with no distinct or constant picture.

Similar differences are observable with regard to memories. Some persons firmly retain what they read, while the memory forte of others is in what they hear; and pathology supports this subdivision of the sense-memories by showing, for example, that all remembrance for seen objects may be lost while that for sounds remains intact. A case, remarkable in several aspects, is recorded by M. Charcot. The subject in question could accurately call up, in full detail, all the scenes of his many travels, could repeat pages of his favorite authors from the mental picture of the printed page, and by the same means could mentally add long columns of numbers. The mere mention of a scene in a play, or of a conversation with a friend, immediately brought up a vivid picture of the entire circumstance. Through nervous prostration he lost this visual memory. An attempt to sketch a familiar scene now resulted in a childish scrawl; he remembered little of his correspondence, forgot the appearance of his wife and friends, and even failed to recognize his own image in a mirror. Yet his eyesight was intact and his intellect unimpaired. In order to remember things he had now to have them read aloud to him, and thus bring into play his undisturbed auditory centre — to him an almost new experience.

The function of vision in dreams is doubtless subject to similar individual variations, though probably to a less extent. Seeing, with rare exceptions, constitutes the typical operation in dreams; it is this sense, too, that, under the influence of drugs or of other excitement, is most readily stimulated into morbid action, and most easily furnishes the basis of delusions and hallucinations to a disordered mind. The dependence of the nature and content of dreams upon the waking experiences is so clearly proven that it would be surprising not to find in them the individual characteristics of our mental processes; and if Aristotle is right in saying that in waking life we all have a world in common but in dreams each has a world of his own, we may look to the evidence of dream-life for indications of unrestrained and distinctive psychological traits.

II

With regard to the blind, much of what has been said above is entirely irrelevant. However intimately we appreciate the function of sight in our own mental development, it is almost impossible to imagine how different our life would have been had we never seen. But here, at the outset, a fundamental distinction must be drawn between those blind from birth or early infancy, and those who lose their sight in youth or adult life.[1] " It is better to have seen and lost one's sight than never to have seen at all," is quite as true as the sentiment which this form of statement parodies. Expressed physiologically, this means, that to have begun the general brain-building process with the aid of the eye insures some further self-development of the visual centre, and thus makes possible a kind of mental possession of which those born blind are inevitably deprived.[2]

[1] A noted blind teacher of the blind says. " Wenn wir . . . den Einfluss der Blindheit auf die geistige Thätigkeit des Blinden beobachten, so haben wir Blindgeborene und Blindgewordene . . . streng auseinander zu halten."

[2] This applies mainly to intellectual acquirements. The emotional life of those who have lost their sight is often, and with much truth, regarded as sadder and more dreary than that of the congenitally blind ; the former regretfully appreciate what they have lost ; the latter live in a different and more meagre world, but have never known any other. It is interesting in this connection to trace the influence of the age of "blinding" (sit venia verbo) on the mental development of eminent blind men and women. Of a list of 125 blind persons of very various degrees of talent, which I have been able to collect, the age of blinding was (approximately) ascertainable in 114 cases. Of these about 11 are really very distinguished, and 10 of them (the exception is the wonderful mathematician, Nicholas Saunderson) became blind either in ad-

A fact of prime importance regarding the development of the sight-centre is the age at which its education is sufficiently completed to enable it to continue its function without further object-lessons on the part of the retina. If we accept as the test of the independent existence of the sight-centre its automatic excitation in dreams, the question can be answered by determining the age of the onset of blindness, which divides those who do not from those who still retain in their dream-life the images derived from the world of sight. The data that enable me to answer this question were gathered at the Institutions for the Blind in Philadelphia and Baltimore. Nearly 200 persons of both sexes were personally examined, and their answers to quite a long series of questions recorded. All dates and ages were verified by the register of the institution, and the degree of sight was tested.

Beginning with cases of *total* blindness (including under this head those upon whom light has simply a general subjective " heat-effect," enabling them to distinguish between night and day, between shade and sunshine, but inducing little or no tendency to project the cause of the sensation into the external world), I find on my list fifty-eight such cases. Of these, thirty-two

vanced youth, middle life, or still later ; of the group next in eminence (about 25) the average age of the onset of blindness is in early youth (at nine or ten years) ; and those earliest blind are generally musicians, who least of all require sight for their calling. The average age of blinding of the rest of the list — whose achievements would for the most part not have been recorded had they not been those of blind persons — is as low as seven years, while that of the musicians (about 15 in the group) is little over three years. All this speaks strongly for the permanent intellectual importance of sight in early education.

became blind before the completion of their fifth year, and *not one* of this group of thirty-two sees in dreams. Six became blind between the fifth and the seventh year : of these, four have dreams of seeing, but two of them do so seldom and with some vagueness ; while two never dream of seeing at all. Of twenty persons who became blind after their seventh year *all* have " dream-vision " — as I shall term the faculty of seeing in dreams. *The period from the fifth to the seventh year is thus indicated as the critical one.* Before this age the visual centre is undergoing its elementary education ; its life is closely dependent upon the constant food-supply of sensations ; and when these are cut off by blindness, it degenerates and decays. If blindness occurs between the fifth and the seventh years, the preservation of the visualizing power depends on the degree of development of the individual. If the faculty is retained, it is neither stable nor pronounced. If sight is lost after the seventh year, the sight-centre can, in spite of the loss, maintain its function ; and the dreams of such an individual may be hardly distinguishable from those of a seeing person.

It was a very unexpected discovery, to find, after I had planned and partly completed this investigation, that I had a predecessor. So long ago as 1838, Dr. G. Heermann studied the dreams of the blind with the view of determining this same question, the physiological significance of which, however, was not then clearly understood. He records the answers of fourteen totally blind persons who lost their sight previous to their fifth year, and *none* of these has dream-vision. Of four who lost their sight between the fifth and the seventh year, one has dream-vision; one has it dimly and occasionally; and two do not definitely know. Of thirty-five who became blind after their seventh year *all* have dream-vision. The two independent researches thus yield the very same conclusion. Dr. Heermann includes in his list many aged persons, and from their answers is able to conclude that, generally speaking, those who become blind in mature life retain the power of dream-vision longer than those who become blind nearer the critical age of five to seven years. He records twelve cases where dream-vision still continues after a blindness of from ten to fifteen years, four of from fifteen to twenty years, four of from twenty to twenty-five years, and one of thirty-five years. In one case dream-vision was maintained for fifty-two, and in another for fifty-four years, but then faded out.[1]

With regard to the *partially* blind, the question most analogous to the persistence of dream-vision after total blindness, is whether or not the dream-vision is brighter and clearer than that of waking life; whether the sight-centre maintains the full normal power to which it was educated, or whether the partial loss of sight has essentially altered and replaced it. To this rather difficult question I have fewer and less satisfac-

[1] Dr. Heermann's observations also enable us to trace the anatomical conditions underlying the power of dream-vision. From ten cases in which post-mortem examinations were held, he concludes that, allowing for much individual difference, after about twenty years the optic nerves degenerate, and often as far back as the chiasma. This shows that the nerve is not necessary for dream-vision, and thus goes to prove that the process is dependent on cerebral organs — a valuable piece of evidence fifty years ago. Esquirol records a case of sight-hallucinations in a blind woman, again indicating the same conclusion.

tory answers than to the former inquiry; but the evidence is perfectly in accord with the previous conclusions. Of twenty-three who describe their dream-vision as *only as clear* as waking sight, *all* became blind *not later* than the close of their *fifth year*; while of twenty-four whose dream-vision is more or less markedly *clearer* than their partial sight, *all* lost their full sight *not earlier* than their *sixth year*.[1] The age that marks off those to whom total blindness carries with it the loss of dream-vision from those whose dream-vision continues, is thus the age at which the sight-centre has reached a sufficient stage of development to enable it to maintain its full function, when partially or totally deprived of retinal stimulation. The same age is also assigned by some authorities as the limiting age at which deafness will cause muteness (unless special pains be taken to prevent it); while later the vocal organs, though trained to action by the ear, can perform their duties without the teacher's aid. This, too,

---

[1] A further interesting question regarding the dream-vision of the partially blind is, How much must they be able to see in order to dream of seeing? In answering this question, the blind give the name "seeing" to what is really a complex of sensations and judgments, and this same complex may enter into their dreams. Cases occur in which there is only the slightest remnant of sight, and yet this forms a factor in dream-life. It is a very imperfect kind of vision, and acts more as a general sense of illumination, and as an anticipatory sense. Generally speaking, those who know color have more frequent and brighter dream-vision than those who distinguish light and shade only. For example, of those partially blind from birth, such as see color tolerably well (there are sixteen such) have regular dream-vision — of course, no clearer than their best days of sight. Of eleven who have some faint notion of color, three have dream-vision regularly; six have it rarely, while two (almost never or) never have it. Of eleven who can see no color at all, ten have no dream-vision, and one has it occasionally.

is assigned as the earliest age at which we have a remembrance of ourselves. This last statement I am
able to test by one hundred answers, collected among
these blind persons, to the question, "What is your
earliest remembrance of yourself?" The average age
to which these memories go back is 5.2 years; seventy-
nine instances being included between the third and
the sixth years. At this period of child development
— the centre of which is at about the close of the fifth
year — there seems to be a general declaration of independence of the sense-centres from their food-supply
of sensations. Mr. Sully finds sense, imagination, and
abstraction to be the order in which the precocity of
great men reveals itself; and the critical period which
we are now considering seems to mark the point at
which imagination and abstraction as permanent mental powers ordinarily come into play. M. Perez likewise recognizes the distinctive character of this era of
childhood by making the second part of his "Child
Psychology" embrace the period from the third to the
seventh year.

III

The general fact thus brought to light — that the
mode in which a brain-centre will function depends so
largely upon its initial education, but that, this education once completed, the centre can maintain its function, though deprived of sense-stimulation — is sufficiently important to merit further illustration.[1] This

[1] That even a comparatively slight disturbance of vision, affecting
only a small portion of the visual experience, can leave a permanent
trace upon the sight-centre is made very probable by a case (recorded
by Dr. McCosh, *Cognitive Powers*, p. 106) of a young man whose defect

fact, though very clear and evident when stated from a modern point of view, has not always been recognized. So ingenious a thinker as Erasmus Darwin inferred from two cases (the one of a blind man, the other of a deaf-mute) in which the wanting senses were also absent in dreams, that the peripheral sense-organ was necessary for all perception, subjective as well as objective ; and entirely neglected the age at which the sense was lost. Such noted physiologists as Reil, Rudolphi, Hartman, Wardrop (who says, " when an organ of sense is totally destroyed, the ideas which were received by that organ seem to perish along with it as well as the power of perception "), more or less distinctly favored this view; while some teachers of the blind and the physiologists Nasse and Autentreith rightly drew the distinction between those born, and those who became, blind. An experimental demonstration of the original dependence of the perceptive and emotional powers upon sense-impressions was furnished by Boffi and Schiff, who found that young dogs whose olfactory bulbs had been removed failed to develop any affection for man.

What is true of the visual, is doubtless equally true of the other perceptive centres. The dreams of the

consisted in his seeing everything double, — a defect which a subsequent operation removed. " If I attempt," he writes, " to recall scenes that I saw while my eyes were out of order, I invariably see them as they appeared during that time, although I may have seen them many times since the operation. For instance, in the case of the minister in the pulpit at home, I see two images of him, no matter how much I may try to get rid of one of them. . . . My recollection of the office in which the operation was performed, as also of everything in it, is double, although I saw it only twice before the restoration of my sight, and many times after. The objects which I have seen since the operation are always single when recalled."

deaf-mute offer an attractive and untouched field for such study.[1] The few accounts of such dreams that I have met with, fail to give the age at which deafness set in; in one case, however, in which deafness occurred at thirty years, the pantomimic had replaced the spoken language in the dreams of thirty years later. Similarly, cripples dream of their lost limbs for many years after their loss; in such cases, however, stimulation of the cut nerves may be the suggestive cause of such dreams. A man of forty, who lost his right arm seventeen years before, still dreams of having the arm. The earliest age of losing and dreaming about a lost limb, of which I find a record, is of a boy of thirteen years who lost a leg at the age of ten; this boy still dreams of walking on his feet. Those who are born cripples must necessarily have their defects represented in their dream consciousness. Heermann cites the case of a man born without hands, forearms, feet, or lower legs. He always dreamt of walking on his knees; and all the peculiarities of his movements were present in his dream-life.

The dreams of those both blind and deaf are especially instructive. Many of Laura Bridgman's dreams have been recorded; and an unpublished manuscript by Dr. G. Stanley Hall places at my service a valuable account of her sleep and dreams. Sight and hearing were as absent from her dreams as they were from the dark and silent world which alone she knew. The tactual-motor sensations, by which she communicated with her fellow-beings, and through which almost all

[1] I have gathered considerable data in regard to the dreams of the deaf, but they are not ready for definite formulation.

her intellectual food reached her, also formed her mainstay in dreams. This accounts for the suddenness and fright with which she often waked from her dreams; she is perchance dreaming of an animal, which to us would first make itself seen or heard, but to her is present only when it touches and startles her — for she lacks any anticipatory sense. Language has become so all-important a factor in civilized life, that it naturally is frequently represented in dreams. We not only dream of speaking and being spoken to, but we actually innervate the appropriate muscles and talk in our sleep; this Laura Bridgman also did. "Her sleep seemed almost never undisturbed by dreams. Again and again she would suddenly talk a few words or letters with her fingers, too rapidly and too imperfectly to be intelligible (just as other people utter incoherent words and inarticulate sounds in sleep), but apparently never making a sentence."[1]   So, too,

[1] From Dr. Hall's manuscript. Dr. Hall had the opportunity of observing her during three short naps, and has incorporated a part of his manuscript into a paper on Laura Bridgman, republished in his *Aspects of German Culture*, pp. 268–270. From this manuscript I take the following illustrations of her dreams, and her method of describing them. They are recorded verbatim.

"*Question.* 'Do you dream often?' *Answer.* 'Very often, many things.' *Q.* 'Did you think hard yesterday to remember dreams for me?' *A.* 'I did try, but I always forget very soon.' *Q.* 'Did you ever dream to hear?' [Her idiom for 'that you could hear.'] *A.* 'Only the angels playing in heaven.' *Q.* 'How did it sound?' *A.* 'Very beautiful.' *Q.* 'Like what?' *A.* 'Nothing.' *Q.* 'Was it loud?' *A.* 'Yes, very.' *Q.* 'What instrument?' *A.* 'Piano.' *Q.* 'How did the angels look?' *A.* 'Beautiful.' *Q.* 'Had they wings?' *A.* 'I could not know.' *Q.* 'Were they men or women?' *A.* 'Don't know.' *Q.* 'Can you describe their dress?' *A.* 'No.' *Q.* 'Was the music fast or slow?' *A.* 'I cannot tell.' On another occasion she was

all the people who enter into her dreams talk with
their fingers.   This habit had already presented itself
at the age of twelve, four years after her first lesson
in the alphabet.   " I do not dream to talk with mouth ;
I dream to talk with fingers."   No prettier illustra-

asked, 'Did you ever dream to see ? '   *A.*   'I could see the sun.'   *Q.*
'How did it look ? '   *A.*   'Glorious.'   *Q.*   'What color ? '   *A.*   'I cannot tell ' [with a sign of great impatience].   *Q.*   'Was it very bright ? '
A.   'Yes.'   *Q.*   'Did it hurt your eyes ? '   *A.*   'Yes, they ached.'   *Q.*
'What was it like ? '   *A.*   'Nothing.   I saw it with my eyes' [much
excited, breathing hard and fast, and pointing to her right eye].   Some
days later, after some promptings from her attendants, she renewed
the subject of her own accord, as follows : 'I remember once a dream.
I was in a very large place.   It was very glorious and full of people.
My father and mother were standing by.   The glorious piano was
playing.   When I heard the music I raised up my hand so ' [standing
and pointing impressively upward and forward with the index finger,
as the letter g is made in the deaf and dumb alphabet] ' to my heavenly
Father.   I tried to say God.'   *Q.*   'With your fingers ? '   *A.*   'Yes.'
Q.   'Where was God ? '   *A.*   'So' [pointing as before].   *Q.*   'Far
away ? '   *A.*   'No.'   *Q.*   'Could you touch him ? '   *A.*   'No.'   *Q.*   'How
did you know he was there ? '   *A.*   'I cannot tell.'   *Q.*   'How did you
know it was God ? '   *A.*   'I cannot explain.'   *Q.*   'What was he like ? '   *A.*
[After a pause] 'I cannot tell everything to everybody ' [half playfully,
whipping her right hand with her left, and touching her forehead sig-
nificantly, to indicate that she was unable adequately to express what
was in her mind].   *Q.*   'Could he touch you ? '   *A.*   'No.   He is a
spirit.'   *Q.*   'Did he see you ? '   *A.*   'He sees everything.   See how
melancholy I look because I do not feel interested.'   On another occasion she said, 'I often dream that Doctor Howe is alive and very sick,'
but no details could be elicited.   Again, after imitating the gait of
different people, she said, 'I dream often of people walking.   I dream
many things, but do not remember what I really dream.   I used to
dream of animals running around the room, and it woke me.' "

It is evident that her dreams of hearing and seeing were either
merely verbal, or the substitution and elaboration of kindred sensations (sense of jar and heat) which she experienced.   For further examples of her dreams see her *Life and Education*, by Mrs. Lamson,
pp. 88, 154, 166–168, 218, 223, 224, 226, 286, 290, 303, 304.

tion could be given of the way in which her fancy built upon her real experiences, than the fact recorded by Charles Dickens, that on picking up her doll he found across its eyes a green band such as she herself wore. The organic sensations originating in the viscera, though often prominently represented in dreams of normal persons, seemed especially prominent in her dreams. She tells of feeling her blood rush about, and of her heart beating fast when suddenly waking, much frightened, from a distressing dream. One such dream she describes as " hard, heavy, and thick ; " terms which, though to us glaringly inappropriate in reference to so fairy-like a structure as a dream, form an accurate description in the language of her own realistic senses. In short, her dreams are accurately modeled upon the experiences of her waking life, reproducing in detail all the peculiarities of thought and action which a very special education had impressed upon her curious mind.

I have had the opportunity of questioning a blind and deaf young man whose life-history offers a striking contrast to that of Laura Bridgman, and illustrates with all the force of an experimental demonstration the critical educational importance of the early years of life. He was, at the time of my questioning him, twenty-three years of age, and was earning a comfortable living as a broom-maker. He had an active interest in the affairs of the world, and disliked to be considered in any way peculiar. His eyesight began to fail him in early childhood ; and in his fifth year the sight of one eye was entirely lost, while that of the other was very poor. After a less gradual loss of hearing, he became completely deaf in his ninth year. At the age of twelve he was (practically) totally blind, deaf, and nearly mute. The small remnant of articulating power has been cultivated; and those who are accustomed to it can understand his spoken language. He also communicates as Laura Bridgman did, and has a further advantage over her in possessing a very acute sense of smell. He remembers the world of sight and hearing perfectly, and in a little sketch of his life which he wrote for me vividly describes the sights and sounds of his play-days. He usually dreams of seeing and hearing, though the experiences of his present existence also enter into his dreams. Some of his dreams relate to flowers which he smelled and saw; he dreamt of being upset in a boat; shortly after his confirmation he dreamt of seeing God. When he dreams of making brooms, his dream is entirely in terms of motion and feeling, not of sight. His history thus strongly emphasizes the importance which a variety of evidence attributes to the period of childhood, and perhaps especially to that from the third to the seventh year.

The remarkable powers which Helen Keller has exhibited throughout her phenomenal education give to an account of her dream life an especial interest. I am fortunate in being able to present her own account as she prepared it at my solicitation. The wealth and brilliancy of her imagination frequently lead to modes of expression which seem to brusquely contradict her sightless and soundless condition. But a careful observation of her mental activities brings out the verbal or literary character of such allusions, in certain cases essentially aided by associations with impressions of the senses that remain to her. In such cases her familiarity, through literature and through intercourse, with the experiences of the hearing and seeing and with the emotional and intellectual associations that ordinary persons might have with definite scenes or occasions, enables her to realize, and her vivid imagination to construct, a somewhat idealized account of her vicarious experiences, though perhaps real emotions. Her dream life seems in complete concordance with her waking condition ; but this imaginative factor must be constantly borne in mind in reading her report of her dream life. The intrinsic interest of this human document, and the charm of the narrative, present so lifelike and almost confidential a portrayal of her world of dreams, that any elaborate comment would be unnecessary. It should be remembered that Helen Keller became totally blind and deaf at nineteen months ; that her instruction began at the age of seven years ; that she learned to speak orally from her eleventh year ; that at present she speaks orally almost exclusively, although very proficient in the use of the finger alphabet ; that she is able to understand what is said to her by placing her fingers upon the lips and throat of the speaker, but that the more expeditious and certain mode of communicating with her is by making the letters of the finger-alphabet in the palm of her hand. This latter method she uses entirely with her teacher and with all who are conversant with it. This account of her dreams was prepared in August, 1900, when she was twenty years of age ; it was written off-hand by her on a type-writer, and is presented in its original form.

My Dreams

"It is no exaggeration to say that I live two distinct lives, — one in the everyday world and the other in the Land of Nod! Like most people I generally forget my dreams as soon as I wake up in the morning; but I know that when I dream I am just as active and as much interested in everything — trees, books and events — as when I am awake.

"My dreams have strangely changed during the past twelve years. Before and after my teacher first came to me, they were devoid of sound, or thought or emotion of any kind, except fear, and only came in the form of sensations. I would often dream that I ran into a still, dark room, and that, while I stood there, I felt something fall heavily without any noise, causing the floor to shake up and down violently; and each time I woke up with a jump. As I learned more and more about the objects around me, this strange dream ceased to haunt me; but I was in a high state of excitement and received impressions very easily. It is not strange then that I dreamed at that time of a wolf, which seemed to rush towards me and put his cruel teeth deep into my body! I could not speak (the fact was, I could only spell with my fingers), and I tried to scream; but no sound escaped from my lips. It is very likely that I had heard the story of Red Riding Hood, and was deeply impressed by it. This dream, however, passed away in time, and I began to dream of objects outside of myself.

"I never spelled with my fingers in my sleep; but I have often spoken, and one night I actually laughed.

I was dreaming of a great frolic with my schoolmates at the Perkins Institution. But, if I do not use the manual alphabet in my dreams, my friends sometimes spell to me. Their sentences are always brief and vague. I obtain information in a very curious manner, which it is difficult to describe. My mind acts as a sort of mirror, in which faces and landscapes are reflected, and thoughts, which throng unbidden in my brain, describe the conversation and the events going on around me.

" I remember a beautiful and striking illustration of the peculiar mode of communication I have just mentioned. One night I dreamed that I was in a lovely mansion, all built of leaves and flowers. My thoughts declared the floor was of green twigs, and the ceiling of pink and white roses. The walls were of roses, pinks, hyacinths, and many other flowers, loosely arranged so as to make the whole structure wavy and graceful. Here and there I saw an opening between the leaves, which admitted the purest air. I learned that the flowers were imperishable, and with such a wonderful discovery thrilling my spirit I awoke.

" I do not think I have seen or heard more than once in my sleep. Then the sunlight flashed suddenly on my eyes, and I was so dazzled I could not think or distinguish anything. When I looked up, some one spelled hastily to me, ' Why, you are looking back upon your babyhood ! ' As to the sound I heard, it was like the rushing of a mighty cataract, and reminded me forcibly of my visit to Niagara Falls. I remembered as if it were yesterday how I had come very close to the water and felt the great roar by placing my hand on a soft pillow. Now, however, I knew I was far away from the place whence the sound came, and the vibration fell clear, though not loud, upon my ear-drums; so I concluded in my sleep that I really heard. What happened next I have entirely forgotten; but in the morning I was deeply impressed by the only instance in which I had dreamed of hearing, and I wished I could go back to Dreamland, just to hear that far-off, inspiring sound.

"Occasionally I think I am reading with my fingers, either Braille or line print, and even translating a little Latin, but always with an odd feeling that I am touch-ing forbidden fruit. Somehow I feel that the spirits of sleep are displeased if any thoughts of literature cross my mind. Still I am free to enjoy everything else — I can wander among flowers and trees and be with my friends, especially those who live at a distance from where I happen to be. Sometimes I am with my mother, and at other times with my sister Mildred. My teacher scarcely ever appears in my dreams; but I know she would very often if a cruel fate should tear her away from me. I shall never forget the morning seven or eight years ago, when I dreamed that my dear friend, Bishop Brooks, was dying. A few hours later I found that my dream was a terrible reality. It is probable that I thought of him at the very moment when he was passing away, and I certainly wept in the same manner and in the same place while I dreamed, that I did afterwards!

"I hardly ever dream of anything that has happened the day before, although I sometimes have several dif-ferent dreams on the same night; nor do I dream of

the same things often.   However, I dream oftenest of
the unpleasant and horrible, no matter how happy and
successful the day may have been.   Indeed, I have
found it unadvisable to read terrible stories or tragedies
often, or in the evening.   They impress me so painfully, and retain so firm a hold of my imagination that
they sooner or later force themselves into my dreams.
About two years ago I read in ' Sixty Years a Queen '
the story of the awful massacre at Cawnpore, which
took place during the Indian Mutiny.   It filled me
with a horror that haunted me persistently for several
days.   At last I managed to banish these disagreeable
feelings ; but one night a frightful distortion of the
selfsame story appeared before my mind.   I thought I
was in a small prison.   At first I only noticed a skeleton hanging up on one of the walls ; then I felt a
strange, awful sound, like heavy iron being cast down,
and the most heartrending cries ensued.   I was informed that twenty men were being put to death with
the utmost cruelty.   I rushed madly from one room to
another, and, as each ruffian came out, I locked the
door behind him, in the hope that some of the victims
might thereby be saved.   All my efforts were futile,
and I awoke with a sickening horror weighing down
on my heart.   I have also fancied that I saw cities on
fire, and brave, innocent men dragged to a fiery mar-
tyrdom.   One instant I would stand in speechless
bewilderment, as the flames leaped up, dark and glar-
ing, into a black sky.   The next moment I would be
in the midst of the conflagration, trying to save some
of the sufferers, and seeing in dismay how they slipped
away beyond my power.   At such times I have thought

myself the most wretched person in the world; but in the morning the bright sunshine and fresh air of our own dear, beautiful world would chase away those horrible phantoms.

" On the whole, my dreams are consistent with my feelings and sympathies; but once I thought I was engaged in a great boat-race between Yale and Harvard. Now, in reality I am always on Harvard's side in the great games; but at that time I dreamed that I was a thorough Yale man! Perhaps this inconsistency arose from the fact that a long time ago I had declared how glad I was of Harvard's failure to win a certain boat-race, because the Yale men rowed with the American stroke and the Harvard men had learned the English stroke. At any rate, sleeping or waking, I love my friends, and never think they change or grow unkind. From time to time I make friends in my dreams; but usually I am too busy running around and watching other people to have any long conversations or ' reveries.'

" I am often led into pretty fantasies, of which I will give an illustration. Consternation was spread everywhere because the news had been received of King Winter's determination to establish his rule permanently in the temperate zones. The stern monarch fulfilled his threat all too soon; for, although it was midsummer, yet the whole ocean was suddenly frozen, and all the boats and steamers were stuck fast in the ice. Commerce was ruined, and starvation was unavoidable. The flowers and trees shared in the universal sorrow, and bravely strove to keep alive through the summer. Finally, overcome by the intense cold, they dropped their leaves and blossoms, which they had kept fresh and spotless to the last. Slowly the flowers fluttered down and lay at King Winter's feet, silently supplicating him to show mercy, but all in vain. They froze unheeded, and were changed into pearls, diamonds, and turquoises.

"Another time I took it into my head to climb to the stars. I sprang up into the air, and was borne upward by a strong impulse. I could not see or hear; but my mind was my guide as well as my interpreter. Higher and higher I rose, until I was very close to the stars. Their intense light prevented me from coming any nearer; so I hung on invisible wings, fascinated by the rolling spheres and the constant play of light and shadow, which my thoughts reflected. All at once I lost my balance, I knew not how, and down, down I rushed through empty space, till I struck violently against a tree, and my body sank to the ground. The shock waked me up, and for a moment I thought all my bones were broken to atoms.

"I have said all that I can remember concerning my dreams; but what really surprises me is this; sometimes, in the midst of a nightmare, I am conscious of a desire to wake up, and I make a vigorous effort to break the spell. Something seems to hold my senses tightly, and it is only with a spasmodic movement that I can open my eyes. Even then I feel, or I think I feel, a rapid motion shaking my bed and a sound of light, swift footsteps. It seems strange to me that I should make such an effort to wake up, instead of doing it automatically."

This faithful and dramatic sketch is replete with

specific as well as with generic corroborations of the
distinctive results of the present inquiry.   The differences between the dream experiences of Helen Keller
before and after education are quite consistent with
comparable results in the cases of other defectives —
although dreams of her uneducated period seem to
occur rarely if at all, and it is not possible to determine how soon after she began to speak, such speech-
communication made its appearance in her dreams.   It
is interesting to note that oral speech, when once acquired, speedily superseded manual talking, and that
automatic talking aloud in her sleep appeared; the
finger alphabet became almost obsolete in her waking
life, and likewise in her dreams.   Yet the persistence
of early acquired habits is strikingly shown in her occasional unconscious tendency to talk to herself by forming the letters with one hand against the palm of the
other.   These processes she seems to utilize quite automatically and unconsciously as aids to composition or
to " thinking aloud."

In regard to the source and content of her dreams,
the more realistic episodes reflect their perceptional
origin in tactile and motor experiences; such are the
attack of the wolf, the fall from a height, the reception
of information through the palm, reading the raised
print, — while dreams of flying naturally present the
same elaboration of sensory elements as in normally
equipped individuals.   The dreams of seeing and hearing probably reflect far more of conceptual interpretation and imaginative inference than of true sensation;
yet they are in part built up upon a sensory basis, —
in the former case, that of the heat sensations radiat-

ing from a brilliant illumination (witness the flames of the conflagration, the "intense light" of the stars), in the latter of vibrational or jarring sensations communicated to the body (as in the torrent of Niagara). But, on the whole, the direct sensory tone of her dream life is weak; while for this very reason, possibly, the imaginative and "transferred" components are unusually dominant. The associative elaboration of fancies in dream life is rarely capable of simple analysis, and commonly reveals results, and not the processes or stages by which the results were reached. Dependent, as Helen Keller is so largely, upon the communication of others for her knowledge of what is going on about her, it is natural that this transferred communication should be important in her dream knowledge. That her consciousness of the process of such acquisition should be vague and difficult to express is natural; and the phrases "my thoughts declared," "my mind acts as a sort of mirror," "I was informed," are as satisfactory psychologically as could be expected. It is, however, in dreams not of external incidents involving vaguely transferred or directly communicated information, but in the free roamings of creative imagination, that the dream life of Helen Keller finds its most suitable *métier*; it is in this direction that this dream narrative, reflecting, as it does, her rich emotional nature and enthusiastically sympathetic temperament, presents its most distinctive and attractive aspect.

IV

Returning to the general data regarding the dreams of the blind, the question that next suggests itself is whether and how, in cases where blindness ensued after a remembered period of vision, the pre-blindness period is distinguished from the post-blindness period in dream-imagery. It was noticed, for instance, that the blind and deaf young man mentioned above, though seeing in his dreams, never thus saw the shop in which he worked. It is easy to imagine that the more or less sudden loss of sight, the immersion into a strange and dark world, would for a time leave the individual living entirely upon the past. His remembered experiences are richer and more vivid (we are supposing his blindness to occur after childhood) than those he now has ; he is learning a new language and translates everything back into the old. His dreams will naturally continue to be those of his seeing life. As his experiences in his new surroundings increase, and the memory of the old begins to fade, the tendency of recent impressions to arise in the automatism of dreaming will bring the events of the post-blindness period as factors into his dreams. I find in my list only seven who do not have such dreams ; and in these the blindness has been on the average of only 2.8 years standing. The average age of "blinding" of the seven is fifteen years, making it probable that the adaptation to the new environment has here been a slow one, and that such dreams will occur later on. On the other hand, cases occur in which, after three, two, or even one year's blindness, when the persons so afflicted were young, events happening within that period have been dreamed of. Heermann cites a case of a man of seventy who never dreamed of the hospital in which he had been living for eighteen years, and to which he was brought shortly after his blindness. This and other cases suggest that the more mature and settled the brain-tissue, the more difficult is it to impress upon it new conditions sufficiently deeply to have them appear in the automatic life of dreams.

Whether there is a difference in the vividness, or any other characteristic which sight would lend, in the dreams of events before and after blindness, is a question to which I could obtain few intelligent and satisfactory answers; but, as far as they go, the tendency of these replies is to show that when blindness ensues close upon the critical period of five to seven years of age, the power of vivid dream-vision is more exclusively limited to the events of the years of full sight; and, as Heermann pointed out, this power is often subject to a comparatively early decay. Similarly, I find that those who lose their sight near the critical age are not nearly so apt to retain color in their dream-vision as those who become blind later on. The average age of "blinding" of twenty-four persons who have colored dream-vision, is 16.6 years, including one case in which blindness set in as early as the seventh year. All who see enough to see color, have colored dream-vision.

I also asked those who became blind in youth, or later, whether they were in the habit of giving imaginary faces to the persons they met after their blindness, and whether they ever saw such in their dreams. Some answered in very vague terms, but several undoubtedly make good use of this power, probably somewhat on the same basis as we imagine the appearance of eminent men of whom we have read or heard, but whose features we have never seen. When we remember

how erroneous such impressions often are, we can
understand how easily it may mislead the blind. Such
imaginary faces and scenes also enter into their dreams,
but to a less extent than into those of the sighted. Dr.
Kitto [1] quotes a letter from a musician who lost his
sight when eighteen years old, but who retains a very
strong visualizing power both in waking life and in
dreams. The mention of a famous man, of a friend,
or of a scene, always carries with it a visual picture,
complete and vivid. Moreover, these images of his
friends are reported to change as the friends grow old;
and he feels himself intellectually in no way different
from the seeing.

This leads naturally to the consideration of the
power of the imagination in the blind. It is not difficult to understand that they are deprived of one
powerful means of cultivating this faculty, that the eye
is in one sense the organ of the ideal. Their knowledge is more realistic and tangible, and so their dreams
often, though by no means always, lack all poetical
characteristics, and are very commonplace. Ghosts,
elves, fairies, monsters, and all the host of strange
romance that commonly people dreams, are not nearly
so well represented as in the dreams of the sighted.
What is almost typical in the dreams of the latter is

[1] *The Lost Senses*, by John Kitto. Dr. Kitto draws an ingenious inference from the sonnet addressed by Milton to his deceased (second)
wife, whom he married after the onset of his blindness. From the
lines, "I trust to have | Full sight of her in Heav'n without restraint,"
and "The face was veiled, yet to my fancied sight," etc., he argues
that the poet was unable to imagine the face of his wife, which he had
never really seen, and so saw the face veiled; but hoped in the
future world to have "full sight of her without restraint."

unusual in the dreams of the blind, especially of those early blind. Many observe that such dreams grow rare as they outgrow their youth,[1] which is probably true of the sighted. When the blind dream of ghosts they either hear them, and that usually not until they are close at hand, or they are actually touched by them. A blind man, describing a dream in which his friend appeared to him, said : " Then I dreamt that he tried to frighten me, and make believe he was a ghost, by *pushing me down sideways*," etc. By some the ghost is heard only ; it has a rough voice, and its bones rattle ; or it pursues the victim, humming and groaning as it runs.

Contrary to the opinions of some writers, I find hearing, and not the group of tactual-motor sensations, to be the chief sense with the blind, both in waking and in dreams. That hearing owes very much of this supremacy to its being the vehicle of conversation, goes without saying. Many of the blind dream almost exclusively in this sense, and it is quite generally spoken of as the most important. Even those who see a little, often regard hearing as their most useful sense ; those who see well enough to see color, almost invariably claim for their partial sight an importance exceed-

---

[1] I have evidence to indicate that among the blind (as probably amongst persons at large) women dream more extensively than men, that is, they have more " frequent " and fewer " occasional " dreamers than men. The period from five to nine years is richer in dreams than the period from ten to fourteen years, and from then on a slight decrease with age occurs. It is to childhood, the period of lively imagination and of a highly tinged emotional life (and to women, who present these characteristics more prominently than men), that dream-life brings its richest harvest.

ing that of hearing. Next in importance to hearing is the group of sensations accompanying motion. An important item in the dreams of the sighted is furnished by this complex of sensations, and the same is true of the blind ; almost all remember such dreams, and some make this their most important avenue of sensation. Yet such a purely artificial movement as reading the raised type with the finger almost never occurs in dreams. The boys dream of playing, running, jumping, and so on; the men of broom-making, piano-tuning, teaching, and similar work; the girls of sewing, fancy work, household work, and the like.

There is often ascribed to the blind a somewhat mystical sense, by which they can tell the presence and even the nature of objects, and can feel their way. As far as such a power exists, it depends upon a complex group of sensations, and includes the cultivation of the irradiation sense, which we all possess. It is not at all difficult to tell whether a large object is within a few inches of the hand, by the fact that it modifies the air currents and heat radiations reaching the hand. This is especially the case if the temperature of the object be somewhat different from that of the room, or if it be an object like metal, which rapidly exchanges its heat. In sunlight the shadows of stones and posts can be thus detected ; and the illumination of a room, both as to its source and extent, can be judged. This sense the blind carefully, though often unconsciously, cultivate, and I have heard it spoken of by them as " facial perception," because the face seems to be most sensitive to this kind of change. Many mention that the power fails them under the influence of a headache or similar nervousness. The question whether the position of a door, whether opened or closed, could be told at a distance was variously answered; about half testified that they could do so mainly by the aid of this facial perception. This enters in a vague way into their dreams, but seldom plays an important rôle.

The stories attributing to the blind rather wonderful notions of color have, on careful examination, been readily explained by natural means; the use of words referring to color is often merely verbal (of this both Laura Bridgman and Helen Keller furnish many excellent examples), while the knowledge of the colors of special objects is obtained by inference, based upon texture, appropriateness, and similar characteristics. The analogies between color and sound have been frequently described within recent years. Mr. Galton has recorded many cases in which the sounds of the vowels, of words, of musical notes, and the like, immediately summon to the mental eye an appropriate color, often with a peculiar outline and shading. One person could actually read sounds out of a wall-paper pattern, or write the sounds in the name *Francis Galton* in colors. It seemed possible that the blind might obtain or receive some dim notions of color by a similar process; and Dr. Kitto and the blind teacher, Friedrich Scherer, mention that such is the case, though to a very slight extent. The latter calls musical instruments the bridge across which color comes to him. (He became blind when two years old.) The flute is his symbol of green, the swelling organ tones of blue. The trumpet is red, the hunter's horn dark green and violet, a general confusion of tones is gray, while pink and crimson are associated with the feeling of velvet. In my list occurs the record of a young man twenty years old, and blind for three years. He saw colors on hearing certain sounds soon after his blindness, and claims that he is thus able to keep alive his notions of color. To him an alto voice is gray; a soprano, white; a tenor, yellow; a bass, black. My own voice suggested a dark background. A few words are also colored to him; the sound of *Smith* seems yellow. These analogies, however, are fanciful and rare. They belong to a region of mental phenomena, of great complexity, in which associations and idiosyncracies have free play, and seem as little capable of definite explanation as much of the stuff that dreams are made of.

A brief selection of instances from the collection of dreams and parts of dreams which these blind people have put at my command, may serve to reinforce the several factors of the dream-life of the blind which have been commented upon. Many of the dreams present no special differentiation from those of the seeing, but the most carefully recorded ones usually reveal some traces of a defective or peculiar apperception. A blind boy with more than usual imagination dreamed that he was in a battle in which Alexander the Great put the Gauls to flight; he heard the thunder of the cannon, but saw no flash. A young man dreamed that his mother was dead; this he knew by the cold touch of her body. He next heard the chanting of the Mass at her funeral. This young man at times improvises airs in his dreams. A partially-sighted girl dreams repeatedly of a wide river, and is afraid of being dashed across it, while anxious to

secure the flowers on the opposite bank, which she
dimly sees. A boy dreamed of being picked up by
some mysterious agency, and then suddenly allowed to
fall from a tremendous height. Here he awoke, and
found his head at the foot of the bed. Another dreamed
of the Judgment Day, mainly in terms of hearing.
He was drawn to heaven by a rope, clinging to a pole
used for exercising ; he heard the trumpets sounding,
and the voices singing, and so on. One dreamed that
he was on a steamboat which suddenly sank, whereupon he quietly walked ashore. Another, that his
father saw some wild people in the water, and swam
out and rescued them; another, of a large conflagration, of which he saw nothing, but was constantly receiving reports from the bystanders. A girl dreamed
that she was sent by her aunt to get a loaf of bread
from the cellar, and was cautioned not to step too far
down in the cellar, because there was water there ;
upon arriving at the dangerous place she stood still,
and called for her aunt. Another dreamed of chivalry,
as the result of reading " Ivanhoe ; " another of visit-
ing Lincoln and being much impressed with the strange-
ness of the place ; another of her examination in
physics — she placed a piece of glass on her finger,
and showed its centre of gravity, when the glass fell
and broke with a crash ; on another occasion she
dreamed that she was sick, went to the doctor, and
recovered her full sight, and things looked strange and
unfamiliar when compared with the knowledge she
had derived from touch.

V

The study of the dreams of the blind thus emphasizes many points of interest in the nature and development of the cortical centres of the human brain ;
it graphically illustrates the explanatory power of the
modern view of their functions; and it presents in a
new aspect certain characteristics of their constitution.
It shows beyond a question that the power of apper-
ceiving sight-images is in no true sense innate, but is
the product of slow development and long training.
That the same holds true of other centres is proved by
a mass of evidence gathered from many quarters ; with
regard to the motor centres, it is even experimentally
determined by the observation that stimulation of the
central convolutions of the brains of puppies fails to
excite the appropriate movements of the legs, unless the
puppies are already nine or ten days old.   These facts
will be utilized in the formulation of an important developmental law applicable alike to physiological and
to psychological processes.

The " critical period," revealed by the above research, must not be understood as marking the point
at which the visual centre begins its life ; this indeed
occurs at a much earlier age, and this centre from the
outset and continuously increases in complexity and
stability.   Nor was the statement made that there was
no difference here relevant, between the loss of vision
at different ages before the critical period.   That a
child who has seen up to the fourth, or the third, or even
the second year of life, probably retains some traces
of visualizing not attainable by those who attended

the school of vision for a shorter time or not at all, is believed on evidence of a general, but not as yet of a specific nature. Among other facts it is indicated by the influence of the age of blinding on the future development of noted blind persons. Similarly, after the critical period, the same processes of growth and assimilation continue, as is evidenced by the vague character and comparatively early decay of the dream-vision of those becoming blind close upon the end of the seventh year. The more time spent in gathering in the provisions, the longer do they hold out. The significance of the critical period lies in its demon-strating a point in the growth of the higher sense-centres, at which a divorce from sense-impression is no longer followed by a loss of their psychical mean-ing; a point at which imagination and abstraction find a sufficiently extended and firmly knit collection of ex-periences to enable them to build up and keep alive their important functions; a point where the scholar dispenses with the object-lesson and lives off his capital; a point at which the scaffolding may be torn down and the edifice will stand.

The indication of such a period in the development of the human mind brings clearly into view the de-pendence of the higher mental processes upon the basis furnished them by the experiences of sensation; it strongly suggests a rational order and proportion in the training of the several faculties of the child's mind; and finally, it prevents the formation and sur-vival of false notions, by substituting certain definite though incomplete knowledge for much indefinite though very systematic speculation.

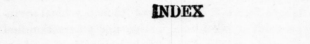

INDEX

INDEX